BEYOND DEATH

Beliefs, Practice, and Material Expression

EDITED BY PATRICK RYAN WILLIAMS, GARY M. FEINMAN, AND LUIS MURO YNOÑÁN

In association with the exhibition *Death: Life's Greatest Mystery*

FIELDIANA

Published in 2022 by
BAR Publishing, Oxford, UK

BAR International Series 3104

Fieldiana: Anthropology, volume 47
Beyond Death

ISBN 978 1 4073 6043 0 paperback
ISBN 978 1 4073 6044 7 e-format

DOI https://doi.org/10.30861/9781407360430

A catalogue record for this book is available from the British Library

COVER IMAGE *Ceramic skeleton figure from Mexico (FM 355626). Photo by Michelle Kuo, © 2022 Field Museum*

This book is available in printed format at http://www.barpublishing.com.

BAR titles are available from:

BAR Publishing
122 Banbury Rd, Oxford, OX2 7BP, UK
info@barpublishing.com
www.barpublishing.com

Contents

List of Figures

1

Introduction

Patrick Ryan Williams and Gary M. Feinman

Field Museum

Abstract: Death is universal, though it is experienced in diverse ways by different peoples and cultures. It has different meanings and implications to each community. Through reflection on death from various perspectives, we gain insight into the meaning of life. Death is a biological, social, and spiritual phenomenon and we explore those different meanings across time and place. It is about the body, but also the essence of one's being, and about the living who carry on the memories and the genes of those who passed. It is about the human endeavor to forestall death, our capacity for injustice in that search, and our humanity in coping with loss. Finally, it is about how we live on in the face of death as individuals who are intimately connected to one another through social ties and whose existence is disrupted by the disappearance of those closest to us. Death, in its ultimate rendition, creates life anew.

Resumen: La muerte es universal, aunque esta se experimenta de diversas maneras por cada sociedad y cultura. Desde una perspectiva global e histórica, la muerte tiene diferentes significados e implicancias para cada comunidad. Reflexionando sobre la muerte, desde diversas perspectivas, obtenemos una mejor idea del significado de la vida. La muerte es un fenómeno biológico, social y espiritual; y exploramos en este capítulo sus diferentes significados, a través del tiempo y el espacio. La muerte se refiere al cuerpo, pero también a la esencia del propio ser; además, a los vivos quienes llevan los recuerdos y los genes de aquellos que fallecen. Se refiere al esfuerzo humano para prevenirla; a nuestra capacidad para cometer injusticias con tal de evitarla, y a nuestra humanidad para hacerle frente a la pérdida. Finalmente, se trata de cómo seguimos hacia adelante pese a la muerte como individuos íntimamente conectados unos a los otros a través de lazos sociales, y cuya conexión se ve interrumpida por la desaparición de aquellos más cercanos a nosotros. La muerte, en su último acto, crea nuevamente vida.

The authors of this volume explore the role of death in our lives, how it is understood from various perspectives, and how it intersects with life: past, present, and future. Although neither the exhibition nor this volume can be completely comprehensive, we aim to illustrate a diversity of perspectives, behaviors, and beliefs. We live in a society that adopts an outlook in which nature is separate from humanity; this perspective views life and death in ways distinct from the religious and cultural perceptions of many other human groups past and present. For many in the US, death is a biological endpoint. It represents a specific moment in time in which life expires definitively and is bounded, a finite path with a beginning and an end. It is rooted in an empiricism that pervades our modernist view, rooted in science and medical knowledge as the overarching prospect of our time.

Yet, even in our own society, alternative perspectives on death pervade many of our understandings. And in societies across the globe, this empirical perspective of death as a finite moment in time, an end without renewal, and a fatalist viewpoint is challenged by both religious thought and lived realities of what happens to living beings as we move through death. For many, death is not an endpoint or a grand finality but has meaning much deeper in the cycle of life.

The exhibition built from this volume's scholarship leverages knowledge across cultures and the natural world to pose diverse answers to and vantages on several existential questions about death (see Miller and Whitfield in this volume). What is death? Do I have to die? What will happen to my body? What will happen to my spirit? How will my death affect others? Answers to these questions are not addressed sequentially in this volume, for every story has multiple responses to the questions about one's own death and that of others. Yet, certain themes represented in this collection address certain questions more directly than others. The treatment of the body, for example, reverberates in the essays on the biology of the life cycle and the performance of grieving rituals while the potential of the spirit has lasting invocation in the essays on religion, vitality, and life force.

This volume is organized around five thematic essays, each with four short case studies that elaborate on themes from the exhibition (Figure 1.1). The authors are leading scientists, Indigenous scholars, and museum professionals who have contributed to the exhibition as consultants, developers, designers, and co-curators or are museum curators themselves. Many of the objects displayed in the exhibition and photographed in exquisite form by exhibition photographer Michelle

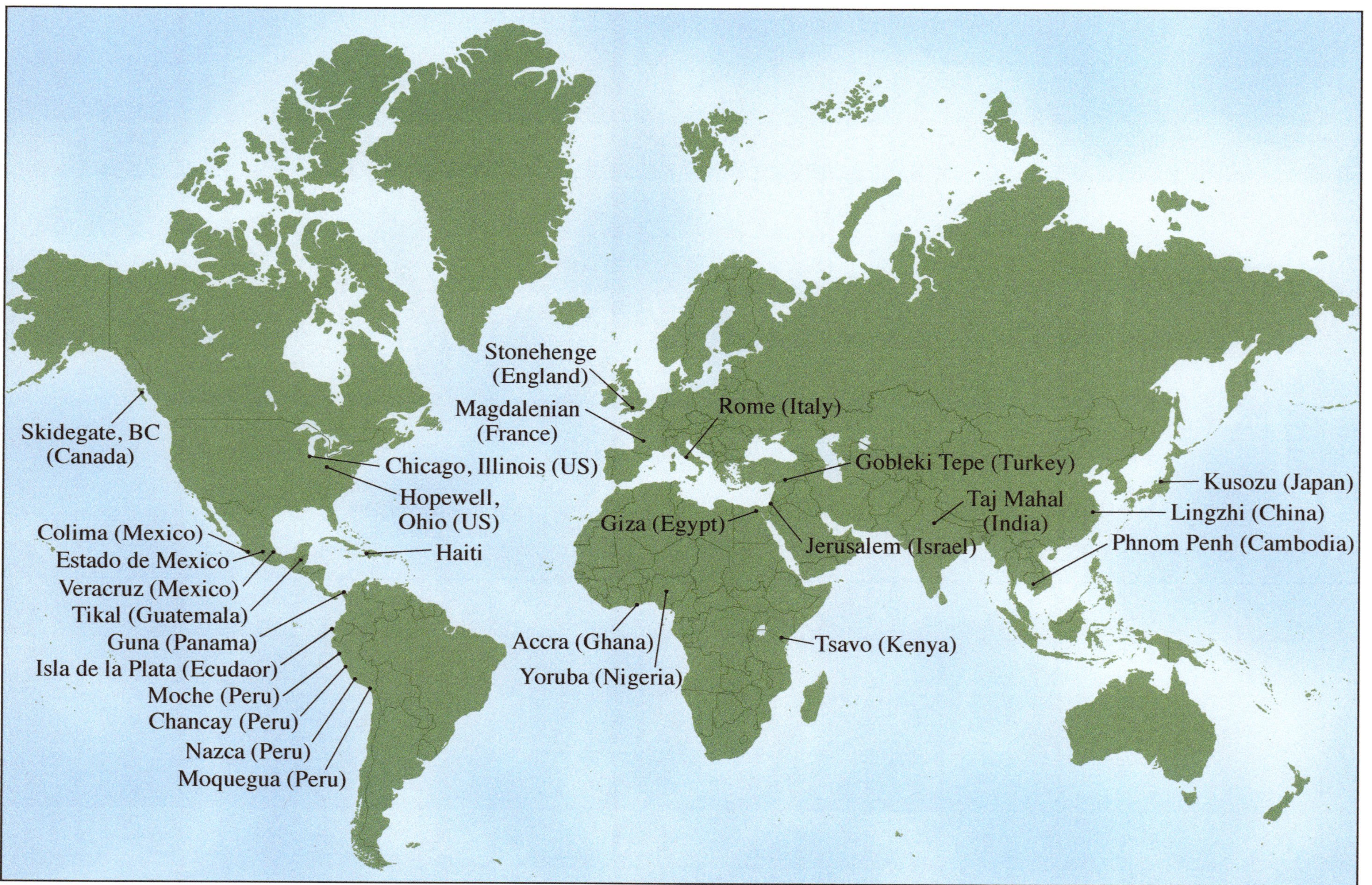

Figure 1.1. World Map of the Peoples, Places, and Stories in this volume. Map by Jill Seagard.

Kuo are part of the Field Museum's permanent anthropology collection. Several of the objects were acquired for the exhibition and have become part of the permanent collection through the exhibition. These include the Ghanian coffin by Seth Kane Kwei and the Haitian *drapo* flags and *govi* and *kanari* pottery created by Ronald Edmunds' workshop. We are grateful for loans from the Jewish Museum and the Art Institute of Chicago, as well as Mitch Hendrickson, Tory Hambly, and Life Gem.

The chapters represented here are based on the stories chosen for the exhibition, which in turn were selected following extensive research in the Field Museum's collections and selected stories and objects obtained especially for the exhibit. The museum's extensive collections were key to identifying which stories we could tell through the exhibition and thus through this work. We strove to take a global approach as we worked to address the five questions posed; most of the world's continents are represented here. We also attempted to incorporate diverse religious faith perspectives, including those of the distant past and the modern day. In the end, this is not a comprehensive look at humanity's take on death. Still, it does incorporate perspectives from long ago and through the present, from across distinctive cultural experiences, and from reflections on the diverse religious faiths of today and yesteryear. The thematic essays that open each of the five chapters help synthesize the particular perspectives on death, while the short case studies elaborate on the diversity of perspectives different peoples bring to bear on the questions about death.

The first of the thematic essays, by Robert Martin, explores the biological view in his examination of the Journey from Life to Death. He takes us through the conception of the human life-cycle, and how it parallels those of our animal cousins, and explores the artificial extension of life and the hope of some for immortality. He questions whether modern medicine can drastically alter the human lifespan, or if we are not restricted to the physical limitations of the human body. Longevity, it turns out, is heavily dependent on our biological and physical realities and on our lived social experience. Martin considers how scientists examine the bodies of the dead in order to assess their lives and their deaths. He also reflects on how we care for the bodies of the dead, a theme that other authors in this volume also explore. Notably, several of the case studies that accompany this thematic essay reflect on the injustices in death that our society imposes on certain members based on sex, race, and other categorizations of identity.

Accompanying Martin's essay, Japanese Buddhist meditations on the biological decay of the human body are explored through the *Kusōzu* watercolors (*Nine Stages of Bodily Decay*). While the exhibition focuses on the watercolors as a depiction of what happens to the body, Chelsea Foxwell brings our attention to how the *Kusōzu* reflected the morals of Buddhist thought. In the nineteenth century, when the watercolors were likely originally created, most Japanese Buddhists were cremated. Yet, the *Kusōzu* reflects on the body's impermanence and its change through the stages of death. While we are drawn to the biological process of death in the exhibit, this story brings to light the more complex nature of Buddhist thought around death and the search for *nirvana*.

The search for immortality in ancient and present China illustrates the difficulties in defying death and the ways in which it has been approached. This story appears in the exhibition section on longevity, and Deborah Bekken tells the story of Daoist practices that seek to prolong life using elixirs and natural elements. A particular focus on the *lingzhi* fungus as a purveyor of life illuminates how the human body may be maintained and/or preserved and foreshadows the use of medicines today to stave off death. *Lingzhi*'s life-giving properties go back more than 2000 years and are widely available today in teas, powders, or dietary supplements.

And in modern US society, social inequalities that lead to early death for mothers of color, as well as the deaths of victims of Covid, bring us to understand that social injustice and death are intimately related. Kimberly Mutcherson details the appalling death rates among Black women in the US due to drastic disparities in maternity care. While the US has one of the worst morbidity rates among developed nations for mothers in general, mothers of color are affected even more profoundly. It is the racist ways in which Black bodies are treated and the indifference to a woman's own knowledge of her health and well-being that create these high morbidity rates. It is a crisis that threatens the future of ourselves as a human population that needs immediate redress.

The COVID-19 pandemic likewise has had vast and differential effects on world populations, and Alaka Wali details how the Field Museum initiated a project to document the impacts on people worldwide, and particularly in Chicago. One object in particular, a banner thanking essential workers, tells the story of resilience and injustice in who was exposed to the virus and how race and class structured who lived and who died. This textile, made by Chicagoan Andrea Martinez, tells the story of those courageous workers who continued to help us all at great risk to themselves during the pandemic's early weeks and months.

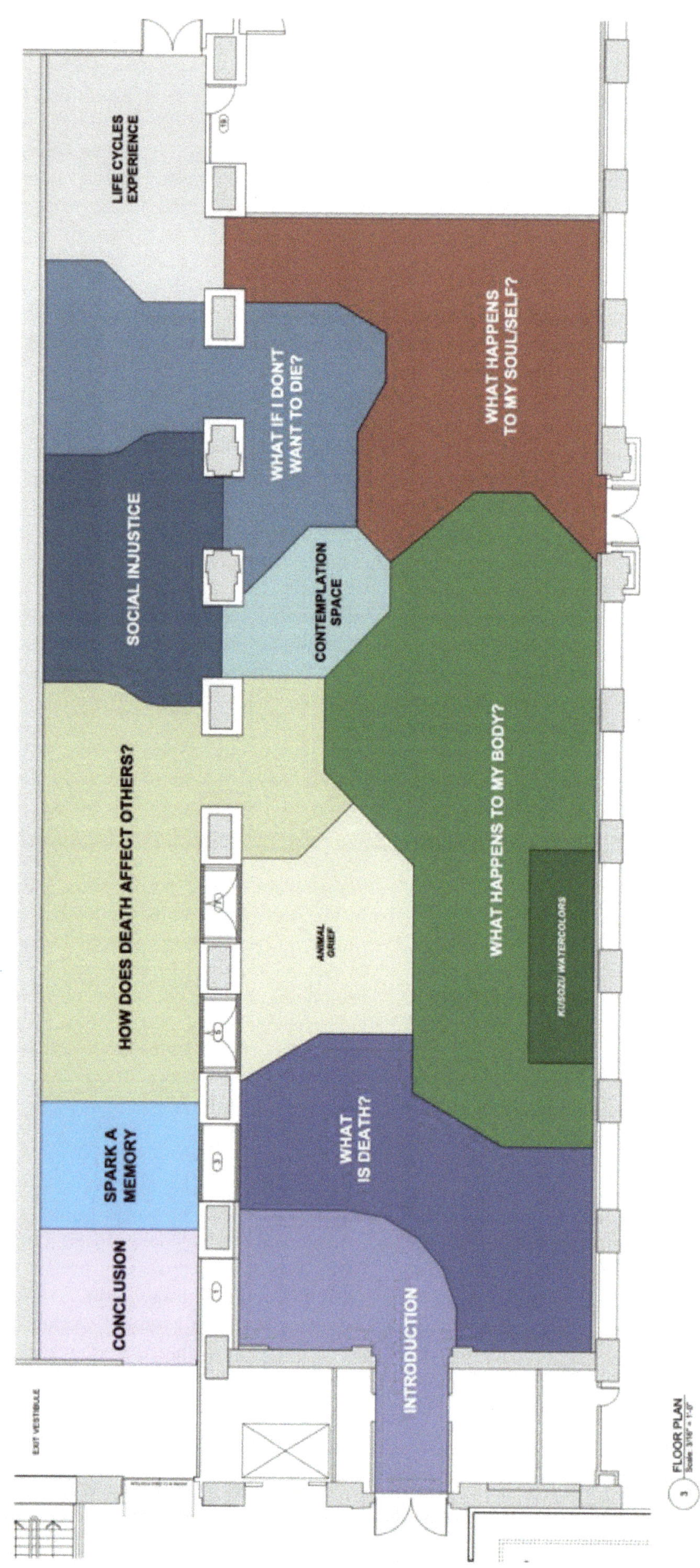

Figure 1.2. Schematic floorplan of *Death: Life's Greatest Mystery* at the Field Museum.

1A Big Questions: A Framework for Exploring Death

Benjamin Miller and Meredith Whitfield
Field Museum

Death is an incomprehensibly vast subject, extending to virtually every facet of our lives. It pervades our news: disease, mass shootings, war. We encounter it when beloved characters are killed off in books, films, and television shows. The dead surround us when we trace our ancestry or study history. And inevitably, we experience the deaths of loved ones—a grandparent taken by cancer, a friend suddenly lost in a car crash, or a beloved pet that needs to be put down.

Nevertheless, Americans often struggle to talk about death (Doughty 2019). Many of us are sheltered from thinking about death as children, and we deny its inevitability as we age. The alarming result is that about 63 percent of American adults have not made formal end-of-life plans (Yadav et al. 2017).

This was the challenge we faced when developing *Death: Life's Greatest Mystery*, a new traveling exhibition from the Field Museum of Natural History. How do we inspire our audience to engage with a topic they are so reluctant to acknowledge? How can we create an environment where visitors are comfortable pondering their own death, and discussing it openly with friends and family? And how can we explore this broad topic in a way that feels satisfyingly diverse but not overwhelming?

Why Questions?

As Michael Spock, former Public Programs Director at the Field Museum, once said, the best exhibitions are "for someone, not about something." With a topic so broad and sensitive, we paid special attention to understanding who this exhibition was *for*. We interviewed death professionals—hospice nurses, hospital chaplains, funeral directors, suicide hotline workers, and others who deal with death regularly. They offered valuable insight into how people imagine death: *personally*, in relation to themselves or their loved ones.

Further, visitor tracking data from other Field Museum exhibits demonstrated that displays organized around questions resulted in longer dwell times than other organization schemes, such as timelines (Roberts et al. 2018). Synthesizing these findings, we opted to organize the exhibition around five universal but personal questions:

What is death?
Do I have to die?
What will happen to my body?
What will happen to my spirit?
How will my death affect others?

Each gallery in the exhibition is devoted to one of these Big Questions, which serve as launchpoints for stories told with objects from the Field Museum's collections (Figure 1.2). Of course, none of these questions can be answered comprehensively or definitively, so each display is a case study that provides a potential answer to the gallery's question. *What will happen to my body?*, *What will happen to my spirit?*, and *How will my death affect others?* emerged quickly as questions that framed the topics that most intrigued visitors during audience surveys. We arrived on "What is death?" and "Do I have to die?" more gradually; many versions of these questions were explored as we worked to unify more existential ideas like social death and concepts of immortality.

Balancing Culture, Making Space for Nature

Visitors enter each gallery with a key personal question in mind, and each display, a possible answer from nature or culture, is an opportunity to reinforce or challenge their preconceptions about death. Visitor surveys demonstrated strong interest in both cultural views of death and examples from nature. The Big Questions framework was an opportunity to produce an explicitly interdisciplinary exhibition, pulling from nearly every collection at the Field Museum and blending multiple realms of expertise and ways of knowing.

Several cultural stories were co-curated or advised on by descendant community members. For example, community members in Skidegate provided critical context to Haida memorial and mortuary poles, and Seth Kane Kwei's grandson advised us on the legacy of Ghanaian fantasy coffins. Additionally, a few stories showcase works created especially for the exhibition, such as an *ofrenda* by Norma Rios Sierra.

Although cultural stories form the majority of displays in *Death: Life's Greatest Mystery*, natural history examples are an important complement. Audience surveys demonstrated that this balance was correct: in a survey of nearly 2000 visitors, 90 percent were somewhat or very interested in how animals deal with death. Examples from nature provide an approachable on-ramp for visitors to grapple with challenging concepts inherent to discussing death. For instance, early in the exhibition visitors encounter a diorama of a whale fall ecosystem (Figure 1.3). When a whale dies, its body becomes host to a unique collection of deep-sea organisms that live off the remains for decades. The underlying concept—death is not an endpoint, and is frequently a beginning—is simple but essential, and applicable to many of the cultural traditions explored elsewhere.

Creating Space to Engage

Our roundtables with death professionals yielded other valuable insights. Advisors told us about the value of humor, which can break tension and help people cope. They also stressed the importance of ritual action—

opportunities to do something or leave something behind as an outlet for grief. We incorporated this advice throughout the exhibition. Moments of levity, such as a display where a cartoon chicken demonstrates different forms of cremation, provide breaks between heavier topics. We incorporated ritual action in two key areas: the "spark a memory" interactive display allows visitors to contribute memories of their loved ones to a tree of light, and a version of artist Candy Chang's community art project *Before I Die* invites visitors to share their hopes and dreams for their lives and afterlives.

Conclusion

To inspire engagement with a difficult topic, we organized this exhibition to meet visitors where they are: thinking about their own deaths, and the deaths of those close to them. Starting from this very personal place, we positioned stories from nature and culture as possible answers to their big questions—answers that will either reinforce or challenge their existing ideas about death. To keep the exhibition approachable and emotionally satisfying, we interspersed humor, areas to take breaks, and opportunities to take ritual action.

References

Doughty, C. 2019. *Will My Cat Eat My Eyeballs? And Other Questions About Dead Bodies.* New York: W. W. Norton and Company.

Roberts, J., Banerjee, A., Hong, A., McGee, S., Horn, M., and Matcuk, M. 2018. "Digital Exhibit Labels in Museums: Promoting Visitor Engagement with Cultural Artifacts." *Proceedings of the 2018 CHI Conference on Human Factors in Computing Systems* 623: 1–12. https://doi.org/10.1145/3173574.3174197.

Yadav, K. N., Gabler, N. B., Cooney, E., Kent, S., Kim, J., Herbst, N., Mante, A., Halpern, S. D., and Courtright, K. R. 2017. "Approximately One in Three US Adults Completes Any Type of Advance Directive for End-of-Life Care." *Health Affairs* 36, no. 7: 1244–51. https://doi.org/10.1377/hlthaff.2017.0175.

Alternative perspectives on the relationship between life and death are addressed by Kyrah Malika Daniels and William Schweiker, who reflect on religious traditions from Africa and its diaspora on one hand, and on the Jewish and Christian worlds on the other. In the former essay, Daniels takes us through the ways in which communities in Africa and its diaspora in the Atlantic world understand death and its place in the human experience. She draws on and references several of the stories told in the exhibit, with a special focus on African-descended peoples in Haiti and contemporary Haitian Vodou, which emphasizes core principles of longevity, livity, and the vibrancy of life. Examining these principles reveals how life's vital force is sustained through balance, ritual, and the fortification of souls and divine energies in Africana religions.

This perspective from Africana religions is complemented by perspectives from the Indigenous cultures of Latin America. The Atlantic World Diaspora is often seen as the European exploitation of African bodies, and rightly so. But it also involved the appropriation of the lands of Indigenous peoples of the Americas and the usurpation of their bodies and labor as well. Daniels' essay and the stories that accompany it highlight the perspectives on death that African, African Diaspora, and native Latin American peoples contribute to understanding death and beyond.

Daniels' work is accompanied by other perspectives on death from Africa and the Americas. From the Yorùbá traditions around twins in West Africa, the *ere ibeji* ("born twice") statues explore the powerful spiritual forces present in twin births, which are highly elevated in Yorùbá society. Wooden figures representing a twin become important representatives of the deceased in the rites and rituals of the living. Foreman Bandama examines how the loss of a twin or of twin children reverberates within Yorùbá society. Since the soul of a twin is shared between them, maintaining balance requires the soul of the departed to have an *ibeji* statue to dwell in. Failing to provide one could have catastrophic consequences for those who remain.

From the other side of the world, the importance of life force is explored in Moche (200–900 CE) representations of death, sexuality, and being that challenge our conceptions of how life animates the world. Luis Muro Ynoñán reveals insights into the nature of life and death through an interpretation of Moche ceramic figurines from Peru. They are engaged in sexually explicit acts that help us understand that death, procreation, and bodily fluids are all entwined in Moche cycles of life. In fact, it is not sexual acts that are the focus, but the passing of vital fluids between entities that is important. And these entities were not only humans, but animals, skeletons, and other beings intimately connected to the reproduction of life.

Figure 1.3. The life-sized whale fall diorama. Blue Rhino Studios.

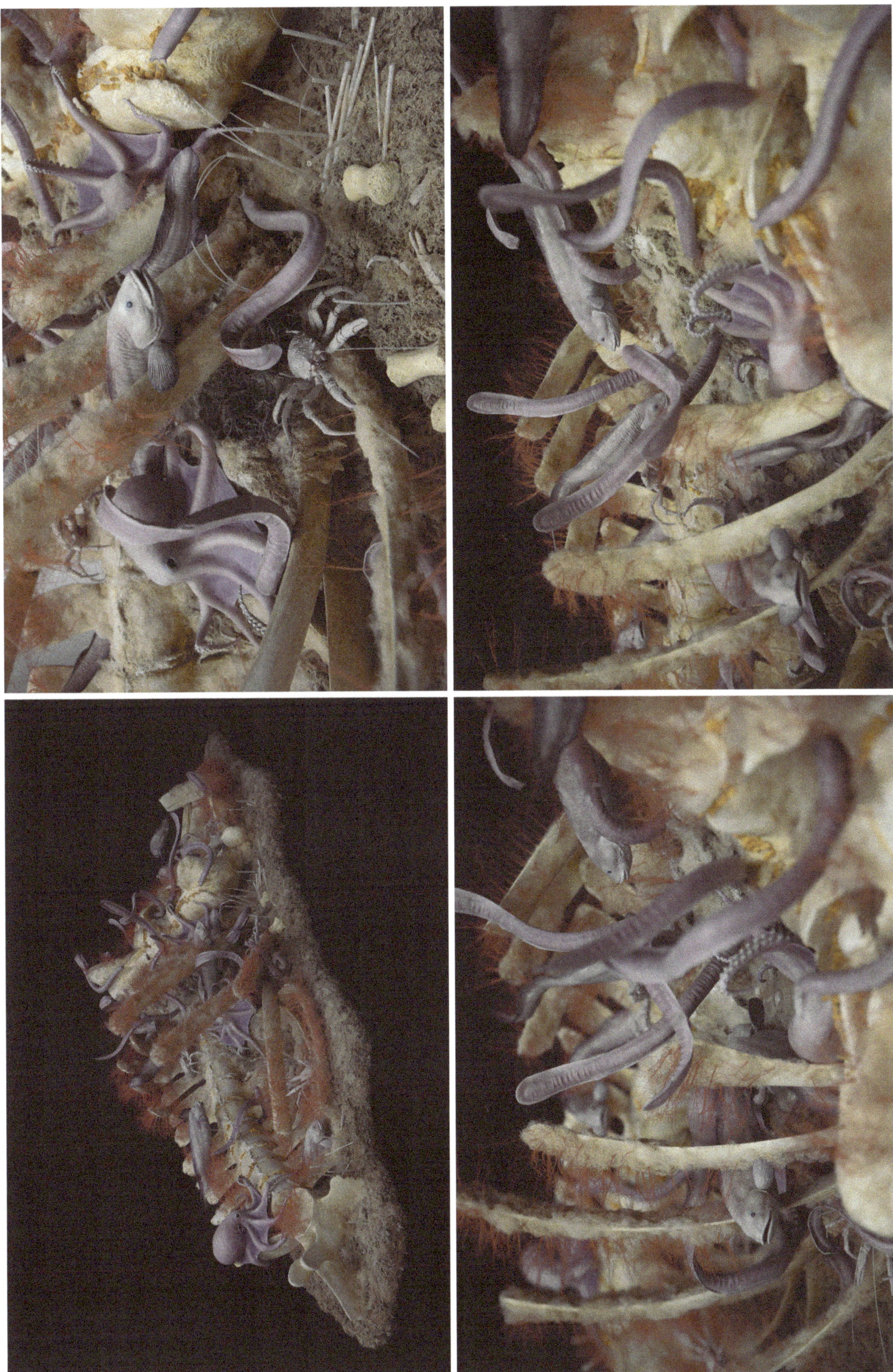

The Inca *capac hucha* presents a South American Andean perspective on the meaning of death, where the sacrifice of noble children shows us that the moment of death is not always easily defined. Patrick Ryan Williams explores the meaning of the *capac hucha* to the Inca (1400–1532 CE) understanding of death. Here, the line between life and death is also challenged as it is in the Haitian and Yorùbá cases. As the children are removed from their communities, they begin the transition to a new existence weeks or months before their biological death. They become different social beings in that transition. Even interred on a snow-capped mountain peak or an island in the middle of the Pacific Ocean, they continue to play a role as messengers to the ancestors. Even in death, they continue to serve the Inca.

Taking the concept of life trajectories anew, the peoples of pre-Hispanic Mesoamerica conceived of distinct realms inhabited by the living and dead. Certain beings and places facilitated the communication and movement between these realms, between living and dead, and thus blurring the distinction between life and death. Gary Feinman discusses the three realms of the Mesoamerican universe: the overworld, middleworld, and underworld and the portals that connect them. It is not unlike the conception of the universe in the Andean world of *hananpacha*, *kay pacha*, and *ukhupacha* that Luis Muro Ynoñán relates. Life, death, and renewal are all connected in the Mesoamerican world, and places like the pre-Hispanic Mesoamerican ballcourts (1200 BCE–1520 CE) or beings such as dogs assisted in passage through those realms. Maize was also a central metaphor in this worldview, and the seeds of life are embedded in the growth and death of maize from seed to corn to stalk.

In his essay, Performing Death, Luis Muro Ynoñán takes us through how ritual and grief help us cope with death in different cultural and social contexts. In the final two chapters of this volume we see the social impacts of death on individuals and communities. In the final essay, Gary Feinman and Patrick Ryan Williams take this perspective further to examine the long-term impacts of death on society writ large. In Muro Ynoñán's essay, however, grief and ritual take center stage in elaborating how we deal with the loss of a loved one in the immediacy of their passing, both physical and spiritually. Muro Ynoñán highlights funerary behaviors in the human past and present as how humans uniquely deal with the grief through ritual. Mortuary ritual also involves the transformation of the person and the body, and that process involves both the personal wishes of the deceased, but especially the inscription of their surviving community's meanings on them. The dead are washed, dressed, feted, and buried in accordance with prescribed identities by those who inter them. Some of the deceased become important ancestors and, in some cases, in the absence of a body, representations of the deceased take on new meanings to their communities.

The ritual treatment of the dead is explored through the ways in which bodies were prepared and buried in coastal Peru 600 years ago among the Chancay. Nicole Slovak discusses how the Chancay treated the bodies of the deceased and the importance of preserving the body in Chancay society (1000–1400 CE). In particular, the deceased continued to engage with the living, even after interment, as deceased individuals were re-dressed, fed, and commemorated multiple times after their burial. Before the arrival of the Europeans, numerous other Andean communities also returned to commiserate with the dead, and to care for the ancestors' bodies for years after their burial. Life, it seems, does not entirely leave the body on death, or at least the physical self continues to be fed and clothed long after clinical death has occurred.

Mummification, preserving the body for the afterlife, was a key means of performing death in ancient Egypt as well. The circumstances of Egyptian mummification were very different from the Andean case, as Emily Teeter explains. In Egypt, while the spirit requires an earthly home, and a preserved body to inhabit, the spirit is transformed into an imperishable god that dwells forever in the afterlife. Not all those who died were mummified in Egyptian society, and it was an elaborate process in its most developed form among the elites; most of the aspects described here date to ca. 1000 BCE. For them, the preservation of the bodily remains was key to the spirit living an eternity in the afterlife. Unlike the Andean case, the mummified deceased no longer actively participated in the world of the living. However, disturbance of their earthly remains could imperil their existence in the hereafter.

In present-day Accra, Ghana, a tradition of burial in elaborate coffins representing professional or personal aspirations, character, or status has emerged from a ritual celebrating chiefly power. Foreman Bandama discusses changes in burial traditions under British colonial rule that removed the deceased from burial in their homes to public cemeteries and the simultaneous adoption of a new burial practice in elaborate fantasy coffins. Beginning with the Ga people, and spreading to many other Ghanian peoples, the tradition grew out of the sedan chairs used by Ghanian chiefs. Today, these coffins are made for both burial and as works of art specifically for museum display. The Ghanian coffin tradition shows how much can change in the course of a century in mortuary tradition and also reminds us that death is about remembering and honoring the deceased.

And in Tsavo, Kenya, an ancestor lost to slaving whose body could not be claimed for inclusion in an ancestral shrine is represented by an animal skull. Chapurukha M. Kusimba describes the migration of the peoples of the Tsavo plains to the upland hills as they fled the slave trade, drought, and disease in the sixteenth to nineteenth centuries CE. They took their ancestors' skulls with them and built shrines in their new mountain homes, where they lived nomadic lives as refugees for several centuries. Among these crania, one was that of a sheep or goat, which represented an ancestor who was lost in a slave raid and whose skull could not accompany those of his kin. Contact with the physical remains of the ancestors kept the continuity between generations. A loved one who was ripped from their social group died a social death in the eyes of those they would never see again and needed to be represented despite knowledge of their bodily death and lack of their physical remains.

In the penultimate essay, William Schweiker's treatise on death in the Christian and Jewish traditions brings us closer to an understanding of death from "the West," that of two of the prominent religions of the Indo-European world. It reminds us that the medical definitions of death are accompanied by rich theologies of thought on the finality of death and the continuation of the being on the demise of the body. In particular, the religious perspective articulated here examines why death exists and its theological origins, how life and death are intertwined, how to prepare for death, and what lies beyond our bodies' death. Schweiker reminds us that, in Christian doctrine, the origin of death was due to the sin of Adam and Eve being exiled from the Garden of Eden to live and die in a sinful world. Death exists because all humans are born with original sin, and only through Christ's atonement for sin can humans be saved. Ultimately, Christ's resurrection from the dead is the victory over death by God.

Christian and Jewish religious traditions also relate the challenges of mortality and living as mortal beings to morality and the importance of following a moral life in the Church. The first Christian sacrament, baptism, is seen as a ritualized death when the individual is raised into a new life in the body of Christ. And in both Jewish and Christian religions, the ideal is to love one another and be a light to the world. Preparing for one's death or the death of a loved one espouses this perspective of love and understanding. Allowing for confession of sins before death, accompanying the dying and mourners in their grief, and providing consolation are all important tenets of preparations for death. Finally, religious doctrine speaks to what lies beyond death, and Schweiker outlines the perils and possibilities of different religious perspectives on the afterlife. Here, the potential of a Second or Eternal Death in Christian and Jewish thought, in which the soul is forever separated from the divine, represents a far more terrifying fate than death itself. These ideas are explored in more depth in several of the stories that accompany the essay.

When the spirit passes, the body remains and must be buried quickly in the Jewish tradition. Those who clean the body before burial perform a solemn duty, the *chevra kadisha*. Laurie Zoloth takes us through a personal reflection on this rite and an analysis of its meaning in Jewish life. She reminds us that once medical death is proclaimed, the body in modern society is treated as an empty vessel, sent to a morgue as an item stored. The ritual rehumanizes the body for burial, as she so eloquently describes, and reminds the participants that they, with the deceased, are part of a community with God. The *chevra* also enlightens us about the rituals and performances surrounding death and their meaning to the communities of practice that envelop them. This discrete tradition reminds us that death is a humbling and humanizing experience, and one that also brings one in touch with the shared experience.

The Guna of Panama bring the Christian story of the Garden of Eden into their own interpretation in the elaborate *molas* they weave. Alaka Wali shares the meaning of the *molas* with us, noting that the story of Adam and Eve as depicted in the *mola* was built on the concept of "original sin," but that likely does not conform or resonate with the Guna weavers over the past 150 years. Some Christian denominations would argue that being spiritually alive requires an acceptance of Christ into one's life. The rejection of God, and Christ his Son, means that one no longer lives in the light of the lord; that one is spiritually dead without God. The Guna artist who created this *mola* may not have been invested in that theology, Wali argues, but appreciated how the elements of the design accorded with Guna principles: the balance of male and female and the representation of the natural world (manifested by a palm native to Panama instead of an apple tree). The meanings of stories can be adapted and changed to meet the realities and traditions of adopting groups.

The Day of the Dead reminds us in another way that the Catholic religion as practiced in Mexico and other parts of Latin America is a rich syncretism of the Christian faith and the traditions of Indigenous belief systems that existed in the New World millennia before that religious conversion. Álvaro Amat shares his personal experience growing up in a Mexican family with a Spanish–Cuban matriarch. The contradictions of Indigenous practices adopted by many Mexican Catholics were in discord with a conservative perspective.

We see an alternative theology to the Judeo-Christian one as practiced in Asia through the lens of Buddha's teachings. Buddhists do not see the body's demise as the ultimate death. For Buddhists ultimate enlightenment comes after many lives lived and many bodies passed. Mitch Hendrickson brings us through Buddha's (sixth to fifth century BCE) teachings and the representation of the final death that Buddha passed through in the many depictions of his *parinirvana* state. The cycle of death, rebirth, and suffering continues until one achieves enlightenment. A being can experience many physical deaths, but they are fleeting, as it is the final spiritual release in which enlightenment is obtained. We learn that the moment of physical death (or deaths) is not the end of existence or suffering; that requires reaching *nirvana*.

Finally, Gary Feinman and Patrick Ryan Williams explore the role of society as a living entity in which death is part of and a challenge to the ongoing social networks that define us as members of a community and collective with an existence that transcends the individual. We delve into the history of human commemorations of the dead and their meaning to societies across thousands of years. In exploring the earliest examples of memorials to the deceased by human ancestors, we find no clear answer to what precipitated these traditions. However, their increasing complexity and scale may be linked to increasing population densities. This behavior certainly pre-dates settled village life, but it may be related to habitual return to certain places in the landscape of our early ancestors. As social aggregation increases, more elaborate memorials take hold and, in some cases, vast amounts of resources and labor are invested in tombs to the dead.

The origins of social remembrance delve deep into our human past. The burial of the Magdalenian Woman reminds us that well before the advent of agricultural societies, human ancestors convened to commemorate the dead in an effort to build a community. The burial took place in the Cap Blanc rock shelter in current-day France, probably between 9000 and 17,000 years ago (there is some ambiguity in the different radiocarbon dates processed from the remains). The rock shelter also contains an incredible sculptured frieze more than 40 feet long, depicting horses, bison, and reindeer. The young woman was likely deliberately interred here as her body was arranged in a flexed fetal position that suggests her body was arranged when placed for burial. No grave goods are associated with her burial, though the placement of her body and the locale in which she was placed may indicate an early concern with memorialization.

The Haida Gwaii show us how their ancestors continue to play essential roles in the community through the placement of mortuary and memorial poles from the nineteenth century to the present. As Luis Muro Ynoñán and Gary Feinman explain, both mortuary and memorial poles help communities remember and keep ancestors connected to their kin who dwell here. They are real manifestations of the rights and the histories of the families that own them, and they are intimately related to the family ancestors as a bridge to the afterlife. Mortuary poles, for example, place the ancestral remains high in the air and help push them into the next realm. In a future generation, those same poles help the soul of the ancestor return to the village in the form of a spirit or reincarnated being. Memorial poles serve a similar purpose in assisting the ancestor's spirit to find their way back to the village, especially in cases where they died while away. They are a beacon that brings the ancestors home and continues to rejuvenate life in the community through the ancestors' return. The Haida have thus perpetuated their communities for thousands of years, reinvigorated by the ancestors who are always a part of them.

Hopewell society 2000 years ago built inclusive and extensive social networks with great burial mounds for their dead (100 BCE–500 CE) in what is today the state of Ohio. These were not just cemeteries, as Brad Lepper describes, they were central places on the landscape of the mobile Hopewell groups dedicated to world renewal ceremonies. Linked not only to the renewal of the living world, these Hopewell earthworks were also the engines of renewal for the entire cosmos. And of course, for the living who came to bury their dead and participate in these ceremonies, they reaffirmed their social ties to the larger Hopewell community. This may have been the place where life partners were found, where inter-community relationships were confirmed, and where distant kin were reacquainted. Death and renewal became central to the social network that constituted Hopewell life. Without these ceremonies and places, Hopewell as a society could not exist.

And across the world past and present, memorials to the dead anchor their descendants and forge the basis for social ties that last for generations. Donna Nash helps us understand the difference between collective memorials and those monuments dedicated to elite rulers. She reminds us that the monuments to the dead can be sources of collective inspiration that draw societies together like the Hopewell, Stonehenge, and Göbekli Tepe. Powerful rulers may also expend great resources to memorialize themselves and reinforce the dominance of their lineage and descendants for generations. Here Khufu's pyramid at Giza, Shah Jahan's Taj Mahal, and Tikal's Temple 1 built by Jasaw Chan K'awiil are evocative examples. Regardless of their original purpose, these memorials take on a life of their own in society as they are used to project ideas about nationhood, power, and social unity. The dead continue to exert their influence on the living through their impacts on generations to come.

Acknowledgments

Our thanks to the community members and scholars who consulted on the stories in the exhibition: Kyrah Malika Daniels, Laurie Zoloth, Robert DeCaroli, Chelsea Foxwell, Kostas Arvanitis, William Schweiker, Betsy Williams, Troy Hambly, Emily Teeter, Chap Kusimba, Kim Mutcherson, Brad Lepper, Ben Barnes, Mitch Hendrickson, Aay Aay Hans, Nika Collison, Sean Young, James McGuire, Colette Lee, Elizabeth Kvale, Fr. Eddie DeLeon, Geraldine Gorman, Jim Brown, Patrick Belligarde-Smith, Robin Wright, and William Gblerkpor.

Ashley Vance provided invaluable editorial assistance. The Lilly Endowment provided funding for the development of the exhibition.

2

The Journey from Life to Death: Biology of the Human Life Cycle and Our Attempt to Control It

Robert D. Martin
Field Museum

Abstract: Like most other many-celled animals, every mammal species has a characteristic life cycle, beginning with a sperm fertilizing an egg and ending with death. For mammals generally—including humans—major milestones are conception, birth, attainment of sexual maturity, and the end of life. Typically, before they die, individuals experience a period of physical decline in old age (senescence), which may be brief but is quite extensive in humans. And in each mammal species those principal life stages have typical durations, beginning with gestation in the mother's womb and then proceeding through infant and juvenile development into adult life. In every mammal species, the overall lifespan also has a typical duration. Death from natural causes is universal among mammals and its timing is fairly predictable for any particular species, given the existence of a species-specific maximum lifespan. Nevertheless, artificial extension of the lifespan—perhaps culminating in immortality—has long been a cherished goal in human societies. With the advent of modern medicine, it may seem as though long-term postponement of death has become a realistic prospect for the future. But this may well be a vain hope. The much-vaunted "improvement" in human longevity attributed to continued improvements in medical care may be an illusion. In the end, we all must learn to live with death. Content articles explore decay, immortality, and longevity in human societies.

Resumen: Como la mayoría de los animales multicelulares, cada especie de mamífero tiene un ciclo de vida característico, que comienza con un espermatozoide que fertiliza un óvulo y termina con la muerte. Para los mamíferos en general-incluidos los seres humanos-los principales hitos son la concepción, el nacimiento, el logro de la madurez sexual, y el final de la vida. Por lo general, antes de morir, las personas experimentan un período de deterioro físico en la vejez (senectud), el cual puede ser breve, pero es bastante extenso en los humanos. Y en cada especie de mamífero, esas etapas principales de la vida tienen duraciones típicas, comenzando con la gestación en el útero de la madre y luego avanzando a través del desarrollo infantil y juvenil hasta la vida adulta. En cada especie de mamífero, las etapas de vida en general también tienen una duración típica. La muerte por causas naturales es universal entre los mamíferos y su momento es bastante predecible para cualquier especie en particular, dada la existencia de una esperanza de vida máxima específica de la especie. Sin embargo, la extensión artificial de esta esperanza de vida, quizás culminando en la inmortalidad, ha sido durante mucho tiempo un objetivo preciado en las sociedades humanas. Con el advenimiento de la medicina moderna, puede parecer que el aplazamiento a largo plazo de la muerte se ha convertido en una perspectiva realista para el futuro. Pero esto bien puede ser una esperanza vana. La tan deseada "mejora" en la longevidad humana atribuida a las continuas mejoras en la atención médica puede ser una ilusión, y quizás una trampa. Al final, todos debemos aprender a vivir con la muerte. Los artículos contenidos en esta sección exploran la decadencia, la inmortalidad, y la longevidad en las sociedades humanas.

How different are human beings from other animal species? Is there something in our biology that makes us particularly distinctive from them? Each multicellular organism has a characteristic *lifecycle*, beginning when a sperm fertilizes an egg and ending with death. For mammals generally—including humans—major milestones are *conception*, *birth*, *attainment of sexual maturity*, and the *end of life* (Healy et al. 2014). Typically, before dying, mammals experience a period of physical decline in old age (*senescence*) (Finch 1990), which may be brief but, for some reason that will here be explored, can be more extensive in humans. And in each mammal species those principal life stages have typical durations, beginning with gestation in the mother's womb and then proceeding through infant and juvenile development into adult life (Charnov and Berrigan 1993). In humans, pregnancy (*gestation*) lasts nine months, physical maturity is typically reached by about 21 years of age (with sexual maturation somewhat earlier), and an individual can potentially live for over a century (Figure 2.1). However, in spite of the similitude, humans are the only mammals that have developed strategies to extend their natural lifecycles. This chapter will explicitly address biological aspects of human development; how our body progressively degenerates; how our lifecycles can be culturally manipulated; and the potential effects that such actions produce on our biology. Will the manipulation of our lifecycles prevent us from advancing toward our inexorable demise? Can we control all those variables that can potentially affect our chances of survival?

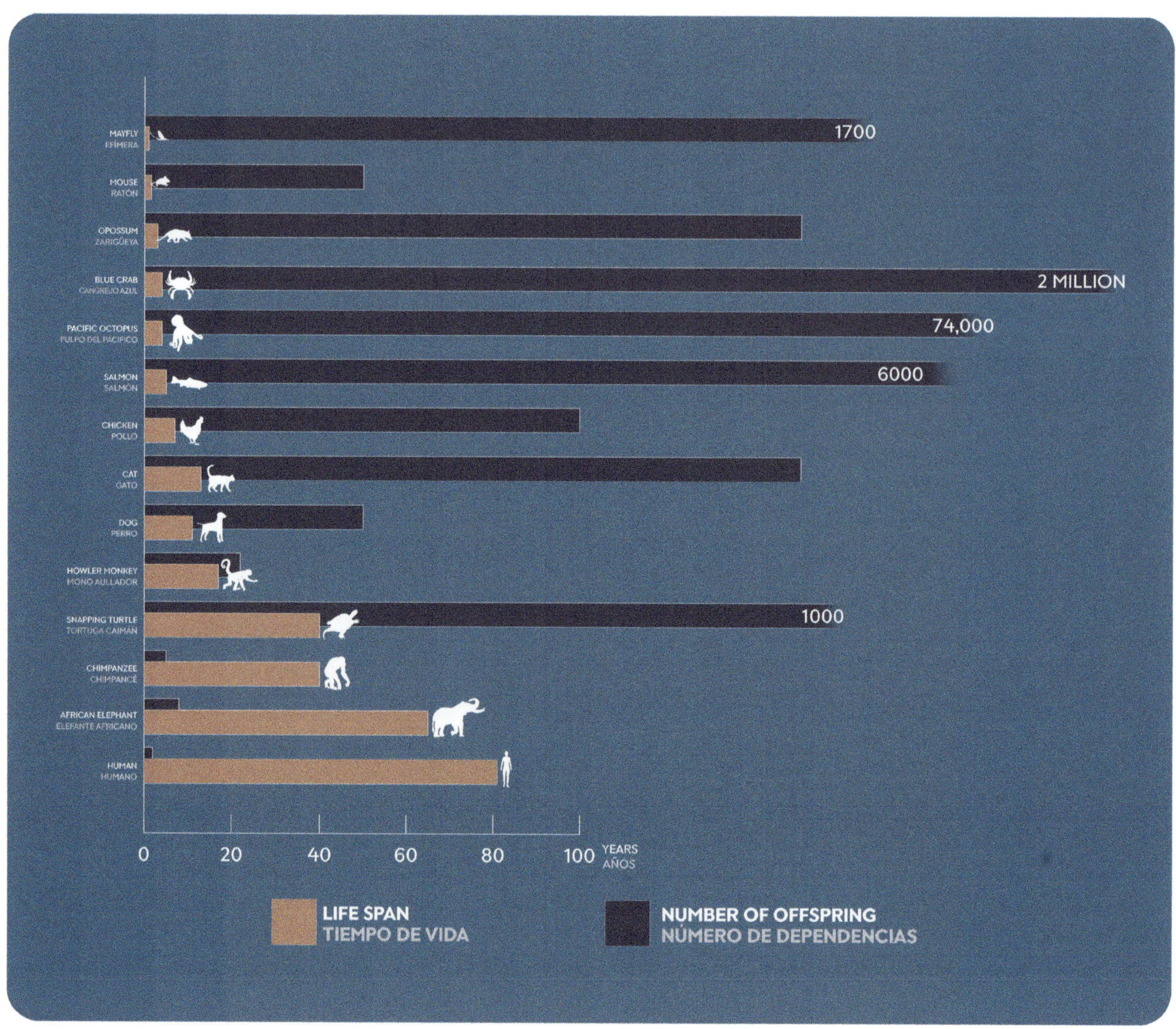

Figure 2.1. Comparative lifespans and offspring for humans and other species.

Overall, in every mammal species, lifespan has a typical duration (Smith 1993). Because of external influences—inadequate resources, accidents, predation and disease—longevity can vary quite widely between individuals of a species (Pokharel, Sharma, and Sukumar 2022). For this reason the *maximum* recorded lifespan (which is far more consistent for any given species) is used for comparisons between species. Across species the gestation period, time taken to reach sexual maturity, and maximum lifespan all tend to increase with increasing body size (Ellis et al. 2018). Typically, small-bodied mammals have short lifecycles, whereas those of large-bodied species are long. In short, some mammal species live in the "fast lane," while others (notably including primates) progress in the "slow lane." However, mammals of similar body size can have different durations of life stages (Lemaître et al. 2020). Among medium-sized mammals, for instance, the fast cycles typical of rodents and carnivores contrast with the slow cycles that characterize primates. In fact, at any given body size, tree-living mammals typically have longer maximum lifespans than mammals that live at ground level. Primates are essentially tree-living and long human lifespans have been retained and expanded from that biological heritage (Alberts et al. 2013; Alvarez 2000).

In contrast to humans, development after birth in other mammals has notably fewer stages. Many fast-breeding mammals are weaned and become sexually mature at about the same time, so they really have only two basic life stages: immaturity and adulthood. Other, more slowly breeding mammals such as nonhuman primates have a juvenile stage inserted between weaning and adulthood. However, and interestingly, humans have more life stages than other primates (Acscadi and Nemeskeri 1970; Carey 2003; Carey and Judge 2000). In particular, a new *childhood phase* intervenes before the juvenile period, and a similarly novel *adolescent phase* follows. American anthropologist Barry Bogin (2009) convincingly argued that the developmental stage of childhood is unique to humans. Adolescence also seems to be more-or-less confined to our species. In other words, the undivided "juvenile period" seen in other mammals consists of three distinct phases in the human lifecycle. This increased complexity of human development before adulthood is associated with an extension of the period between birth and sexual maturity (Westendorp and Kirkwood 1998), and it can also be related to our prolonged period of senescence (see Austad 2015; Hamilton 1968).

With stages of development, as with many other aspects of human biology, comparisons with nonhuman primates yield a revealing perspective (Austad and Fischer 1992). These comparisons allow us to recognize ancient features of our primate origins or general mammalian heritage, and thus to identify more recent innovations that can be uniquely human. And here, valuable clues can be gleaned from the archaeological record, as interpretations of skeletal remains can expand our understanding of human life-histories, sometimes even back to fossil relatives. For instance, Barry Bogin and fellow American anthropologist Holly Smith inferred that the novel stages of childhood and adolescence in the human lifecycle may date back to the emergence of early members of the genus *Homo* around two million years ago, suggesting that these early stages of development could be unique features of the early hominids (Colchero et al. 2016).

It has long been widely accepted that the duration of the life stages is contingent on the development and progress of modern life (Barbi et al. 2018; Caspari and Lee 2006). In pre-industrial societies a typical human lifespan is "three score years and ten," or 70 years. With increasing advances in healthcare in industrialized nations, however, *average* life expectancy at birth has increased by about a decade—to 80 years—in the USA and Europe and other industrialized regions in Asia and Australasia (see Chernew et al. 2016; Olshansky 2008; Olshansky, Carnes, and Désesquelles 2001). Although, as Mutcherson (in this volume) demonstrates, other factors of social inequality in the USA can dramatically reduce life expectancy. As she cleverly asks, could we ever overcome the limitations of a deeply unequal life?

In general, it is usually expected that, accompanying progress in medical sciences, average longevity will continue to increase in future. But an important distinction must be noted. Thus far—although medical progress can substantially increase average human lifespans—it seems that there may be an upper limit (Dong, Milholland, and Vijg 2016; Olshansky, Carnes, and Cassel 1990). It is entirely possible that, while improvements in healthcare have enabled many individuals to survive longer than pre-industrial conditions allowed, there is a natural maximum age. All other mammal species have a recognizable maximum lifespan, so why should humans be any different? Under free-ranging conditions, because of fluctuation in resources, accidents, predation, and disease, individual mammals rarely attain the maximum lifespan (see Finch 2010; Flatt and Partridge 2018; Gavrilov and Gavrilova 1991). In captivity, however, average longevity may approach the species maximum more closely, although increasing signs of senescence become apparent with increasing age (Hawkes 2003; Hawkes and Coxworth 2013).

In fact, several lines of evidence indicate that the human species may have a maximum lifespan of about 125 years. This very long potential lifespan is substantially longer than in any nonhuman primate species. Indeed, it is longer than in any other mammal, not only relative to body size but also absolutely. For a medium-sized mammal, our extended lifespan is a striking outlier. Reliable sources indicate that no human has ever survived beyond the age of 125 years. The current record-holder (and even that has been questioned) is the French woman Jeanne Calment, who reportedly died during her one-hundred-and-twenty-third year in 1997.

Some researchers have concluded that maximal human longevity has actually increased over time, while others have inferred that no such increase is likely. In 2000, American demographer John Wilmoth and colleagues published an impressively detailed study of recent variation in the human lifespan. They reported that the maximum age at death in Sweden increased from about 101 years during the 1860s, in Darwin's heyday, to about 108 years during the 1990s. Over two thirds of that seven-year increase in maximum age at death can be attributed to reduced death rates for individuals more than 70 years old. Wilmoth and colleagues also noted that the rate of increase in maximum lifespan per decade accelerated after 1970. This faster increase in the maximum age reflected a more rapid decline in old-age mortality over the most recent three decades of the study. Wilmoth and colleagues (2000, 2368) concluded that "reductions in death rates at older ages … seem likely to continue and may gradually extend the limits of achieved human longevity even further." In other publications, the Wilmoth group has similarly argued that human maximum lifespan may continue to increase into the future.

九想詩

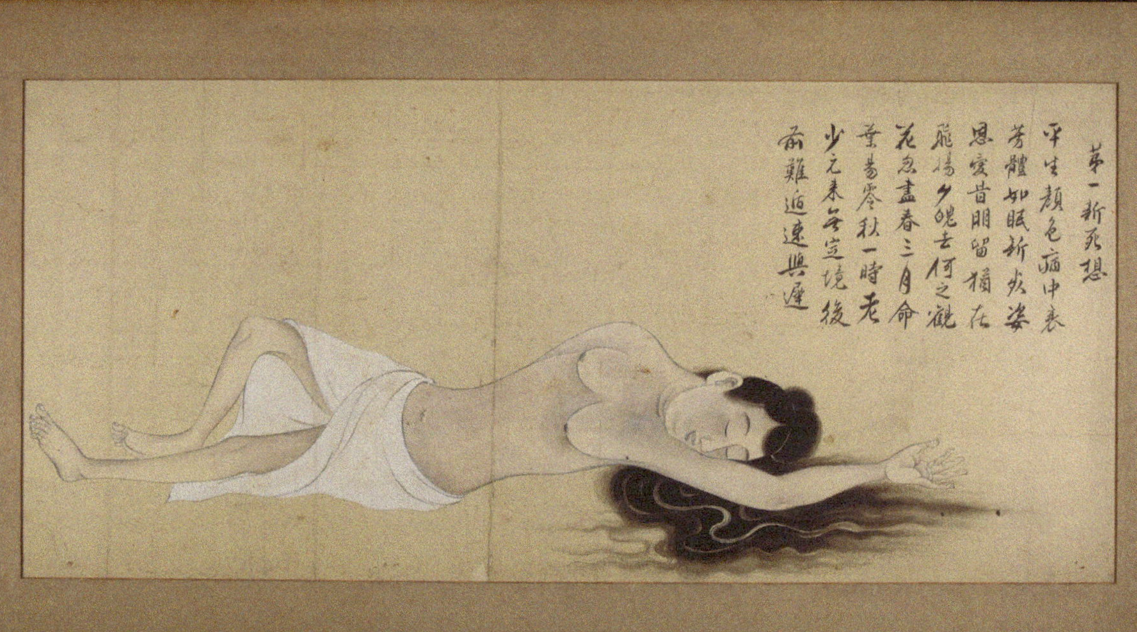
第一新死想

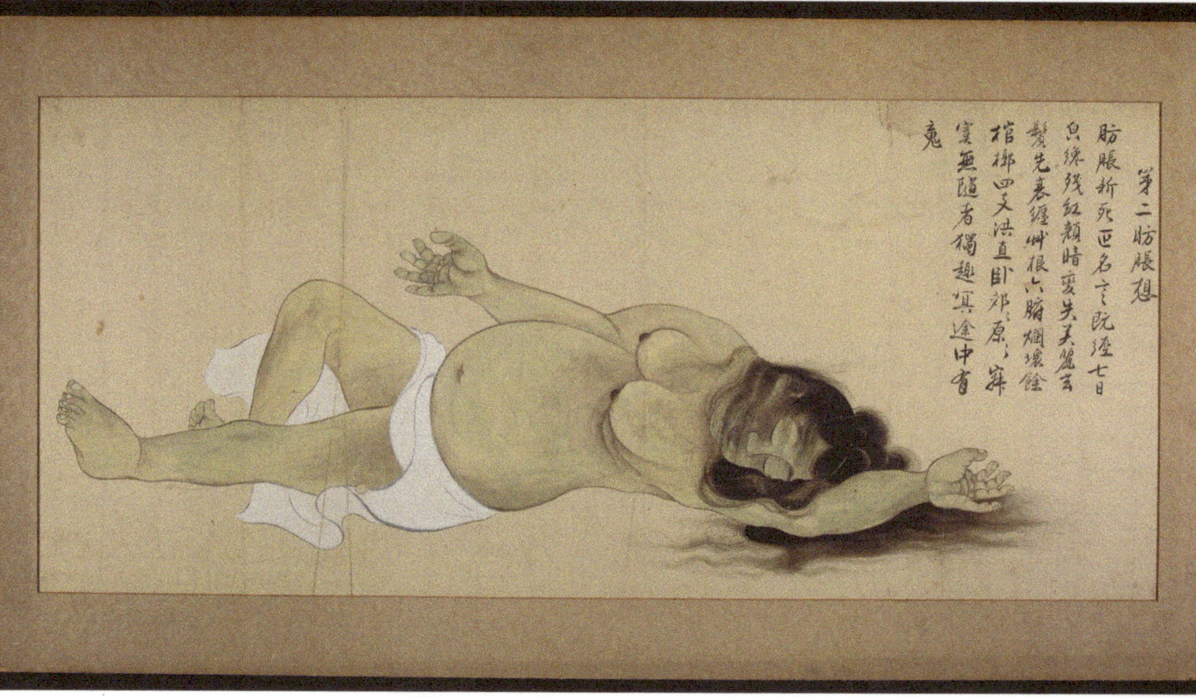
第二肪脹想

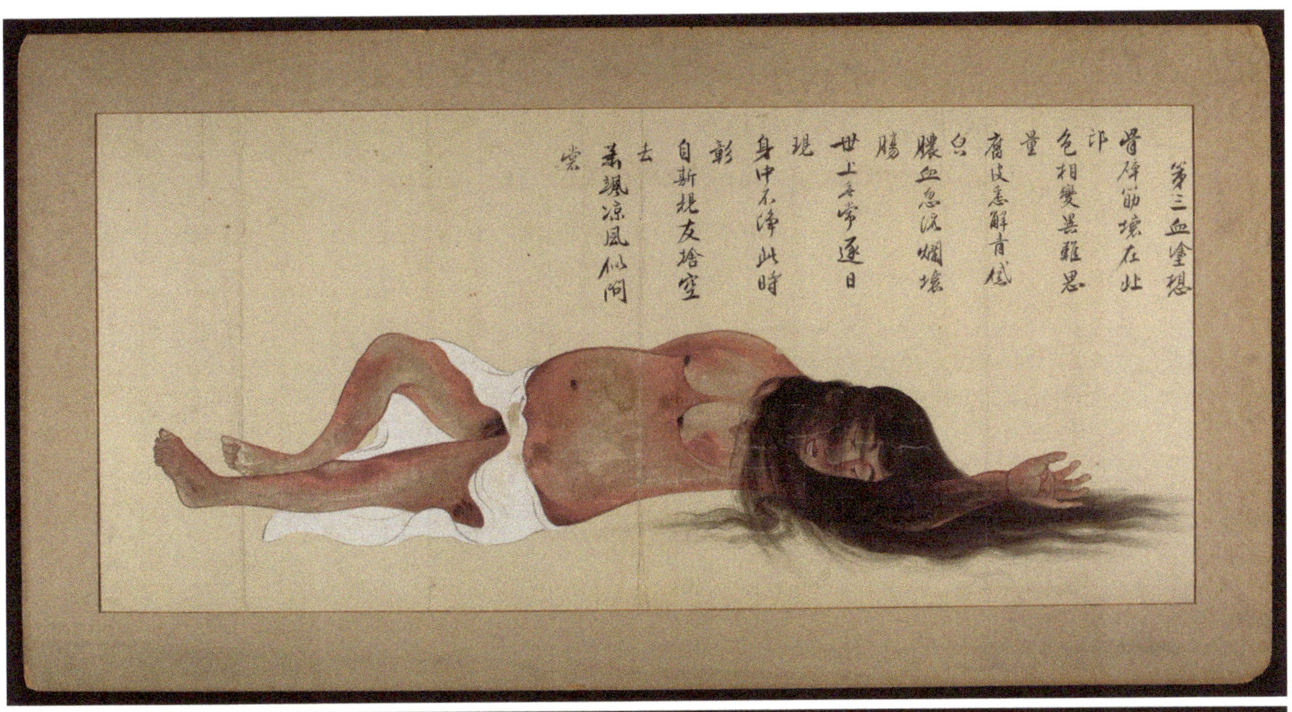

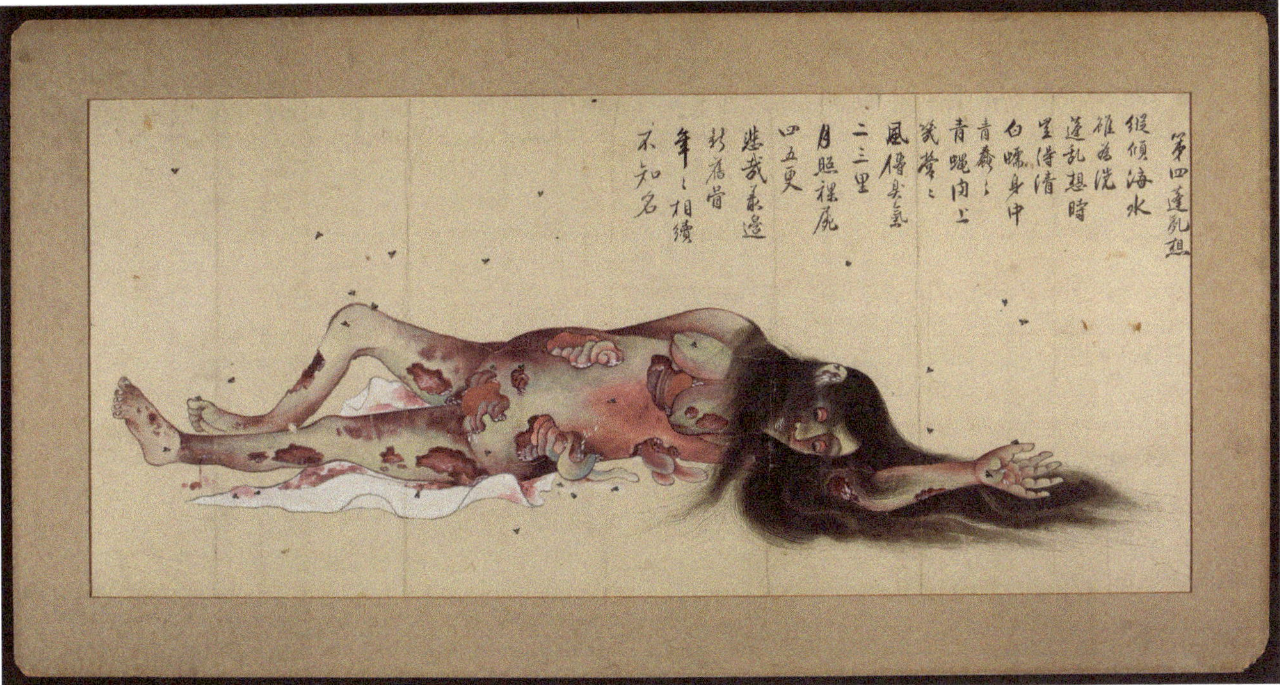

Figure 2.3. The fourth and fifth images of the *Kusōzu* series represent rupture of the body and exudation of blood (FM 125807.4,. 5-A115292d_009, 10).

Figure 2.2. *Kusōzu* watercolors representing a sequence of bodily decomposition: the first three images represent the living woman, the newly deceased, and the distension of the body (FM 125807.1, .2, .3-A115292d_003, 5, 6).

2A Sekishinsai Okada Tadaharu 赤心斎 岡田忠逕: *Nine Stages of Bodily Decay* (Kusōzu)

Chelsea Foxwell
University of Chicago

The *Buddhacarita: In Praise of Buddha's Acts* tells the story of how Siddhartha was raised as a crown prince in a lavish palace. Having received a prophecy that the boy would become an ascetic, Siddhartha's father sheltered him from everything painful and unpleasant. At the age of 29, however, Siddhartha requested to see the outside world. Proceeding in one direction, he encountered an elderly person bowed with the pain and afflictions of old age; in another, a sick man; and in another, a funeral procession. He returned to the palace grief-stricken: "The world is very painful, ruined by old age, illness, and death," he reflected (Aśvaghoṣa 2009, 30). He eventually attained enlightenment after meditating under the bodhi tree and expounded the fourfold truth: all life is suffering; the cause of suffering is desire; the abandonment of all desire will bring liberation from suffering; the path to freedom is brought by the Middle Way, between the extremes of self-indulgence and self-abnegation. By abandoning desire and leaving his earthly body behind, the Buddha achieved *nirvana* and release from the cruel cycle of death and rebirth.

Buddhist scriptures portrayed the body in negative terms as the site of hunger, thirst, and sexual desire: Just as a man who "has lived painfully afflicted in a prison" despises the prison and "seeks only freedom," so, too, should people rid themselves of attachment to this present existence and focus on attaining Buddhahood. Just as sailors would toss a broken, leaking boat to the sand without giving that unseaworthy vessel a further thought, so, too, says the *Buddhavamsa,* should people cast off their impure bodies leaking from nine orifices and seek enlightenment (Horner 1975).

Since ancient times, Buddhist texts advocated meditating on a decaying corpse or on a skull in order to remind followers of the impermanence of the human body in contrast to the eternal nature of *nirvana*. Death's ability to transform even the most beautiful body into a putrid sight was taken as evidence not only of impermanence, but also of the fundamental impurity of the human body itself. Within the male-centered Buddhist worldview, female bodies were considered particularly unclean, both because patriarchal thought blamed them for leading men astray, and because karmic retribution for acts in a previous life were cited as the reason for being born a woman, whose social status at the time was inferior to that of men.

Accordingly, whereas the sight of a beautiful body was known to incite desire, meditating on a repulsive, decaying corpse was seen as an effective means of quelling sexual desire in devout believers, particularly those who had taken the tonsure. The *Discourses on Mahayana Meditation and Contemplation* is one of several Buddhist texts that recommends meditation on the stages of death and decay in this manner. It explains:

> Even a woman with graceful eyebrows, jadelike eyes, white teeth, and red lips is as if covered by a mixture of feces with fat powder, or as if a putrefied corpses were clothed with silk and twill .... [C]ontemplation [on a decaying corpse] is a golden remedy for sensual desire. (Translated and quoted in Kanda 2005, 61)

The stages of bodily decay were devised as an aid to meditation. Believers were encouraged to construct and reflect on detailed mental images of each of the following stages: newly deceased, distention, rupture, exudation of blood, putrefaction, consumption by animals, skeleton, and disjunction of the bones. Scholars have pointed out that beyond quelling sexual desire, the images might also help viewers mourn and come to terms with the loss of a loved one. In the eighth stage of the Field Museum version we see a skull, strands of hair, and a few bones amid flourishing autumn flowers and grass. The ninth stage features a stone stupa with scattered wooden grave tablets, autumn trees and grasses, and small birds. Despite having experienced a gruesome process of decomposition, the body of the deceased young woman ultimately returns to nature, which continues to flourish around the durable stone marker that is used to memorialize her.

The Field Museum *Nine Stages of Bodily Decay* was donated to the museum by Frederick Gookin in 1923 and may date from the nineteenth century (Figures 2.2–2.5). Deceased persons were usually cremated in Japan, and while the sutras taught that leaving corpses in the open for consumption by animals was an expression of compassion, centuries had passed since this practice was common. By contrast, the practice of making *Nine Stages* handscrolls, hanging scrolls, and large horizontal images such as this set remained well known. As in many medieval cases, the images are accompanied by named titles of each stage of bodily decay, accompanied by poetry in literary Chinese. While these poems have been attributed to the eleventh-century Chinese literary figure Su Shi (1037–1101), they were likely composed in medieval Japan and attributed to the Chinese thinker.

Nine Stages pictures often included an image of the deceased woman while still alive. The Field's images are distinctive in their portrayal of a woman in Chinese dress: many other *Nine Stages* paintings and prints depicted the subjects in courtly Japanese robes. The deceased was sometimes interpreted as Ono no Komachi, a courtly Japanese poetess renowned for her beauty and literary gifts. The medieval Japanese Noh drama *Sotoba Komachi* portrays Komachi as an impoverished old woman whose beauty has faded and who is found seated on a burial marker. The living woman in the Field's set of paintings bears an elaborate headpiece with designs of flowers and birds. It has been suggested that she may be Yang Guifei

(719–756), the Chinese beauty who is said to have so monopolized the attention of Tang Emperor Xuanzong as to bring about the downfall of his court. Xuanzong's ministers put Yang Guifei to death, but the epic poem by Bai Juyi (772–846) recounts that Xuanzong experienced everlasting sorrow at her passing. If Japanese viewers identified this elegantly attired Chinese lady as Yang Guifei, then the identification adds layers of moral and poetic sentiment onto the established genre of *Nine Stages of Bodily Decay*.

The Field Museum *Nine Stages* exhibits careful attention to anatomical details, such as to bones in the hands and feet. In the fifth stage, the skin is removed in an almost didactic manner to produce careful windows onto the veins, muscles, and bones below. Other aspects suggest the artist's limited anatomical experience: there seems to be uncertainty about whether a skeleton has a nose, for example, and details such as the number of ribs are incorrect.

The corpse is positioned in a manner that arouses sexual desire only to subsequently negate it. In the first stage, for example, the newly deceased pillows her head on her arm, which is raised to expose the breasts and willowy torso. In stages 2 and 3, the body continues to be depicted in a sensual manner despite the facts of bloating and decomposition: stage 3 clearly depicts the pubic area, which is just visible where the white cloth has fallen away. In stages 5 through 7, by contrast, the body and face appear gruesome, yet in the final two stages order is restored with the whiteness of the bones, the flourishing of nature, and the presence of the stupa.

Acknowledgments

The author thanks Yoon-Jee Choi, Or Porath, and Zinan Wang for their invaluable assistance in this research.

References

Aśvaghoṣa, B. 2009. *Buddhacarita: In Praise of Buddha's Acts.* Translated by C. Willemen. Berkeley: Numata Center for Buddhist Translation and Research.

Horner, I. B. 1975. *The Minor Anthologies of the Pali Canon: Part III, Chroncicle of the Buddhas (Buddhavamsa) and Basket of Conduct (Cariyāpiṭaka).* Translated by I. B. Horner. London: Pali Text Society.

Kanda, F. 2005. "Beyond the Sensationalism: Images of a Decaying Corpse in Japanese Buddhist Art." *Art Bulletin* 87, no. 1: 24–49.

McCausland, S. 2009. *Chinese Romance from a Japanese Brush: Kano Sansetsu's* Chōgonka [Song of Everlasting Sorrow] *Scrolls in the Chester Beatty Library.* London: Scala.

Yamamoto, S. 2015. *Kusōzu o yomu: Kuchite yuku shitai no bijutsushi.* Tokyo: Kadokawa.

Yamamoto, S., and Nishiyama, M. 2009. *Kusōzu shiryō shūsei.* Tokyo: Iwata Shoin.

An opposing viewpoint—championed by American demographers Jay Olshansky and Bruce Carnes in their 2001 book *The Quest for Immortality: Science at the Frontiers of Aging*—is that the human lifespan has a fixed biological limit. Among other things, they suggest that our lives are subject to a certain inherent level of mortality that will remain even if we eliminate or at least drastically reduce all external and disease-driven causes of death. Confirming this interpretation, in a 2009 paper, Korean aging researchers Byung Mook Weon and Jung Ho Je reported results from a mathematical model designed to estimate the maximum possible human lifespan. Using life tables for Swedish women for the period between 1950 and 2005, they derived a figure of about 125 years. At the same time, they determined that the probability of survival is close to its upper limit in datasets for modern human populations in industrialized countries. Accordingly, the expectation is that maximum lifespan in human populations can increase to an upper limit of about 125 years but not beyond.

Moreover, there is now good reason to question the confident expectation that, enabled by medical advances, the average human lifespan will continue to expand into the future. In a 2005 paper, Olshansky and colleagues concluded that estimates of how long Americans are going to live in the twenty-first century could be incorrect because of current trends in obesity, to which we could add the emergence of new diseases and their varied impact on populations (see Wali in this volume, on responses to the pandemic). Kontis and colleagues' analysis of the effect of obesity on longevity indicates that the steady increase in life expectancy observed in industrialized populations over the past 200 years could soon go into reverse gear (Kontis et al. 2017). In a similar manner, the COVID-19 pandemic has demonstrated that the human immunological system provides differentiated levels of protection, leaving some more vulnerable than others, as well as more susceptible to dying because of the emergence of new infectious disease.

A key point concerning differences in interpretation on this issue is the crucial distinction between the maximum lifespan achieved in any human population at a particular time and the *maximum possible* lifespan that any individual, with full access to a good quality health service, can attain (Imai and Soneji 2007). In the oft-quoted words of English philosopher Thomas Hobbes, human life under original gathering-and-hunting conditions is generally perceived as "nasty, brutish and short." Although it is widely accepted that in industrialized societies average life expectancy has progressively increased thanks to a wide array of technological and medical advances, it is not at all clear whether the maximum possible length of the lifespan has also increased.

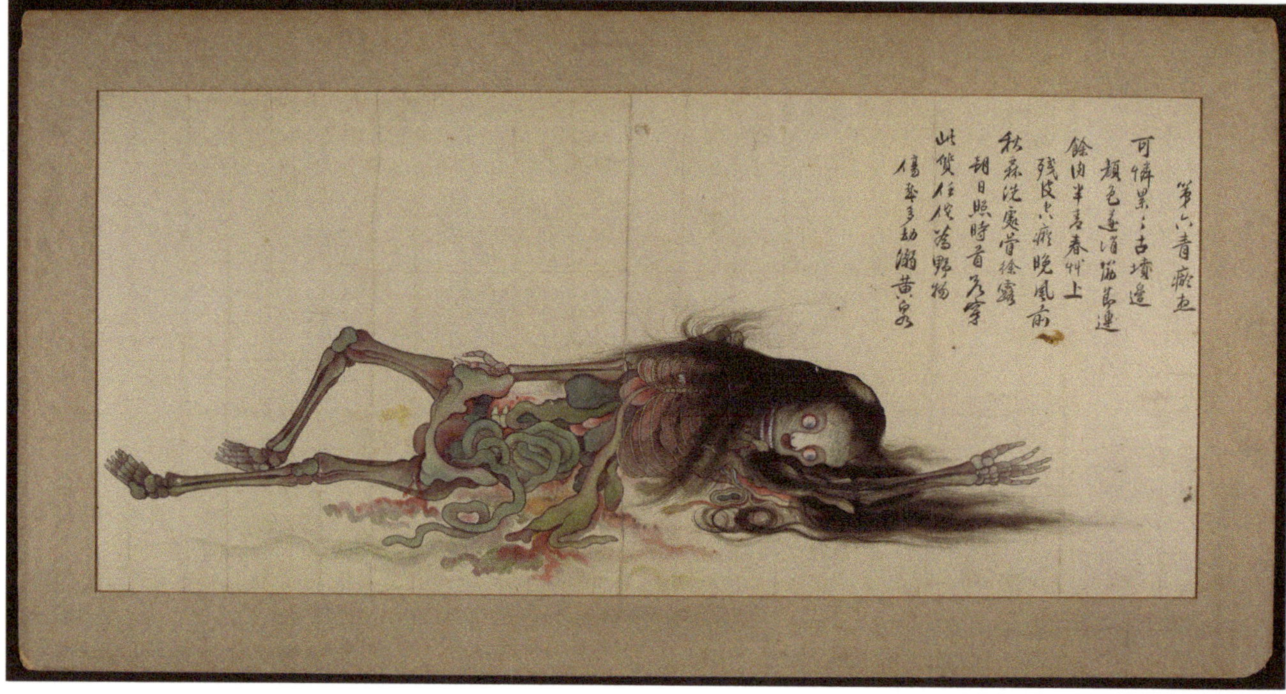

Figure 2.4. The putrefaction stage is followed by consumption by animals in the sixth and seventh images of the *Kusōzu* paintings (FM 125807.6, .7-A115292d_013, 4).

Figure 2.5. The final stages of the *Kusōzu* paintings represent the skeleton, the disjunction of the bones, and the final resting place of the body (FM 125807.8, .9, .10- A115292d_017, 8, 21).

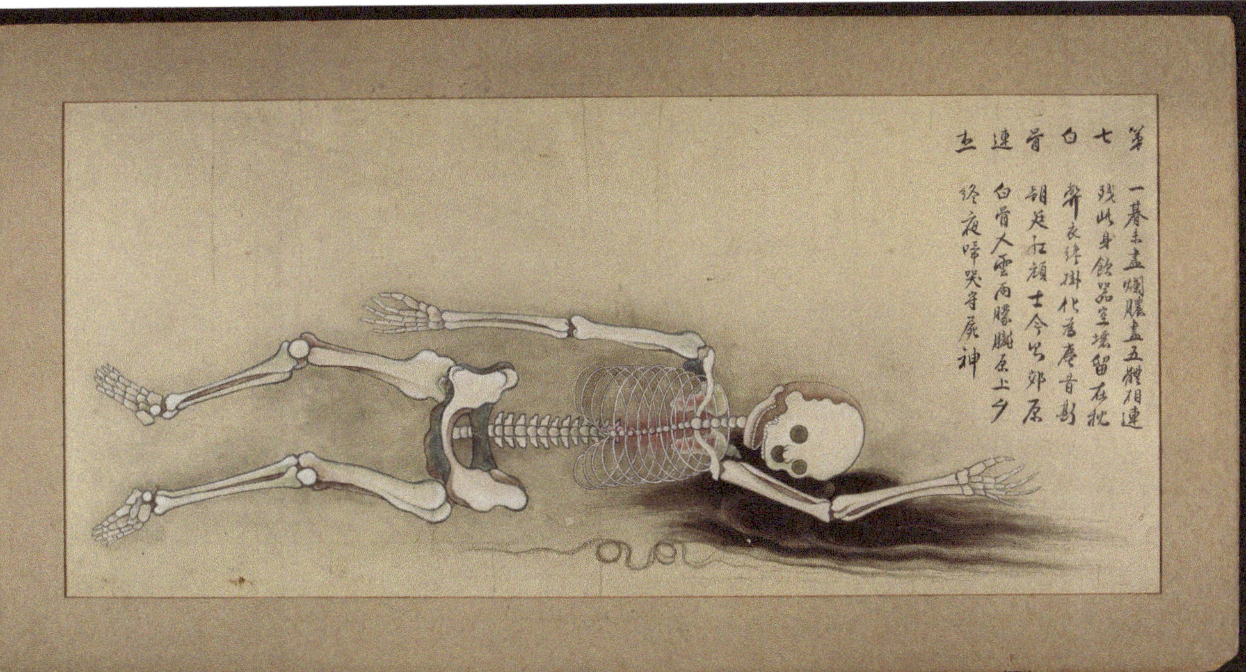

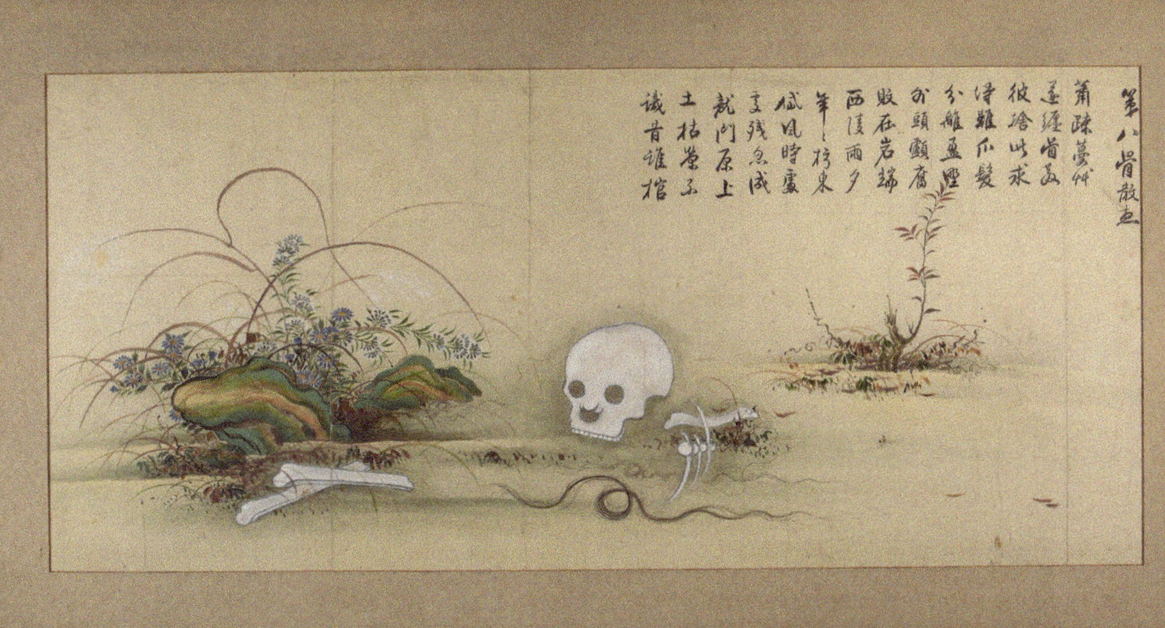

Figure 2.7. Lead pewter plate with brass rim design including examples of animals holding the *lingzhi* (fungus of immortality) in the mouth. Consuming the *lingzhi* was thought to convey energy and immortality (FM 110086).

←

Figure 2.6. Roman basin (reproduction) with representation of immortal gods Mars and Venus (FM 24010).

2B Daoist Immortals, the *Lingzhi* Fungus, and the Search for Immortality

Deborah Bekken
Field Museum

The search for immortality and the extension of the lifespan are often culturally linked, although in concept they represent two somewhat separate activities (Figure 2.6). The transition to immortality requires a transformation in the spiritual realm to free the spirit from the earthly manifestation of the body. Extension of lifespan is tied more directly to the physical body as it experiences aging and senescence. In both cases though, various mixtures of ingredients—elixirs—may play an important role. Almost always ingested either as food, liquid, or in some cases smoke or vapor, elixirs have an important role in mediating and affecting the transition from life to death to afterlife, and potentially the transition to immortality.

The ancient spiritual and ritual practices that coalesced in the later Han period (206 BCE–220 CE) into a more formalized set of religious and philosophical beliefs that became Daoism evolved over centuries (Copp 2018). There are legions of Daoist deities, sages, and wise adepts that inhabit various forms and live in sacred places such as mountains, blessed islands, and celestial places such as the moon. They have achieved immortality either through divine intervention or by extensive study or an extraordinary life or talent. An ancient example is the Queen Mother of the West who lives in the moon with many attendants in the form of animals, including a magical rabbit who pounds elixirs in a mortar and pestle. Many immortals are based on historical or legendary figures. Of later appearance in Daoist literature and practice, a core set of several individuals known collectively as the Eight Immortals is among the most well-known. Drawn from various walks of life and life histories, the Eight Immortals include four pairs of opposites: male and female, rich and poor, military and civilian, and young and old. They reinforce a central idea in Daoism that anyone can pursue mental cultivation.

The nature of beliefs and practices surrounding death and the interest in immortality was more prominent at certain times than at others. Nevertheless, Daoism does recognize a richly detailed and diverse set of beliefs regarding immortality and how it may be achieved (e.g., de Bary and Bloom 1999). Proper burial and the attentive care of one's descendants is important. Achieving immortality is difficult and requires many steps, such as mental cultivation, correct living, and a corresponding incorporation of, or surrender to, the Dao or the Way, a concept that loosely translates as the force and universality of energy that animates everything that happens, all of nature, and the cosmos (Ebrey 2010, 46–49; Watson 2007). Understanding the Dao is the work of several lifetimes, and perhaps truly unattainable, but key concepts include the embeddedness of all things in nature, the interdependence of opposite states, and a focus on yielding to the flow of nature and energy (Watson 2007).

The search for immortality can also include the use of elixirs (e.g., de Bary and Bloom 1999). There is a long history of alchemical attempts to develop elixirs to extend the lifespan, to achieve immortality, or to preserve the mortal remains of the body prior to burial. Many preparations made use of minerals and elements such as cinnabar, gold, sulphur, arsenic, and lead, often in deadly combinations. Many preparations used plant and animal ingredients, of which several are still in wide use such as the *lingzhi*, otherwise known as the fungus of immortality or the mushroom of immortality (Figures 2.7–2.9).

The *lingzhi*, *Ganoderma lucidum*, is also known as the reishi in Japanese. It is widely cultivated and has been a component of traditional Chinese medicine for centuries. It has a glossy brown surface appearance with a firm or woody texture; the exhibition includes a botanical specimen, now dried. All parts of the *lingzhi*, such as the spores or the fruiting body, have medicinal uses. Many health benefits are ascribed to *lingzhi*, including longevity and improvements in energy, as well as regulation of blood sugar, liver function, and other systems. As with many products from nature with traditional uses, it is being investigated today for the degree to which there are clinically measurable effects. It is widely available and marketed as a supplement for longevity and general health, including immune system support.

Given its long association with medicinal benefits of such power as to include immortality in the right preparations, the *lingzhi* is also potent symbolically. Hiding in plain sight in many artworks from East Asia, and especially China, is a stylized depiction of the *lingzhi*. Often depicted as an upside-down heart or kidney bean shape, the *lingzhi* is part of the rich visual vocabulary of Asian art. It is often used both as a symbol of longevity and, due to its similarity in shape to a wish-granting scepter known as a *ruyi*, as a visual rebus that expresses the desire that a wish be granted (Bartholomew 2006).

In the examples from the exhibition, the *lingzhi* appears in several configurations. The rhinoceros horn cup (Figure 2.8) employs motifs of the *lingzhi*, as well as bamboo. Rhinoceros horn libation cups were highly valued gifts made primarily for scholars, but the horn itself

Figure 2.8. Rhinoceros horn cup with stylized *lingzhi* fungus on the body of the cup (FM 110574).

was also considered by Daoists to have magical properties. The pewter tray (Figure 2.7) is surrounded by a border of auspicious motifs that include the *lingzhi* as a symbol of longevity. The ivory figure holds a fly whisk in one hand and a *lingzhi* in the other (Figure 2.9). In all these forms the *lingzhi* functions either as an auspicious symbol of longevity or as a visual rebus for the granting of a wish.

Daoism is certainly not alone in devoting energy and interest to the extension of life and the pursuit of immortality. The richness and detail with which Daoist practitioners have pursued these goals across centuries offers abundant evidence of our collective human desire to live on, to continue to experience the world, and to become a part of nature in a manner that transcends the body and escapes the boundaries of the human lifespan.

References

Bartholomew, T. T. 2006. *Hidden Meanings in Chinese Art.* San Francisco: Asian Art Museum of San Francisco.

Copp, P. 2018. "Daoism and Buddhism in Traditional China." In *China: Visions through the Ages,* edited by L. Niziolek, D. Bekken, and G. Feinman, 205–28. Chicago: University of Chicago Press.

De Bary, W. T., and Bloom, I. 1999. *Sources of Chinese Tradition: From Earliest Times to 1600,* Vol. 1, 2nd ed. New York: Columbia University Press.

Ebrey, P. B. 2010. *The Cambridge Illustrated History of China,* 2nd ed. Cambridge: Cambridge University Press.

Watson, B. 2007. "Introduction." In *Tao Te Ching Lao Tzu,* translated by S. Addiss and S. Lombardo, xvii–xxx. Chicago: Shambhala.

The unusually long average and maximum lifespan of humans is undoubtedly linked, among many other factors, to the universal occurrence of *menopause* in women—the abrupt cessation of fertility at about 50 years of age. Until recently, menopause was regarded as a unique feature of the human lifecycle in comparison to all other mammals. However, new research has revealed that five whale species (Foster et al. 2012) and the Indian elephant (Lahdenperä and Lummaa 2014) also show abrupt cessation of fertility long before the average age at death. Nevertheless, the mammals concerned are all large-bodied, long-lived species whose lifespans are about as long as would be expected for their substantial size, so the human case stands out as being especially unusual.

Death from natural causes is universal among mammals and longevity is fairly predictable, given the existence of a species-specific maximum lifespan for any particular species. Nevertheless, artificial extension of the lifespan—perhaps culminating in *immortality*—has long been a cherished goal in human societies (see Bekken in this volume). Throughout human history, humans have obsessively sought mechanisms to extend life through the use of elixirs, sacred substance, and favors to the gods; and the emergence of religion in itself could be related to this human deep desire (Hall 2003).

Nowadays, with the advent of modern medicine, it may seem as though long-term postponement of death has become a realistic prospect for the future. But this may well be a vain hope. The much-vaunted "improvement" in human longevity attributed to continued improvements in medical care may be an illusion. Whereas it is undoubtedly true that *average human lifespan* has tended to increase in industrialized societies (see Tuljapurkar, Li, and Boe 2000), this may simply reflect the fact that more individuals are living longer and approaching the natural limit more closely. However, across the board, *average human lifespan* is still well below the inferred maximum of 125 years, and there is no reason to expect that even the best medical care, if accessible, will allow anyone to live longer than that. Furthermore, it is important to remember that artificial extension of human life is only worthwhile if the additional years are relatively free of health issues. The total period over which any person enjoys good health without any kind of physical handicap is now called the *healthspan*. It is surely more rewarding to seek ways of increasing human healthspans than to maximize lifespans.

The issue of whether there is an upper limit to human lifespan is directly linked to a key question that has long concerned biologists: Why do senescence and death occur at all? (see also Kirkwood and Rose 1991). The Bible, Shakespeare, and healthcare practitioners all portray aging and dying as inevitable facts of human existence. But why should this be so? Why are we not immortal? As proclaimed in the title of Peter Medawar's 1952 book *An Unsolved Problem of Biology*, this is a fundamental issue that has still not been definitively resolved. We know that various other organisms, notably viruses and bacteria, are potentially immortal, continuously propagating themselves. Individuals may succumb to lack of resources, accidents, predators, or disease, but they never die of old age. In principle, natural selection is expected to promote survival and continued reproduction of individuals. So it is not at all clear why humans and most multicellular animals have a relatively fixed maximum lifespan and do not simply survive indefinitely.

One simple view is that senescence is the unavoidable result of accumulated wear and tear and that we eventually die because we are well and truly burned out. As George Williams noted in a seminal paper in 1957, this view really stems from a simplistic analogy with disintegration of human artifacts. However, unlike a desktop computer or a washing machine, living organisms are equipped with an array of mechanisms for self-repair. So why should deterioration be inevitable? Williams proposed that senescence has actually been built into our genetic make-up through evolution so that we usually remain healthy throughout a standard period of active reproduction but then begin to decline and eventually die.

Numerous hypotheses have been proposed to explain the evolution of aging, but they generally fall into two categories (see Morley 1995). *Error theories* are based on the wear-and-tear notion of chance accumulation of damage to the body's tissues. This may be either environmental—including disruption of DNA and cumulative production of noxious chemical agents in cells—or internal, resulting from progressive failure of genetic systems for maintenance and repair (Stearns 1977). Other theories, by contrast, are founded on the idea that aging has been *pre-programmed by evolution* and is regulated by biological clocks across the lifespan (Szilard 1959). Such regulation is attributed to changes in expression of genes governing systems responsible for maintenance, repair, and defense. A key point is that natural selection should generally become weaker as an organism ages. It is suggested that aging may have evolved because external causes of mortality (resource depletion, predation, disease, accidental death)—which are likely to be largely random—gradually decrease

Figure 2.9. Daoist immortal holding a fly whisk and *lingzhi* fungus (FM 126823).

the probability that an organism will still be alive as age increases. Natural selection could hence favor developments leading to a higher reproductive rate at a young age and a shorter overall lifespan because the net outcome is a higher lifetime breeding success. This introduces the crucial notion, now well established in research into aging, that there is some kind of *trade-off*. It is proposed that aging occurs as a byproduct of investing in breeding rather than in upkeep of the body (Ossewaarde et al. 2005; Pavard, Metcalf, and Heyer 2008; Perls and Fretts 2001), because external causes of mortality will eventually kill an individual regardless of resources committed to maintenance of bodily functions (Harvey and Zammuto 1985).

In his "disposable soma" theory of aging (eloquently portrayed in his 1999 book *Time of Our Lives: The Science of Human Aging*), British biologist Tom Kirkwood proposed that pre-programmed mortality may have arisen as an energy-saving adaptation with reduced regulation of errors in body cells (also see Kirkwood 1999; Kirkwood and Austad 2000). He was particularly influenced by the observation that human fibroblast cells in culture have a finite lifespan, reflecting a constraint on the total number of divisions of any cell to about 60. Furthermore, the lifespan of cultured cells decreases with the age of the donor, indicating that a cellular clock of some kind has been ticking away.

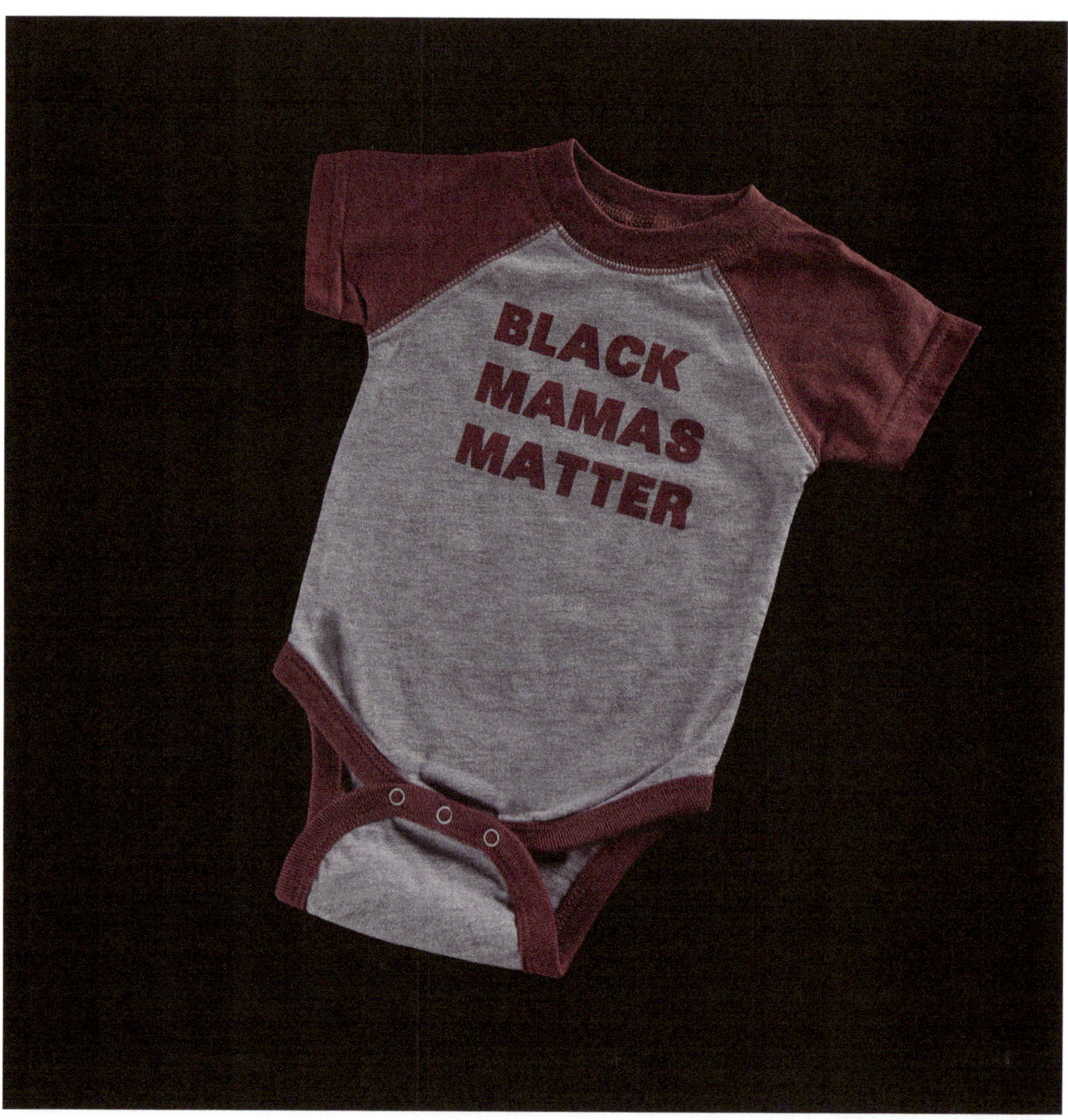

Figure 2.10. Black Mamas Matter onesie that advocates for building awareness about Black maternal health, rights, and justice.

2C On Health Disparities and Motherless Children

Kimberly Mutcherson
Rutgers Law School

Serena Williams, one of the greatest athletes of all time, almost died while becoming a mother. Williams is a global superstar, one of the most dominant women to ever play in the WTA, who even won the 2017 Australian Open title while eight weeks pregnant. She is an entrepreneur, multi-millionaire, fashion designer, wife, sister, friend, daughter, and a mother. She is also a Black woman who, like far too many others in the United States, almost died because of her pregnancy. Williams delivered her daughter via an emergency C-section that initially seemed to go well. But the next day she began to feel short of breath, a worrying sign for a person with a history of blood clots and pulmonary embolisms. She assumed that the difficulty breathing indicated a coming pulmonary embolism. This world-class athlete, whose entire life has centered around being in tune with and control of her body, recognized worrying symptoms and immediately raised the alarm with a nearby nurse. Williams said that she needed a "CT scan with contrast and IV heparin (a blood thinner)" (Haskell 2018). The nurse suggested she was simply having a bad reaction to pain medication, but Williams did not back down. A physician at the hospital performed an ultrasound of her legs, not a CT scan, and found nothing. Still not satisfied, Williams insisted on the CT scan that she'd already requested. The medical team sent her for the CT scan, which revealed several small blood clots in Williams' lungs. She was soon given the drip that she'd asked for and lived to tell the tale.

Black women die or experience significant injury during pregnancy, childbirth, or in the immediate postpartum period far too frequently in the United States (Figure 2.10). The names of these women appear in numerous news reports as the crisis in maternal mortality for Black women has become a more mainstream discussion. Women like Dr. Shalon Irving, a CDC epidemiologist who studied health disparities, who died from complications related to high blood pressure three weeks after giving birth to her daughter (Martin and Montagne 2017). Or Sha-Asia Washington, who died after going into cardiac arrest while in labor (Dickson 2020). Or Dr. Chaniece Wallace, a pediatric chief-resident who died due to complications from preeclampsia two days after giving birth to her daughter (Burke 2020). So much preventable death at a time that should be full of wonder and happiness.

The US is one of the most dangerous countries for a woman who is pregnant or giving birth. In this country, 700 women die annually due to pregnancy or delivery complications. Unsurprisingly, there are significant racial disparities in the maternal mortality rate. According to the Commonwealth Fund, Black mothers in the United States have been more likely to die than white mothers for 100 years (Declercq and Zephyrin 2020). Black women and American Indian/Alaska Native Women are two to three times more likely to die from a pregnancy complication than are white women—a disparity that increases with age. Though higher education levels typically lead to better health outcomes, that is not so when it comes to maternal mortality. Black college-educated women are five times more likely to die from pregnancy-related complications than are white women with similar levels of education (Petersen et al. 2019). Thus, the data alarmingly reveals that education exacerbates the maternal mortality gap. Maternal deaths are more common among Black mothers with a college education than they are among white mothers with less than a high-school education (Declercq and Zephyrin 2020). Even where death does not result, research shows that Black and Latina women experience significantly higher risk of severe maternal morbidity, such as preeclampsia, which is much more common than maternal death (Artiga, Pham, and Orgera 2020). Despite advances in medicine, Black women continue to die at shocking rates because of pregnancy and childbirth, and efforts to combat this disparity have been sporadic and decidedly ineffectual (Declercq and Zephyrin 2020).

To be a Black woman in America is to live within a system that does not invest in your well-being. The historical line of mistreatment of Black women's bodies runs from the father of gynecology who experimented on enslaved women (Khabele et al. 2021), to the forced sterilizations of Black women across decades (Roberts 1999), to incarcerated women who have labored while chained to hospital beds (Goodwin 2020). The dignity of pregnancy and motherhood has frequently been denied to Black women, so it is no surprise to see persistent disparity in birth outcomes for Black women as compared to others.

Critically, it is racism, not race, that increases the risk of death for Black pregnant women. Research shows that the compounding effects of racism and the stress that it brings to the lives of Black women has a deleterious impact on health (Patterson, Becker, and Baluran 2022). Healthcare is an arena where Black women face deeply problematic interactions with clinicians who are blind to their own lack of cultural competence. One study found that, as compared with the white counterparts, Black women were more likely to report: unfair and disrespectful treatment from healthcare providers because of their race; being denied decisional autonomy during labor and delivery; and pressure to consent to a C-section. Low-income women on Medicaid, in contrast to women with private health insurance, were more likely to report no postpartum visit, a return to work within two months after the child's birth, less access to postpartum support (emotional and practical); a lack of decisional autonomy during labor and delivery, and unfair treatment and disrespect because of their insurance status.

As these findings illustrate, the experiences that women have with maternity care and childbirth differ significantly across race, class, and insurance status. The maternal morbidity and mortality gap cannot be narrowed or eliminated without considering the root causes of racial disparities. Those causes can be related to health status (weight, chronic illnesses, nutrition), but the experiences that Black women have with the healthcare providers tasked with keeping them and their newborns safe is equally relevant and harder to quantify (Declercq and Zephyrin 2020).

There is no denying that the United States has a maternal morbidity and mortality crisis, and that crisis is even more pronounced in Black communities. Every pregnant woman or person deserves to have the tools to maximize their own health during pregnancy. As has been true for so much of the history of Black women in the United States, death presents itself in times that should be joyous. This will continue to be the case until there is a sustained commitment to identifying and weeding out bias in medicine, ensuring access to high-quality prenatal care for all pregnant people, providing community-based postpartum services and, most of all, valuing the lives of Black pregnant women as much as this country values those of other pregnant women.

References

Artiga, S., Pham, O., and Orgera, K. 2020. "Racial Disparities in Maternal and Infant Health: An Overview." Kaiser Family Foundation, November 10. https://www.kff.org/report-section/racial-disparities-in-maternal-and-infant-health-an-overview-issue-brief.

Burke, M. 2020. "Death of Black Mother after Birth of First Child Highlights Racial Disparities in Maternal Mortality." NBCNews.com, November 6. https://www.nbcnews.com/news/us-news/death-black-mother-after-birth-first-child-highlights-racial-disparities-n1246841.

Centers for Disease Control and Prevention (CDC). 2022. "Infographic: Racial/Ethnic Disparities in Pregnancy-Related Deaths–United States, 2007–2016." cdc.gov, April 13. https://www.cdc.gov/reproductivehealth/maternal-mortality/disparities-pregnancy-related-deaths/infographic.html.

Declercq, E., and Zephyrin, L. 2020. "Maternal Mortality in the United States: A Primer." Commonwealthfund.org, December 16. https://www.commonwealthfund.org/publications/issue-brief-report/2020/dec/maternal-mortality-united-states-primer.

Dickson, E. J. 2020. "Death of Sha-Asia Washington, Pregnant 26-Year-Old Black Woman, Highlights Devastating Trend." *Rolling Stone*, 13 July. https://www.rollingstone.com/culture/culture-features/shaasia-washington-death-woodhull-hospital-black-maternal-mortality-rate-1026069.

Goodwin, M. 2020. *Policing the Womb: Invisible Women and the Criminalization of Motherhood*. Cambridge: Cambridge University Press.

Haskell, R. 2018. "Serena Williams on Motherhood, Marriage, and Making Her Comeback." *Vogue*, January 10. https://www.vogue.com/article/serena-williams-vogue-cover-interview-february-2018.

Khabele, D., Holcomb, K., Connors, N., and Bradley, L. 2021. "A Perspective on James Marion Sims, MD, and Antiblack Racism in Obstetrics and Gynecology." *Journal of Minimally Invasive Gynecology* 28, no. 2: 153–55. https://doi.org/10.1016/j.jmig.2020.10.027.

Martin, N., and Montagne, R. 2017. "Black Mothers Keep Dying after Giving Birth: Shalon Irving's Story Explains Why." NPR, December 8. https://www.npr.org/2017/12/07/568948782/black-mothers-keep-dying-after-giving-birth-shalon-irvings-story-explains-why.

Patterson, E., Becker, A., and Baluran, D. 2022. "Gendered Racism on the Body: An Intersectional Approach to Maternal Mortality in the United States." *Population Research and Policy Review*, January 27. https://doi.org/10.1007/s11113-021-09691-2.

Petersen, E., Davis, N., Goodman, D., Cox, S., Syverson, C., Seed, K., Shapiro-Mendoza, C., Callaghan, W., and Barfield, W. 2019. "Racial/Ethnic Disparities in Pregnancy-Related Deaths—United States, 2007–2016." *Morbidity and Mortality Weekly Report* 68, no. 35: 762–65. http://dx.doi.org/10.15585/mmwr.mm6835a3.

Roberts, D. E. 1999. *Killing the Black Body: Race, Reproduction, and the Meaning of Liberty*. New York: Vintage.

An alternative suggestion favored by Peter Medawar (1952), who won the Nobel Prize for major contributions to immunology, is that late-acting deleterious mutations may accumulate because there is only weak selection against them (Vijg and Dong 2020). Consider a population of otherwise immortal individuals whose fertility does not decrease over time. Some individuals will still be eliminated because of external factors such as lack of resources, predation, and disease. External risks of mortality are present throughout life, so their effects are cumulative and older age cohorts will contain fewer survivors. As a result, young cohorts make a greater contribution to the next generation than older ones. This is why selection against deleterious mutations that take effect late in life—affecting only a reduced number of older individuals—will be relatively weak. So such mutations may progressively become more prevalent over time.

One advantage of Medawar's hypothesis is that it yields a straightforward testable prediction: species that are subject to high external levels of mortality under natural conditions should age more quickly and have shorter lifespans (Peccei 2001). Testing the prediction is complicated by the fact that, as with most biological features, large-bodied mammals generally live longer than small-bodied mammals. Once appropriate scaling analyses take body size into account, however, it emerges that the predicted inverse relationship between mortality rates and lifespan does indeed exist. Mammal species that are subject to heavy mortality have relatively short lifespans and vice versa. Moreover, analysis of data from field studies has revealed that the age at which sexual maturity is achieved decreases as natural mortality rates increase. So species that are exposed to heavy mortality begin to breed earlier. As already noted, compared to other mammals, primates have relatively long lifespans. Their typical arboreal habits are seemingly associated with lower mortality. However, the development of exceptionally long lifespans in ground-dwelling humans requires a different kind of explanation. Undoubtedly, in our case cultural innovations that reduced death from resource depletion, accidents, predation, and (eventually) diseases played an important part. In any case, according to Medawar's hypothesis the relatively long lifespan of humans indicates that humans are biologically adapted for relatively low mortality.

In 1957, George Williams proposed a somewhat different evolutionary aging hypothesis, based on the fact that a single gene may have a number of different effects (*antagonistic pleiotropy*). Williams suggested that certain effects that positively influence survival early in life might exert negative influences at a later stage. Because there are many more young individuals in a typical population, even quite limited positive effects of a given gene early in life can be subject to strong selection. By contrast, selection against large negative effects that emerge only later in life is likely to be weak. Williams offered an imaginary example in which a gene promoting calcium deposition in bones during development also promotes deleterious accumulation of calcium later in life. Once again, the concept of a trade-off is involved, but Williams' aging hypothesis suffers from the drawback that it is largely theoretical and that very few practical examples have been reported since it was originally proposed. Nevertheless, it is notable that Williams' hypothesis also predicts that—in species with high levels of externally caused mortality—individuals should age more quickly and have shorter lifespans.

A radically different perspective is presented in David Sinclair and Matthew LaPlante's 2019 book *Lifespan: Why We Age—and Why We Don't Have To*. This is based on his *Informational Theory of Aging*, developed over recent decades on the basis of extensive experimental studies at the molecular level conducted on organisms ranging from yeast to mice in his and many other laboratories. As in several other examples, Sinclair's hypothesis depends on a trade-off, in this case between resources needed for reproduction and repair of the fundamental genetic material. However, aging effects are attributed not to accumulating mutational errors in genes themselves but to increasing disruptions of *epigenetic* chemical tags that govern and guide their function. The *Informational Theory of Aging* differs from other proposals in that numerous experiments have indicated ways in which the effects of deleterious changes over time might be mitigated or even reversed. In sum, Sinclair argues persuasively that aging is not an unavoidable fact of life but a *disease* that can be cured (Gavrilov and Gavrilova 2018). The findings that he reports indicate that it should soon be possible to combat aging affects and add healthful decades to human lifespans. But it is not at all clear whether the treatments he envisages could extend the maximum lifespan beyond 125 years. Although Sinclair reports striking increases in age-at-death with experimental animals, there is as yet no evidence for survival beyond the maximum recorded lifespans for any of the species concerned. In a not-too-distant future, we may be enabled to live healthier, longer lives; but the long-sought goal of *immortality* will surely forever remain beyond our grasp.

This contrasts harshly with the way in which humans fantasize with the limits of their own existence and mortality. As this exhibit particularly shows, art has been a remarkable medium through which we express idealized notions of beauty, maturity, and the twilight of life. It is curious that when it comes to art produced to express such notions the number seven is a recurring theme. A superb illustration of this is the renowned painting *Seven Ages of Woman*, crafted in 1544 by the medieval German artist Hans Baldung Grien. This well-known masterpiece depicts seven female life-stages ranging from infancy through puberty and on into maturity and old age. An oft-quoted monologue from Shakespeare's play As *You Like It*, probably written in about 1599, provides a male counterpart. Jaques, a discontented nobleman, lists successive intervals, now widely known as the "seven ages of man": infant, schoolboy, lover, soldier, justice, pantaloon, and second childhood. (The word pantaloon here refers not to trousers but to a person showing signs of senility.) Interestingly, biology similarly leads us to distinguish seven key stages in the human lifespan too, though they are somewhat different: infancy, early childhood, later childhood, juvenile period, adolescence, adulthood, and old age. Similar parallels can be made with how the stages of death have been artistically represented by both ancient and modern cultures. A remarkable example is *the Nine Stages of Bodily Decay* depicted by Japanese Buddhist monks (see Foxwell in this volume). They reflected on the impermanence of the human body, and, opposed to the aesthetic beauty of *nirvana*, envisioned death as a disgusting process of decay and evanescence of the body.

Returning to biology, investigation of longevity and human lifecycles, in general, has been particularly enriched through information derived from archaeological and bio-archaeological research. Human remains found in ancient cemeteries are sometimes preserved under excellent conditions, yielding a large proportion of available data when carefully examined in contexts (*archaeothanatology*). Through them, it is possible to study broad lifecycle characteristics (*palaeodemography*) in such population samples. However, it should not be forgotten that cemetery remains are death assemblages and do not provide a cross-sectional view of lives led in general populations.

Following the discovery of human skeletons at any given site, specialists are confronted with two practical tasks: inference of sex and estimation of age at death for the individuals represented. This information is of importance when trying to reconstruct life-history patterns for prehistoric populations. There is, in fact, a connection between sex and longevity because there is a certain tendency in human populations, other things being equal, for women to live longer than men, despite the challenges of childbirth (see also Mutcherson in this volume, on other factors affecting this tendency). In the USA, for example, the average life expectancy for women is currently around 81 years, whereas for men it is 77 years (Woolf, Masters, and Aron 2022; Woolf and Schoomaker 2019). In Europe, average lifespans are somewhat longer: 83 years for women and 78 years for men (United Nations Department of Economic and Social Affairs Population Division 2017). Information from archaeological sites may yield information about longevity from ancient populations. For example, age at death was estimated on skeletons recovered from graves at the Ukrainian locality of Sredny Stog, dated at about 7000 years ago. The results indicated that average life expectancy at birth was 44 years for women but only 36 years for men, a difference of eight years between the sexes (Wilmoth 1998). Eventually, analysis of information from a large number of well-documented archaeological sites may indicate whether the widely recognized sex difference in age at death in modern human populations dates back to antiquity. In fact, this seems highly likely as a large-scale survey of life histories of 101 wild mammal species has revealed a general tendency for females to live almost 20 percent longer than males, with relatively few exceptions (Lemaître et al. 2020).

Primary information regarding prehistoric life-history patterns comes from age-at-death estimations, derived from similar techniques to those used by forensic scientists today. For infant and sub-adult individuals, age estimation is based on developmental markers, such as the formation and eruption of the dentition, and patterns of long bone fusion. For adult individuals, age estimation is based on increasing signs of degradation of the skeleton, a prime example being tooth wear (*dental abrasion*). However, age estimation for any individual skeleton becomes increasingly unreliable as the lifecycle advances, especially because environmental factors exert effects. For instance, the degree of dental abrasion depends upon physical properties of the food that is masticated, including contamination with wind-borne sand.

Specialists face many more challenges when it comes to the age-at-death estimations, and even more so for identification of the causes of death. For the former, specialists draw on gradual degenerative changes that occur in the skeleton after attainment of physical maturity. Combining both developmental and degenerative aspects, one special example actually overlaps the transition to adulthood: the fusion of skeletal elements that are initially formed from separate centers of bone formation (*ossification*). In humans, the process of gradual ossification of cartilage regions of long bones is completed between ages of 16 and 21 years, depending on the skeletal element concerned. Eventually, bone formation in the skeleton is completed, although faint traces of fusion sites are still visible externally (and especially internally) for a while. With X-rays, traces of the fusion sites can be detected for several years after the attainment of adulthood.

Skeletal information derived from archaeological sites can also be used to study potential causes of disease and death (*palaeopathology*) and to investigate broad dietary habits (*palaeonutrition*) in prehistoric populations. Unfortunately—apart from healed fractures—only a limited number of pathological features are reflected by identifiable lesions or other changes in human skeletons. Notable examples are bone cancers, anaemia, and end-stage syphilis. Thankfully, modern molecular techniques permit direct identification of disease agents in samples from archaeological skeletons. For instance, recent work on genetic traces of the bacterium that causes syphilis has provided confident confirmation of the presence of the disease in certain individuals. Moreover, comparison between samples has permitted reconstruction of an evolutionary tree that throws new light on the origins of syphilis (Xirocostas et al. 2020). In a similar way, modern techniques have also permitted reliable inference about dietary habits in prehistoric populations, notably using assessment of stable isotopes.

2D Response to the Pandemic: Creativity in the Face of Precarity

Alaka Wali
Field Museum

Toward the end of 2019, people in the city of Wuhan, China, started to fall ill in large numbers, affected by a respiratory disease we all soon came to know as COVID-19. Caused by the SARS-CoV-2 virus, the illness spread quickly around the world, and in March 2020, the World Health Organization (WHO) declared COVID-19 a pandemic—a disease that was global in scope. In the United States, states and cities began to take measures to prevent the spread of the virus, shutting down public venues, requiring social distancing and masks, as the Centers for Disease Control (CDC) promoted national guidelines based on epidemiological investigation.

As museums began to recognize the enormity of the crisis, they began to implement programs to document the pandemic moment for the future. One of the earliest was the Victoria and Albert Museum in London, which started to make a collection there of pandemic-related material culture (Wainwright 2020).

The Field Museum also joined the effort and created a small task-force within the Science and Education Division to establish a collection of material culture that reflected the social and cultural responses to the COVID-19 pandemic. In part, this effort was spurred by the curiosity that there was virtually no representation of the material culture of previous pandemics, such as the 1918 influenza pandemic. In part, it was also part of a broader conversation in museums about future directions for collecting and representing practices (cf. Thorner 2022; Rotenberg and Wali 2014). By the early summer of 2020, it became clear that the pandemic was unfolding in tandem with other social and cultural events that represented significant shifts in the public manifestation of underlying tensions created by rising inequality (cf. Caduff 2020; Wahlberg, Burke, and Manderson 2021). The task force—social scientists from the Keller Science Action Center and the Negaunee Integrated Research Center (including scientific affiliates), together with anthropology collections staff—determined that the Field Museum collection should include documentation of the broader social circumstances.

Additionally, because scientific staff were working in venues across the world, the collection could reflect a global perspective on the pandemic. As of May 2022, the collection of objects numbers over 100 and includes: masks, visual art, song and poetry, educational materials, plant medicines, digital media, and more. The collection also includes over 60 interviews with cultural producers and community members. Our team is working with community partners in the Chicago, northwest Amazon, and south Philippines regions to identify creative cultural responses that give meaning to widespread suffering, and to support efforts to repair social well-being. From movements for racial, gender, medical, and environmental justice, to reflections on how to communicate with neighbors and strangers about the things that matter most, the stories and materials collected here demonstrate that even our most challenging moments invite us to connect and remake our world anew.

To find out more about the collection, please see the website: https://www.pandemic-collection.fieldmuseum.org.

One object in the current collection, displayed in the exhibition, encapsulates several themes emerging from the collection and ethnographic documentation. This is a textile made by Andrea Martinez, a life-long Chicagoan, and donated to the museum in 2021. Ms. Martinez is a neighbor of a Field Museum staff member, who happened to see the textile hanging from the fence in front of the house. It is a cotton fabric banner with hand-stitched letters cut out from other fabric scraps to spell out "Thank You Essential Workers." Ms. Martinez kindly donated the piece to the museum when she was contacted by the staff member. Subsequently, she agreed to be interviewed virtually (see Horton 2021 for an interesting perspective on doing remote ethnography during the pandemic) and narrated the story of the banner. She had been furloughed from her job and, with little to do, decided to sew the banner as her contribution to helping neighbors and family, some of whom were continuing to work. The banner stayed on the fence for several months, was photographed and shared on social media. Ms. Martinez was a self-taught seamstress, had a sewing machine, had saved fabric scraps, and obtained the blue cotton cloth for the banner from a neighborhood Facebook group set up as a barter site. The forced absence from her job inspired the creative response of making the banner. As stated in the interview, she "felt bad" that she couldn't do anything, that she wasn't "doing her part." Making the banner and hanging it connected her to her working relatives and friends. She also did a lot of baking and taking care of others. During the pandemic, she and her husband invited a close friend who lived alone to stay with them.

Ms. Martinez's account of her experience of the pandemic was similar to others we heard during ethnographic interviews. There were frustrations because plans had to be changed (her wedding was cancelled and instead became a small ceremony in her family's yard), but also the forging of closer connections to neighbors. Neighbors shared resources and, as the strict lockdowns faded, convened in their yards for shared meals. The experience of time also changed. To replace the routine of work, Ms. Martinez created a "to do" list every day that provided structure and prevented her from feeling idle. She brought a Kindle™ and read more than she had in years. Sewing also occupied her time. Ms. Martinez and her husband wanted to spend more time on their front porch so they could chat with neighbors and passers-by so they purchased outdoor furniture and a heat lamp for cold weather. Neighbors they had not really known for the decade or so they had lived in their home became friends and have remained so. These types of creative responses to the pandemic are reflected in other collection items (cf. TallBear 2019 for an alternative approach to documentation of creativity).

In the ethnographic interview, we asked Ms. Martinez how she defined "essential workers." She included "grocery clerks, delivery people, teachers, healthcare workers" and all who had remained working during the lockdown. The concept of essential workers has emerged in the pandemic to make visible the working class who have largely been neglected in current public discourses. Media captured moments of recognition, such as people standing on their balconies clapping and banging pots as healthcare workers came home from long shifts. Grocery clerks, meat-packing-plant workers, and those who kept the infrastructure of social life going were more vulnerable to the disease and their plight shed light on the accumulated inequalities of late twentieth- and early twenty-first-century capitalism. The intersection of class and race also became more visible as the majority of essential workers are African American and Latinx.

Deeply embedded forms of societal structural racism also became the subject of public discourse as evidence grew that people of color were dying at disproportionally higher numbers. The systemic persecution of African Americans and other people of color by the police and other instruments of the state also became more visible, most notably after the murder of George Floyd by policemen in Minneapolis. Anti-Asian violence took hold as well, as former President Trump and other public officials vilified Chinese people and China as the origin of COVID-19. White nationalism and white supremacist ideologies, historically latent forces in American life, once again became more openly manifest in violent demonstrations and on social media. As with other historical moments when inequalities have disrupted the public square, people subjugated by the discriminatory practices of the intersection of stratifications have risen up to protest and respond. The disruptions are not confined to the United States, but are global. National protests against inequality are erupting in Europe, Asia, and Latin America. The Field Museum's documentation of the pandemic and its impact in this turbulent time continues.

Acknowledgment

Generous support for the Pandemic Collection effort has been provided by The Negaunee Foundation. In-kind support for staff time from the Field Museum's Science and Education Division and volunteer support from our community networks has also been much appreciated.

References

Caduff, C. 2020. "What Went Wrong: Corona and the World after the Full Stop." *Medical Anthropology Quarterly* 34, no. 4: 467–87. https://doi.org/10.1111/maq.12599.

Horton, S. B. 2021. "On Pandemic Privilege: Reflections on a 'Home-Bound Pandemic Ethnography.'" *Journal of North American Anthropology* special issue: *State of the Field* 24, no. 2: 98–107.

Rotenberg, R., and Wali, A. 2014. "Building a Collection of Urban Material Culture." *Museum Anthropology* 37, no. 1: 1–5.

TallBear, K. 2019. "Caretaking Relations, Not American Dreaming." *KALFOU* 6, no. 1: 24–41.

Thorner, S. G. 2022. "Being Called to Action: Contemporary Museum Ethnographies." *Museum Anthropology* 45, no. 1: 3–14. https://doi.org/10.1111/muan.12243.

Wahlberg, A., Burke, N., and Manderson, L. 2021. "Introduction: Stratified Livability and Pandemic Effects." In *Viral Loads. Anthropologies of Urgency in the Time of COVID-19*, edited by L. Manderson, N. Burke, and A. Wahlberg, 1–26. London: UCL Press.

Wainwright, O. 2020. "Museum of Covid-19: The Story of the Crisis Told through Everyday Objects." *The Guardian,* May 4, 2020. https://www.theguardian.com/artanddesign/2020/may/04/museum-covid-19-v-and-a-pandemic-coronavirus-objects.

Use of advanced non-destructive visualization techniques has greatly facilitated investigation of prehistoric human skeletons, leading to notable advances in the study of causes of death and how ancient people dealt with death itself (see chapters 4 and 6 in this volume). Although classical X-rays have long been used to examine skeletal specimens, notably permitting more detailed examination of dentitions, the restriction to two dimensions limits their utility. The advent of CT scanners and three-dimensional reconstructions based on the information recorded, initially developed for medical diagnostics and subsequently applied to archaeological specimens, has literally transformed the study of preserved human remains and, with that, of human corporeality. The non-invasive nature of these techniques has been a particular advantage for renewed investigation of mummies. In this case, much can be learned about the procedures involved in natural or contrived mummification of human remains. Furthermore, much useful information can be extracted from the three-dimensional reconstructions obtained. In addition to permitting non-invasive inference of sex, age at death, and pathological conditions from the skeleton, such reconstructions yield additional information on non-skeletal features, such as preserved hair, wrappings, inclusion of artifacts, and the construction of a sarcophagus.

Mention of sarcophagus construction brings us to the issue of burial and associated funeral rites, as described in other contributions in this book—undoubtedly a unique feature of human societies. They directly indicate that the death of an individual is a recognizable event that evokes strong responses from fellow members of a social group. Such recognition suggests, in turn, that individuals have become aware that they themselves are mortal and will die at some future time. As far as we know, such awareness of death is restricted to humans (see contribution by Martin et al. in this volume), although some primates occasionally show attachment to dead individuals. For instance, for chimpanzees and certain monkeys there have been sporadic reports of a mother carrying the body of a dead infant around for a while—usually just a few days—before abandoning it. As infant chimpanzees and monkeys can actively cling to their mothers from birth onward, carriage by a mother after death indicates her continued active attachment. However, nothing even vaguely similar to burial has been observed in any extant species other than *Homo sapiens*.

Archaeological evidence for human burial (*interment*) has become increasingly abundant since settled communities associated with domestication of plants and animals began to appear around 12,000 years ago (Gurven and Kaplan 2007). Indeed, over that period skeletal remains derived from archaeological sites have provided some of the most direct information that is available regarding past human life-histories, especially during prehistoric times. Deliberate burial accompanied by ritual is clearly evident over those ten millennia, although it is best documented after the end of the Neolithic era, starting at about 5000 years ago. Graves are often specially marked, notably with small and/or large stones, and bodies are often positioned in a special way. For instance, the legs are frequently bent, with the knees close to the chest in the well-known "fetal position," and the arms may be specially arranged. Moreover, recognizable grave goods such as stone tools or seashells and red ocher (the earliest documented natural earth pigment, often associated with burials) may be found on or near a skeleton. As a rule, a grave contains only one individual, but occasionally two or more individuals are buried together. In rare cases, for instance, an adult female skeleton is found buried with the fragile skeletal remains of a late-term or newborn baby, probably indicating the death of both during childbirth. The question that arises in this context is to what extent practices of burial among early groups were conditioned to a specific way of perceiving the physicality of the body, its progressive deterioration and aging, and its subsequent decay.

Given that burial practices are universal among human societies today, it is a reasonable inference that they are deeply rooted in our lineage. However, evidence older than 12,000 years is sparse. As far as *Homo sapiens* is concerned the earliest known potential examples are from the sites of Qafzeh and Skuhl in Israel, dated at about 100,000 years ago. At Qafzeh, two skeletons were found together in a single apparent burial—one from an individual in late adolescence and one from a young child. A more recent example is the skeleton of a human child found at the site of Taramsa 1 in Egypt, dated at around 55,000 years ago. The child's body was found in a sitting posture, with the legs and arms seemingly positioned specially. Several stone blades and flakes were found near the skeleton, but it is unclear whether they were intentionally deposited grave goods. More recently still, in a grave at the site of Nazlet Khater—also in Egypt and dated as about 30,000 years old—the body had evidently been placed on its back, with the knees bent, one arm resting on the pelvis and the other extended lengthwise, suggesting that a sense of orientartion and positionality of the body was already developed. A stone axe had been left in the grave close to the individual's head.

Humans shared a common ancestor with Neanderthals (our closest relatives in the hominid evolutionary tree) somewhere between 500,000 and a million years ago. So it is of particular interest to know whether Neanderthals also practiced deliberate burial (see Martin et al. in this volume, and also Monsó 2022). It has often been claimed that this was indeed the case, a prime example being a skeleton found in Kebara Cave, Israel, and dated as about 60,000 years old. Several feaures indicated that deliberate burial was involved. The skeleton was located in a shallow pit that showed signs of excavation and the body had been positioned on its back, pressed against the sides of the pit. The preserved bones of the fairly complete skeleton were still in their articulated positions and showed no signs of disturbance, indicating that the pit had been covered with vegetation and/or hides. Several Neanderthal skeletons discovered in a cluster of apparent graves in a cave in Shanidar in Iraq, dated at about 70,000 years old, provided additional indications of deliberate burial. One of the graves contained pollen from flowers that occur on a nearby mountain range, indicating carriage from some distance away.

Several other cases of apparent Neanderthal burials have been reported from Eurasia. Indeed, the relatively frequent discovery of fairly complete skeletons in anatomically appropriate configurations has been taken as an indication that protection by intentional burial had been provided. Examples of such burials are La Chapelle-aux-Saints, La Ferrassie, and Regourdou in France, and Teshik-Tash in Uzbekistan. Documentation of apparent burials began in 1908 with the renowned discovery of a skeleton in a cave in La Chapelle-aux-Saints (southwestern France), dated at around 50,000 years ago. The best-preserved Neanderthal skeleton ever found was subsequently discovered at the French site of La Ferrassie, for which an approximate age of 40,000–70,000 years ago has been determined. Here, too, the bones of the skeleton were still in their articulated positions and it was concluded that all of the bodies at La Ferrassie had been intentionally buried.

It must be noted that *all* reports of deliberate burial at Neanderthal sites have been challenged, so it is still uncertain whether our sister species did indeed engage in this practice. Furthermore, the earliest proposed evidence for Neanderthal burials dates back only 70,000 years. This leaves a considerable gap lasting hundreds of thousands of years between the common ancestor of Neanderthals and modern humans and the earliest evidence for burials in either lineage. So, if late Neanderthals did actually bury the dead, we do not know whether this practice developed independently in the two sister lineages or whether it was already present at the common ancestral stage. Whatever the case may be, this leaves us with many intriguing questions about the origins of awareness of death and notions of an afterlife, as well as how perceptions of our own corporeality and our hope to avoid its progressive degeneration played a role in the emergence of an early funerary behavior. Aging is, ultimately, part of the natural process of life, of mammals and other animals, but the contradictory reactions and particular responses that it evokes in humans are perhaps what make us truly unique as species.

References

Acscadi, G., and Nemeskeri, N. 1970. *History of Human Life Span and Mortality*. Budapest: Akademiai Kiado.

Alberts, S. C., Altmann, J., Brockman, D. K., Cords, M., Fedigan, L. M., Pusey, A., Stoinski, T. S., Strier, K. B., Morris, W. F., and Bronikowski, A. M. 2013. "Reproductive Aging Patterns in Primates Reveal that Humans Are Distinct." *PNAS Proceedings of the National Academy of Sciences* 110, no. 33: 13440–45.

Alvarez, H. P. 2000. "Grandmother Hypothesis and Primate Life Histories." *American Journal of Physical Anthropology* 113: 435–50.

Austad, S. N. 2015. "The Evolutionary Basis of Aging." In *Molecular and Cellular Biology of Aging*, edited by J. Vijg, J. Campisi, and G. Lithgow, 15–48. Washington, DC: The Gerontological Society of America.

Austad, S. N., and Fischer, K. E. 1992. "Primate Longevity: Its Place in the Mammalian Scheme." *American Journal of Primatology* 28: 251–61.

Barbi, E., Lagona, F., Marsili, M., Vaupel, J. W., and Wachter, K. W. 2018. "The Plateau of Human Mortality: Demography of Longevity Pioneers." *Science* 360: 1459–61.

Bogin, B. 2009. "Childhood, Adolescence, and Longevity: A Multilevel Model of the Evolution of Reserve Capacity in Human Life History." *American Journal of Human Biology* 21: 567–77.

Carey, J. R. 2003. *Longevity: The Biology and Demography of Life Span*. Princeton, NJ: Princeton University Press.

Carey, J. R., and Judge, D. S. 2000. *Longevity Records: Life Spans of Mammals, Birds, Amphibians, Reptiles, and Fish*. Monographs on Population Aging 8. Odense: Odense University Press.

Caspari, R., and Lee, S. H. 2006. "Is Human Longevity a Consequence of Cultural Change or Modern Biology?" *American Journal of Physical Anthropology* 129: 512–17.

Charnov, E. L., and Berrigan, D. 1993. "Why Do Female Primates Have Such Long Lifespans and so Few Babies? Or Life in the Slow Lane." *Evolutionary Anthropology* 1: 191–94.

Chernew, M., Cutler, D. M., Ghosh, K., and Landrum, M. B. 2016. "Understanding the Improvement in Disability Free Life Expectancy in the US Elderly Population." NBER Working Paper 21681.

Colchero, F., Rau, R., Jonesa, O. R., Barthold, J. A., Conde, D. A., Lenart, A., Nemeth, L., Scheuerlein, A., Schoeley, J., Torres, C., Zarulli, V., Altmann, J., Brockman, D. K., Bronikowskj, A. M., Fedigan, L. M., Pusey, A. E., Stoinski, T. S., Strier, K. B., Baudisch, A., Alberts, S. C., and Vaupela, J. W. 2016. "The Emergence of Longevous Populations." *PNAS Proceedings of the National Academy of Sciences* 113: E7681–E7690.

Dong, X., Milholland, B., and Vijg, J. 2016. "Evidence for a Limit to Human Lifespan." *Nature* 538: 257–59.

Ellis, S., Franks, D. W., Nattrass, S., Cant, M. A., Bradley, D. L, Giles, D., Balcomb, K. C., and Croft, D. P. 2018. "Postreproductive Lifespans Are Rare in Mammals." *Ecology and Evolution* 8: 2482–94.

Finch, C. E. 2010. "Evolution of the Human Lifespan and Diseases of Aging: Roles of Infection, Inflammation, and Nutrition." *PNAS Proceedings of the National Academy of Sciences* 107: 1718–24.

Finch, E. 1990. *Longevity, Senescence and the Genome*. Chicago: University of Chicago Press.

Flatt, T., and Partridge, L. 2018. "Horizons in the Evolution of Aging." *BMC Biology* 16, no. 93: 1–13.

Foster, E. A., Franks, D. W., Mazzi, S., Darden, S. K., Balcomb, K. C., Ford, J. K. B., and Croft, D. P. 2012. "Adaptive Prolonged Postreproductive Life Span in Killer Whales." *Science* 337: 1313.

Gavrilov, L. A., and Gavrilova, N. S. 1991. *The Biology of Life Span: A Quantitative Approach*. Reading: Harwood Academic Publishers.

Gavrilov, L. A., and Gavrilova, N. S. 2001. "The Reliability Theory of Ageing and Longevity." *Journal of Theoretical Biology* 213: 527–45.

Gavrilov, L. A., and Gavrilova, N. S. 2018. "Is Aging a Disease? Biodemographers' Point of View." *Advanced Gerontology* 8: 123–24.

Gurven, M., and Kaplan, H. 2007. "Longevity Among Hunter-Gatherers: A Cross-Cultural Examination." *Population & Development Review* 33: 321–65.

Hall, S. 2003. *Merchants of Immortality: Chasing the Dream of Human Life Extension*. New York: Houghton Mifflin.

Hamilton, W. D. 1968. "The Moulding of Senescence by Natural Selection." *Journal of Theoretical Biology* 12: 12–45.

Harvey, P. H., and Zammuto, R. M. 1985. "Patterns of Mortality and Age at First Reproduction in Natural Populations of Mammals." *Nature* 315: 319–20.

Hawkes, K. 2003. "Grandmothers and the Evolution of Human Longevity." *American Journal of Human Biology* 15: 380–400.

Hawkes, K., and Coxworth, J. E. 2013. "Grandmothers and the Evolution of Human Longevity: A Review of Findings and Future Directions." *Evolutionary Anthropology* 22: 294–302.

Healy, K., Guillerme, T., Finlay, S., Kane, A., Kelly, S. B. A., McClean, D., Kelly, D. J., Donohue, I., Jackson, A. L., and Cooper, N. 2014. "Ecology and Mode-of-Life Explain Lifespan Variation in Birds and Mammals." *Proceedings of the Royal Society, London B* 281, no. 1784: 1–7. https://doi.org/10.1098/rspb.2014.0298.

Imai, K., and Soneji, S. 2007. "On the Estimation of Disability-Free Life Expectancy: Sullivan's Method and Its Extension." *Journal of the American Statistical Association* 102: 1199–211.

Kirkwood, T. B. L. 1999. *Time of Our Lives: The Science of Human Aging*. Oxford: Oxford University Press.

Kirkwood, T. B. L., and Austad, S. N. 2000. "Why Do We Age?" *Nature* 408: 233–38.

Kirkwood, T. B. L., and Rose, M. R. 1991. "Evolution of Senescence: Late Survival Sacrificed for Reproduction." *Philosphical Transactions of the Royal Society London B*, 332: 15–24.

Kontis, V., Bennett, J. E., Mathers, C. D., Li, G., Foreman, K., and Ezzati, M. 2017. "Future Life Expectancy in 35 Industrialised Countries: Projections with a Bayesian Model Ensemble." *Lancet* 389: 1323–35.

Lahdenperä, M., Mar, K. U., and Lummaa, V. 2014. "Reproductive Cessation and Post-Reproductive Lifespan in Asian Elephants and Pre-Industrial Humans." *Frontiers in Zoology* 11: 54.

Lemaître, J.-F., Ronget, V., Tidière, M., Allainé, D., Berger, V., Cohas, A., Colchero, F., Conde, D. A., Garratt, M., Liker, A., Marais, G. A. B., Scheuerlein, A., Székely, T., and Gaillard, J.-M. 2020. "Sex Differences in Adult Lifespan and Aging Rates of Mortality Across Wild Mammals." *PNAS Proceedings of the National Academy of Sciences* 117: 8546–53.

Medawar, P. B. 1952. *An Unsolved Problem of Biology*. London: H. K. Lewis.

Monsó, S. 2022. "How to Tell If Animals Can Understand Death." *Erkenntnis* 87: 117–36.

Morley, A. A. 1995. "The Somatic Mutation Theory of Ageing." *Mutation Research* 338: 19–23.

Olshansky, S. J. 2008. "Longevity in the Twenty-First Century." *Population Studies* 62: 245–49.

Olshansky, S. J., and Carnes, B. A. 2001. *The Quest for Immortality: Science at the Frontiers of Aging*. New York: W. W. Norton & Co.

Olshansky, S. J., Carnes, B. A., and Cassel, C. 1990. "In Search of Methuselah: Estimating the Upper Limits to Human Longevity." *Science* 250: 634–40.

Olshansky, S. J., Carnes, B. A., and Désesquelles, A. 2001. "Prospects for Human Longevity." *Science* 291: 1491–92.

Olshansky, S. J., Passaro, D. J., Hershow, R. C., Layden, J., Carnes, B. A., Brody, J., Hayflick, L., Butler, R. N., Allison, D. B., and Ludwig, D. S. 2005. "A Potential Decline in Life Expectancy in the United States in the 21st Century." *New England Journal of Medicine* 352: 1138–45.

Ossewaarde, M. E., Bots, M. L., Verbeek, A. L. M., Peeters, P. H. M., van der Graaf, Y., Grobbee, D. E., and van der Schouw, Y. T. 2005. "Age at Menopause, Cause-Specific Mortality and Total Life Expectancy." *Epidemiology* 16: 556–62.

Pavard, S., Metcalf, C. J. E., and Heyer, E. 2008. "Senescence of Reproduction May Explain Adaptive Menopause in Humans." *American Journal of Physical Anthropology* 136: 194–203.

Peccei, J. S. 2001. "A Critique of the Grandmother Hypotheses: Old and New." *American Journal of Human Biology* 13: 434–52.

Perls, T. T., and Fretts, R. C. 2001. "The Evolution of Menopause and Human Life Span." *Annals of Human Biology* 28: 237–45.

Pokharel, S. S., Sharma, N., and Sukumar, R. 2022. "Viewing the Rare through Public Lenses: Insights into Dead Calf Carrying and Other Thanatological Responses in Asian Elephants Using YouTube Videos." *Royal Society Open Science* 9, no. 5: 1–16. https://doi.org/10.1098/rsos.211740.

Sinclair, D., and LaPlante, M. D. 2019. *Lifespan: Why We Age—and Why We Don't Have To*. New York: Atria Books.

Smith, D. W. 1993. *Human Longevity*. Baltimore: Johns Hopkins University Press.

Stearns, S. C. 1977. "The Evolution of Life-History Traits—A Critique of the Theory and a Review of Data." *Annual Review of Ecology & Systematics* 8: 145–71.

Szilard, L. 1959. "On the Nature of the Aging Process." *Proceedings of the National Academy of Sciences USA* 45: 30–45.

Tuljapurkar, S., Li, N., and Boe, C. 2000. "A Universal Pattern of Mortality Decline in the G7 Countries." *Nature* 405: 789–92.

United Nations Department of Economic and Social Affairs Population Division. 2017. "World Population Prospects: The 2017 Revision, Key Findings and Advance Tables," 1-46. Working Paper No. ESA/P/WP/248. https://population.un.org/wpp/publications/files/wpp2017_keyfindings.pdf.

Vijg, J., and Dong, X. 2020. "Pathogenic Mechanisms of Somatic Sutation and Genome Mosaicism in Aging." *Cell* 182: 12–23.

Weon, B. M., and Je, J. H. 2009. "Theoretical Estimation of Maximum Human Lifespan." *Biogerontology* 10: 65–71.

Westendorp, R. G. J., and Kirkwood, T. B. L. 1998. "Human Longevity at the Cost of Reproductive Success." *Nature* 396: 743–46.

Williams, G. C. 1957. "Pleiotropy, Natural Selection, and the Evolution of Senescence." *Evolution* 11: 398–411.

Wilmoth, J. R. 1998. "The Future of Human Longevity: A Demographer's Perspective." *Science* 280: 395–97.

Wilmoth, J. R., Deegan, L. J., Hundström, H., and Horiuchi, S. 2000. "Increase of Maximum Life-Span in Sweden, 1861–1999." *Science* 289: 2366–68.

Woolf, S. H., Masters, R. K., and Aron, L. Y. 2022. "Changes in Life Expectancy between 2019 and 2020 in the US and 21 Peer Countries." *JAMA Network Open* 5, no. 4: e227067: 1–9.

Woolf, S. H., and Schoomaker, H. 2019. "Life Expectancy and Mortality Rates in the United States, 1959–2017." *Journal of the American Medical Association* 322: 1996–2016.

Xirocostas, Z. A., Everingham, S. A., and Moles, A. T. 2020. "The Sex with the Reduced Sex Chromosome Dies Earlier: A Comparison Across the Tree of Life." *Biology Letters* 16, no. 3: 20190867: 1–6. https://doi.org/10.1098/rsbl.2019.0867.

3

Soul and Vital Force: Vibrant Life Matters and Mortuary Arts in Africana Religions and Beyond

Kyrah Malika Daniels

Emory University

Abstract: Religious devotees all over the world pray for long and healthy life, one hopefully filled with prosperity and purpose. However, the search for immortality is not a universal quest of humankind. In African and African Diaspora religious communities, few rituals aim to prolong life indefinitely, as this would disrupt the cosmic flow of new and returning souls journeying to earth. Instead, African-derived communities emphasize the quality of a vibrant and well-balanced life, one lived with integrity and intention to fulfill the destiny of the soul(s). This thematic essay highlights core principles of longevity, livity, and the vibrancy of life within Black Atlantic religions. These insights ultimately reveal how life's vital force is sustained through balance, ritual, and the fortification of souls and divine energies. Case studies explore other religious traditions with similar characteristics in Latin America, Africa, and Asia.

Resumen: Los devotos religiosos de todo el mundo oran por una vida prolongada y saludable, llena de prosperidad y propósito. Sin embargo, la búsqueda de la inmortalidad no es una búsqueda universal de la humanidad. En las comunidades religiosas africanas y de la diáspora africana, pocos rituales tienen como objetivo prolongar la vida indefinidamente, pues esto interrumpiría el flujo cósmico de las nuevas almas y de aquellas almas viajeras que retornan a la tierra. Más bien, las comunidades de origen africano enfatizan la calidad de una "vida vibrante" y bien equilibrada, vivida con integridad, y con una intención de cumplir aquel destino del alma. Este ensayo destaca los principios fundamentales de la longevidad, la vitalidad, y el dinamismo de la vida dentro de las religiones del Atlántico Negro. Estas perspectivas, finalmente, revelan cómo la fuerza vital de la vida se sostiene a través del equilibrio, el ritual, y la fortificación de las almas y su energía divina. Los artículos que este ensayo contiene exploran otras tradiciones religiosas con características similares en América Latina, África y Asia.

Death as Initiation

Crouched comfortably before a black-and-white tombstone, the Haitian *lwa* (spirit) Gede Nibo balances on his heels in the cemetery and casts a knowing glance toward the viewer. While the spirit Bawon Samdi is officially regarded as Haiti's lord of the cemetery in the Vodou pantheon, all divinities hailing from the Gede and Bawon spiritual families reside between their spiritual home of Afrik-Ginen (an African realm of ancestors and spirits) and the liminal realm of the graveyard (Figures 3.1–3.4). Such is the case for Gede Nibo, a renowned healer and elder in the Gede family. A wide-brimmed purple hat with a tapered green ribbon dons the spirit's head, and against the backdrop of his full black beard, a curved tobacco pipe emerges from his lips. Ever the dapper dresser, Gede (Guede in French) sports a pressed white dress shirt with purple cufflinks, and a polka-dotted handkerchief peeking out from his breast pocket matches the pattern of his purple pantaloons. A diagonally striped tie incorporates all three of his primary colors—white, black, and purple—symbolizing his dominion over the various stages of life, death, and rebirth.

The tombstone that is often represented behind Gede Nibo in many drapo flags features a prominent black cross with white diamonds and an inverted heart in the very center, both emblems from the Haitian Vodou system of divination cards. While the cross is most commonly identified as the iconic symbol of Christianity in a nation such as Haiti colonized by French Catholics, the motif also has deep historical roots as *dikenga,* an Indigenous symbol of the ancient Kongo Kingdom. In Central Africa, the Kongo cross or *dikenga* signified the cosmic crossroads between mortal and spiritual realms, a cosmogram that represented dimensions of both time and space in the mystic encounter between worlds (Thompson and Cornet 1981; Martínez-Ruiz 2013). Kongolese citizens Africanized the Catholic tradition between the sixteenth and nineteenth centuries, and claimed the cross as their own religious symbol (Thornton [1992] 1998; Fromont 2014). Similarly today in Haiti, the cross represents the nation's plural religious realities, simultaneously embodying the presence of Jesus Christ for Christians as readily as the Gede spirits for Vodouizan, devotees of the African-derived tradition Vodou. And an analogous process of religious *mestizaje* becomes evident in other communities from the Caribbean and Central America (see Wali in this volume, on Guna Christianity).

In the same type of drapo flags, the silhouette of a white candle sits on the first step of the tombstone, an

UN
LE SEISME DU 12 JANVIER 2010
EDMOND

Figure 3.2. ***Drapo*** **flag of Haitian Vodou practitioners making an offering to ancestors (FM 362685). Made by Ronald Edmond artisans.**

←

Figure 3.1. ***Drapo*** **ritual flag showing ancestral spirits (*****lwa*****) protecting people from disaster in the 2010 Haiti earthquake (FM 362683). Made by Ronald Edmond artisans.**

BARON LE MEDCIN DO COVID 19
EDMOND

offering left behind by loved ones visiting cherished ancestors in the cemetery. On his right arm, Gede Nibo cradles a wrapped brown whip over his elbow, perhaps to ward off Death when someone's time has not yet come, or to invoke the hotter Petwò and Kongo spirits of enslavement. In his left hand, he carries a shallow dish, likely a *kalbas* (dried calabash gourd) with popular offerings such as dried fish for the dead. Gede thus engages in an act of ritual reflexivity, generously offering nourishment to the *zansèt* (the ancestors), who are in fact citizens of his own Kingdom of the Dead. Two lilac-colored skulls with otherworldly eyes are perched beneath the spirit, reminding us that despite his manifestation in human form here, Gede indeed expertly balances between the realms of life and death.

In many Black Atlantic communities, as well as of the Indigenous world of the pre-Columbian Americas, death does not signal the end of life, but rather the negotiation of divine energies and new realities of being (see Feinman in this volume, on the balance of the divine forces through the Mesoamerican ballgame). Grieving and mourning naturally occur, but it is generally understood that death affords initiation into the ancestral realm of spirits and may present opportunity for rebirth in a new manifestation. This is how Evelyne Alcide often portrays the Gede spirit of her *drapo*, or ceremonial flag: as arbiter of life and death with the power to navigate both realms. The Gede family of spirits are known for their tremendous healing powers, and are frequently called upon to help ease one's transition into the afterlife. Loved ones seek strength and courage from the Gede spirits, and may call for help to heal family members who are unwell in the event that their time has not yet come. However, the Gede do not barter for souls, and Vodou offers no promises of eternal life. Humans are meant to fulfill their purpose on earth as related to the destiny of their soul(s) and to honor the ancestors and spirits through rituals that cultivate vital force (*fòs* or *nanm*), all while recognizing the inevitability of their mortality.

Religious devotees all over the world pray for long and healthy life, one hopefully filled with prosperity and purpose. However, the search for immortality is not a universal quest of humankind. In African and African Diaspora religious communities, few rituals aim to prolong life indefinitely, as this would disrupt the cosmic flow of new and returning souls journeying to earth. Instead, African-derived communities emphasize the quality of a vibrant and well-balanced life, one lived with integrity and intention to fulfill the destiny of the soul(s). This essay highlights core principles of longevity, livity, and the vibrancy of life within Black Atlantic religions, which are also present in other Indigenous religious traditions from the ancient Americas and beyond. These insights ultimately reveal how life's vital force is sustained through ritual balance, the fortification of souls, and the sustenance of divine energies.

Origin Stories and Sacred Arts of Death

Death is conceptualized differently in various regions of the Black Atlantic, and numerous African myths of origin describe how death was brought into the world, often due to human foils or epic battles between spirits. Among Efik nations of southern Nigeria and western Cameroon, death was administered as punishment to defiant humans. The Efik creator spirit Abasi emerged as arbiter of life and death. He initially created the earth, followed by the first humans: a man and a woman, possibly named Esefe and Okporo, who were destined to live with other spirits in the divine realm. The human couple expressed their desire to live on earth, but Abasi forbade this as they might come to challenge his authority. Abasi's wife, Atai, proposed that humans be permitted to live on earth under strict guidelines, and after some persuasion, Abasi agreed to a comprise: the first humans could live on earth under two conditions: they would not cultivate their own food, but rather would return to the divine realm to eat every day, and they would not procreate out of respect for Abasi (Hackett 1998; Scheub 2000).

The new humans respected this divine law of their Efik creator spirits for a time, but eventually both promises were broken: woman desired greater independence and began to cultivate her own crops, while man desired to procreate; they conceived and woman gave birth to many children. Though they tried to conceal their transgressions, Abasi and Atai soon learned of the humans' offenses and deliberated on a fitting punishment. In order to prevent humans from becoming too powerful as masters of their own destiny, the wise wife Atai sent death and discord into the world so that humans would forever remain humbled as a result of their disobedience (Beier 1966). This Efik story of origin reveals an Indigenous theodicy, illustrating how Efik communities theorized the problem of evil in the world. In this narrative, an onslaught of death and chaos was brought about by a goddess who challenged the divine order by first advocating for her mortal children, and who later unleashed her wrath on her defiant progeny.

Other West African myths also describe human failings as the reason for death's emergence in the world, but, unlike those from Judeo-Christian religions (see Schweiker in this volume) West African origin narratives

Figure 3.3. ***Drapo*** **ritual flag depicting Bawon Kowona, an ancestral spirit who protects Haitian people from COVID-19/ coronavirus (FM 362686). Made by Ronald Edmond artisans.**

acknowledge the distinct fate of humans as juxtaposed with other natural beings of the universe. In Central Africa, Tchokwe nations of Angola and the Democratic Republic of Congo distinguish humans' experience of death (and rebirth) as compared to the lifecycle of the sun and moon as celestial bodies. In the Tchokwe graphic writing tradition of Lusona (or Tusona), a myth of creation describes how the sun, the moon, and first human are all given a chicken as a test from the creator God. Upon being instructed to hold the chicken and return to God the next day, both the sun and moon fulfill their tasks with the chicken unharmed, and God rewards them by instructing them to return either every day or every 28 days, respectively. This is why the sun circles the earth to rise and set every day, and why the moon follows a 28-day cycle of rebirth. However, when given the same task, the human became hungry and ate his chicken. Upon the human's remorseful return, God punished him with death (a fate not bestowed upon sun or moon), proclaiming that all humans would eventually return to God upon their death (Olúpọ̀nà 2014). Such myths remind us that in so many Indigenous narratives of origin, humans exist in relationship to other living beings (such as animals, the sun and moon) over whom they cannot claim superiority. Such is the case, for example, for the Incas of Peru, whose actions were always subordinated to the desire of the mountain spirits (see Williams in this volume). This is due partly to humans' transgressions and irreverent disobedience, which leads to their subsequent humbling.

Still other West African traditions describe death as the unfortunate result of spirits' divine rivalries which likely precede humans' arrival on earth. The Akan river spirit (or *abosom*) Tano is a great healer and protector in southern Ghana, and engages in perpetual (im)mortal combat with his nemesis, Death. When someone falls ill, the *abosom* Tano and Death race to the person's side to compete for the individual's soul. Should Death arrive first, the person will become a new citizen of the ancestral realm, but should Tano win the race, the person will be healed and granted a new lease on life. As in many African and African Diaspora traditions, Death therefore does not constitute an inherently maleficent force, because few if any spirits embody pure notions of good or evil. Rather, as a specter of the ancestral realm, Death represents a destructive but inevitable cosmic force to be respected and even feared, but not abhorred.

Southern Ghana's Akanland boasts a powerful aesthetic tradition of funerary arts. Notably, this includes the production of intricate *kente* fabric and other textiles embroidered or embossed with Adinkra, another African Indigenous graphic writing system that dates back at least to the 1600s. These graphic writing systems serve as communication modes for both secular and religious purposes based on ideograms, pictograms, and cosmograms (Mafundikwa 2007; Martínez-Ruiz 2013). Historically, Akan funerary fabrics carried distinct Adinkra symbols with encoded proverbs and historical events in honor of the deceased, and decorated regalia would be coordinated among funeral attendees and family members (Hackett 1998; Ross 1998).

In the mid-twentieth century, a new mortuary arts tradition of Ghana has emerged known as fancy funerals, in which elaborately decorated coffins are constructed for the dead to ensure a safe and "vibrant" passage to the afterlife. Artist Seth Kane Kwei constructed this coffin in the shape of a canoe populated with many rowers who will presumably steer the dead home (see Bandama on Ghanaian fantasy coffins in this volume and Figure 4.14). Often the themes featured in fancy coffins honor a certain vocation, skill, or pastime of the deceased, leading us to imagine that the deceased person honored here may have been a fisherman or a lover of the open waters. As a coastal region, the importance of fishing in southern Ghana cannot be understated, though the rowers' matching blue and yellow uniforms may also suggest that they belong to a team. The bottom of the canoe has been painted black and the words "Sweet Not Always" and "Time Will Tell" have been inscribed on one side of the boat, reminding us that death may not always be sweet, but that time will tell as descendants live on in memory of the deceased.

Painted in gold in the very center of the canoe are three Adinkra symbols, the middle a traditional golden stool (*sika 'dwa*) said to have descended from the sky and landed on the lap of the first Asante king, Osei Kofi Tutu I, to mark his rightful heirship in the newly established kingdom; thereafter, the royal successor would be known as Asantehene, religious and political ruler of the Asante/Ashanti people (Hackett 1998). To the right is a ceremonial sword used in many parts of West Africa as a symbol of allegiance to the throne, while the left icon could be a royal baton, all signaling the likelihood that the coffin was crafted for a community leader of great prominence. In this mortuary rite, it becomes evident that not only must the dead be propitiated and properly cared for as an ancestor in the spirit world, but their passage to the afterlife must be made as smooth as possible. In this newer Akan tradition with finely carved coffins in the shapes of cars, planes, food, animals, and sacred objects, fancy funerals attest to the desire for a triumphant conclusion to one's mortal life as the spiritual life begins anew.

Figure 3.4. Vodou tradition *kanari* and *govi* pots which the deceased's soul returns to inhabit (FM 362680, 362681, 326682). Made by Ronald Edmond artisans.

Figure 3.5. Huastec stone yoke, a representation of ballgame attire (FM 48101).

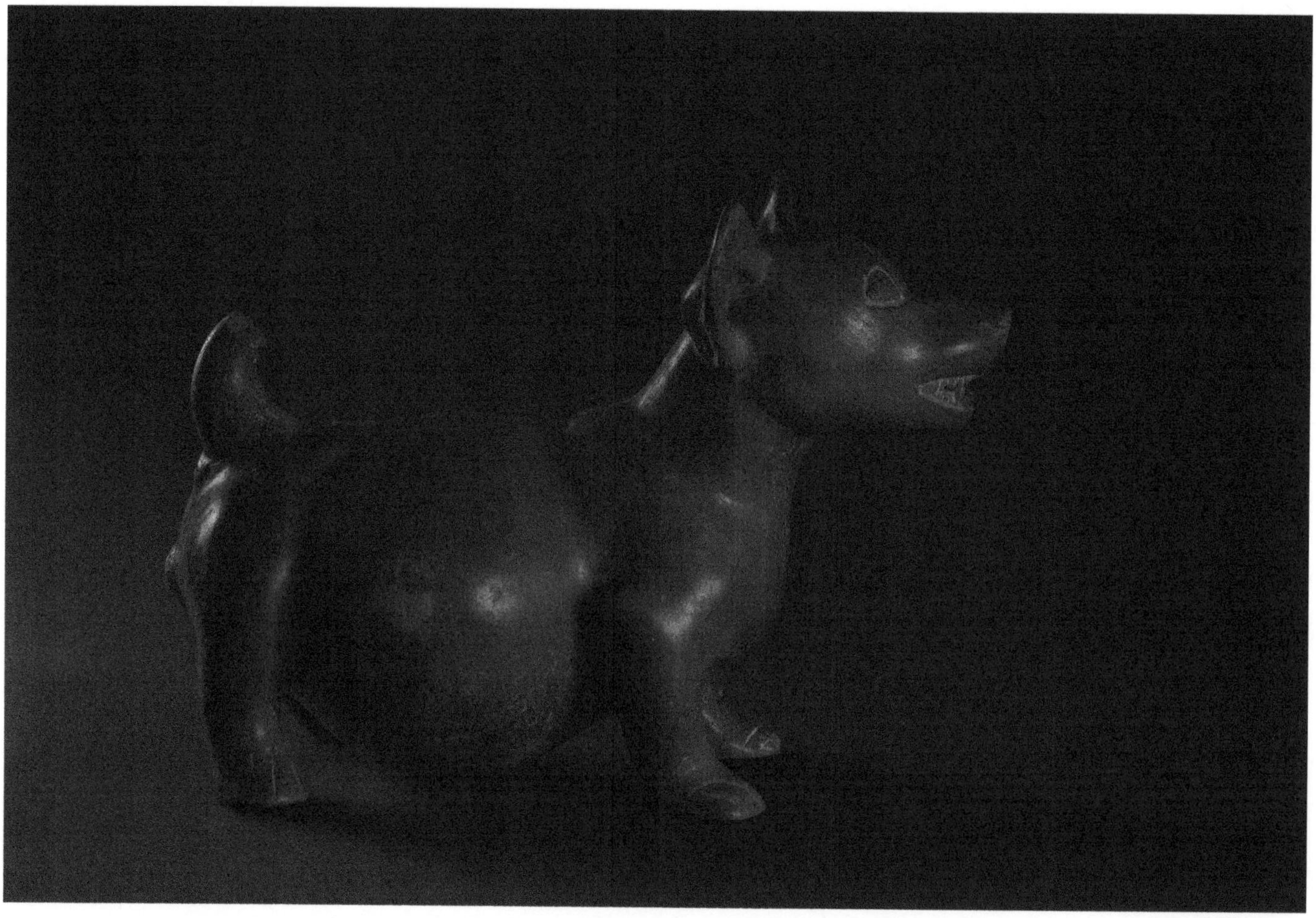

Figure 3.6. Colima dog, likely from a funerary context, side view (FM 95615).

3A Mesoamerican Cosmologies: Death, Maize, and the Ballgame

Gary M. Feinman
Field Museum

Pre-Hispanic Mesoamerica, a world or cultural region that stretched from the southern limits of the deserts of north Mexico down through much of what is now Central America, was a mosaic landscape that was highly differentiated by rugged mountains, wide, flat valleys, and coastal lowlands. Linguistically and culturally, this world also was characterized by diversity, with scores of languages spoken and many different local and regional traditions. Over the 15 or so millennia between the region's first human inhabitants and Spanish invasion (ca. 1520 CE), political boundaries, economic networks, and spheres of interaction shifted markedly across time and geographic space. This pre-Hispanic world was never entirely unified politically.

Central places and urban settlements in pre-Hispanic Mesoamerica also rose and fell over time (e.g., Feinman and Carballo 2018). Despite the rough terrain, geographically restricted opportunities for water-borne transport, absence of effective beasts of burden, and lack of wheeled vehicles, pre-Hispanic Mesoamerican peoples, as a whole, shared certain key cosmological elements and belief systems. From group to group and one temporal phase to another, pre-Hispanic Mesoamerican cosmologies were by no means entirely uniform or static, and this variability underpinned differences in practice. Nonetheless, fundamental tenets of worldview were widely held.

For example, the pre-Hispanic Mesoamerican universe was divided into three general realms or levels—a celestial space or overworld, the earthly level or middleworld, and the underworld or "place of the dead" (Carrasco 1990, 51). The conception of these tiered realms should not be equated with Judeo-Christian concepts of heaven and hell. In Mesoamerica, each tier of the universe was associated with different conditions and even animals. In each domain, time and events passed at their own tempos. Across Mesoamerica, dogs were viewed as companions who could lead the dead to the underworld. Representations of dogs, such as the West Mexican ceramic canine in the exhibition, or sacrificed dogs frequently accompanied the dead at interment.

In pre-Hispanic Mesoamerica, movement across these tiered levels of the universe was believed possible for humans, the dead, and supernatural forces, often along some kind of *axis mundi*, like the trunk of a great tree, that stretched vertically through these tiered domains. Passage from one horizontal realm to others also was seen as possible through caves, fire, sunlight, or the center points of architectural ballcourts where rubber ballgames were played (Carrasco 1990, 52–53). Pre-Hispanic Mesoamerican ballgames were not played with precisely the same rules, or the same accompaniments. Although many ballplayers may have worn padded yokes of leather or rubber around their waists to protect their torso and propel the heavy rubber ball that was used in the game, stone yokes, such as the one exhibited, were limited to the Classic period (500–900 CE) along the Gulf Coast (Veracruz State). Stone yokes (Figure 3.5) were too heavy to wear during the game and likely served as ceremonial emblems or were incorporated into ritual events. Despite differences in the form of the court and the associated artifacts, the game always had a tie to life, death, and a portal between realms of the universe.

In pre-Hispanic Mesoamerican belief systems, death was closely connected to the world of the living. Life and death were conceived to be part of a dynamic and complementary opposition. Pre-Hispanic Mesoamerican thought recognized that the maintenance of the cosmos required both supernatural action and nourishment provided by humans through offerings and other ritual practices (Figures 3.6–3.9). Bloodletting, death, and sacrifice were seen as necessary aspects of life to maintain cosmic order. Furthermore, deceased ancestors had a powerful impact on the living. Not only could they send malevolent forces and disease if not treated properly, but they served as conduits between the living and the supernatural world (Miller and Taube 1993, 74).

Thus, in pre-Hispanic Mesoamerica, the deceased remained social actors. The biological dead continued to be socially alive. For example, in certain representations, they were shown to dance at weddings or bear witness to successions of leadership. The death of an individual began a process of rebirth and renewal in which the deceased was seen as instrumental to what befalls the living (Fitzsimmons 2012, 776–77).

Maize was a key staple crop of most pre-Hispanic Mesoamerican peoples, and the plant's agricultural cycle, from seed to cob to stalk, served as a metaphor for human life and death (Miller and Taube 1993, 28–32). Humans were viewed analogously to maize and other plants grown on the surface of the Earth, born to perish, serving a role on Earth, but also embodying the seed of regeneration (like the corn kernel that gives rises to the next generation crop). This metaphor, portrayed in distinct ways, was a persistent theme in pre-Hispanic Mesoamerican artistic representations.

Pre-Hispanic Mesoamerican conceptions of life, death, sacrifice, and renewal foster traditions that remain alive today. The active role of ancestors in the world of the living undoubtedly is part of the traditional legacy for contemporary rituals associated with the Day of the Dead. Likewise, Mesoamerican farmers let drops of their own or animal blood and spill alcohol in their nascent maize fields as a sacrifice to the Earth and supernatural world when planting to ensure a fertile harvest.

References

Carrasco, D. 1990. *Religions of Mesoamerica*. San Francisco: Harper.

Feinman, G. M., and Carballo, D. M. 2018. "Collaborative and Competitive Strategies in the Variability and Resiliency of Large-Scale Societies in Mesoamerica." *Economic Anthropology* 5: 7–19.

Fitzsimmons, J. L. 2012. "The Living and the Dead." In *The Oxford Handbook of Mesoamerican Archaeology*, edited by D. Nichols and C. A. Pool, 776–84. Oxford: Oxford University Press.

Miller, M., and Taube, K. 1993. *The Illustrated Dictionary of the Gods and Symbols of Ancient Mexico and the Maya*. London: Thames and Hudson.

Figure 3.7. Colima dog, likely from a funerary context, front view (FM 95615).

Figure 3.8. Classic-period Zapotec (Oaxaca, Mexico) effigy vessel (FM 51884), generally recovered from funerary contexts.

In Haiti, ritual flags known as *drapo* serve as a primary sacred art tradition of Vodou (Figures 3.1–3.3), and many feature spirits of the dead. *Drapo* derive from a blended tradition of European military banners and West African processional tapestries of ritual and warfare. Early Haitian *drapo* may have simply included different colored fabric sewn together, but beginning in the mid-twentieth century, factory textile workers collected discarded beads and sequins and began incorporating them in innovative new styles of flagmaking (Girouard 1995; Polk 1997). Ritually speaking, *drapo* play a central role within Vodou communities as emblems of a temple's protective patron *lwa*, and when processed around a temple's sacred center post (the *potomitan*), their sequins capture the essence of spirits in motion. As ceremonial tapestries, *drapo* energize the spirits into action, dancing to welcome newly made initiates to a spiritual family and carried as mystic banners to honor the spirits in sacred outdoor processions. This is strikingly similar to the way the ancient Moche ancestors from northern Peru were represented dancing, celebrating, and even copulating for the successful passage of the deceased into the world of the dead (see Muro Ynoñán in this volume, on Moche death and sex). Today's *drapo* often portray *vèvè*, sacred symbols unique to each *lwa*, or artistic interpretations of the spirits in the Vodou pantheon. Perhaps due in part to the harsh realities of life and death in Haiti, the Gede family of spirits are frequently portrayed in *drapo*.

Gede spirits typically manifest in Vodou ceremony through ritual mountings as powerful yet playful spirits with great wisdom and healing abilities; they tell bawdy jokes and tease uptight devotees about all manners of procreation but as arbiters of life and death, they never tell a lie. In *drapo* such as those by Haitian artist Ronald Edmond, the Gede are portrayed in their signature top hats, black, white, and purple attire, wearing sunglasses to see simultaneously into visible and invisible worlds, and are often depicted dancing lasciviously to bring in new life. Grann Brijit, the Queen of the Gedes, may be portrayed with a headscarf, broad-rimmed hat, pipe, and sacred liquor offerings in the cemetery. The Gede can also be represented as skeletons performing everyday actions, resembling the pantheon of Mexico's own vibrant mortuary art traditions of animated skeletons (see Amat in this volume). Spirits of the dead are ceremonially honored in Haiti on November 1 and 2 for All Saints' Day and All Souls Day, recognized as feast days for the Gede spirit family and all ancestors (*zansèt yo*). The skeletal Gede portraits very much parallel Mexican ancestors and skeletons honored in Día de los Muertos (Day of the Dead) festivities, some of whom have even taken on sacred personas in a skeleton pantheon such as the well-known La Catrina. Ultimately, Haiti's Gede spirits remind devotees to live their lives meaningfully and with vitality, maintaining a sense of humor in facing the precarious nature of death.

Soul Journeys and the Multi-Soul Complex

A common philosophical quandary in Western society unfolds in considering what happens to the soul when someone transitions in death. In many West African and African Diaspora traditions, this query becomes exponentially more complex with the introduction of the multi-soul complex: the common Africana philosophy that each person possesses multiple souls. In several West African cosmologies, certain soul-selves are embodied in the physical body itself such as the Yorùbá *orí odè* of southwestern Nigeria and Kongo *nitu* of northwestern Angola and western Congos (Daniels 2022). Other souls are immaterial, such as the Igbo *chi* (southeastern Nigeria), Akan *kra*, Yorùbá *orí inù*, and Kongo *kini*, which all manifest a person's cosmic double in the invisible realm of spirits. In certain contexts, the soul is regarded as a divine breath as in the Fon *sè mèdo* (southern Benin), Yorùbá èmí, Akan *honhom*, and Kongo *vûmunu*. In all of these regions, this divine breath comprises an aspect of one's selfhood and is eventually extinguished in death (Daniels 2022). Further, the Akan *honhom* and Yorùbá *orì inú* souls have the power to fly, and upon one's death they transform into bird-like creatures as a person makes their way to the spiritual realm (Ogunnaike 2012). At times, the soul makes its own way to the ancestral world upon someone's transition to the afterlife, while in other communities, specific rituals such as the smashing of clay pots occurs to release the soul from its human shell. The notion of a fractal or divisible soul that partitions, travels, and transits from one entity to another, either human or nonhuman, is interestingly present in Andean pre-Columbian societies, suggesting some shared notions about the soul(s) and personhood among Indigenous American and African societies (see Williams and also Muro Ynoñán in this volume, on Inca and Moche death rituals, respectively). Consistently across Black Atlantic religious communities however, death liberates the soul(s), and an individual's personhood as it was once known ceases to exist.

Figure 3.9. Incense burner from the pre-Hispanic valley of Oaxaca (FM 191593).

3B The Inca *Capac Hucha*

Patrick Ryan Williams
Field Museum

The Inca rite of *capac hucha*, the "royal obligation," brings into question the fundamental aspects of death in society. It involves the offering of young children as sacrifices to important sacred entities in the Inca world. It is, in many ways, the sacrifice of the future potential of humanity. The *capac hucha* is not a moment in time, however, as it involves an extensive process of transformation. Those chosen for the ritual of *capac hucha* may have been removed from their home months or a year or more before their biological deaths in many cases. And they were conceived of as intermediaries to the ancestral deities. The Inca empire prepared for these cases well in advance. Some of the young women may have been taken into service as *aqllakuna* (chosen women) and destined for this rite. Other girls and boys were chosen from communities throughout the empire. While often the sacred entities to whom they were sacrificed were lofty mountain peaks, in at least one case it was a sacred island in the Pacific Ocean.

In 1892, George Dorsey, future curator at the Field Museum, conducted excavations on the Isla de la Plata off the coast of Ecuador for the World Columbian Exposition. On a triangular point of land between two ravines, at 16 feet below the surface, the excavations revealed the remains of two poorly preserved skeletons and numerous grave offerings (Dorsey 1901). Based on the grave offerings, we presume these were the remains of two young women, although their bodies were not collected nor identified on site. The excavations revealed many ceramics and stone sculptures of the local Chorrera culture and the remains of a sacred Inca child sacrifice, the *capac hucha* (McEwan and Silva 2000).

The grave offerings accompanying the two individuals included five female figurines (three of gold, one of silver, and one of bronze), six *tupu* pins (used to fasten a women's shawl), and several Inca ceramic vessels which were made in the Inca capital of Cusco, over 1000 miles to the south (Bray et al. 2005) (Figure 3.10). This assemblage of grave offerings is characteristic of the *capac hucha*, a rite of sacrifice that took place on important occasions in the Inca empire. Such occasions may have been on the coronation or death of the emperor, the birth of a royal heir, a great victory in battle, or in response to a natural disaster. The ceremony did not always involve human sacrifice, which was reserved for the most powerful sacred places, often the peaks of great mountains, or *apu*.

According to early Spanish accounts, a *capac hucha* ceremony was preceded by a call to all the provinces of the empire to send as tribute boys and girls between the ages of four and ten years old. Some were required to be children of local lords, and all were to be examples of physical perfection. In some cases, the children were paired as male/female couples and buried as a pair. The children and visiting dignitaries that accompanied them participated in ceremonial feasts, performances, and ritual events for days or weeks in Cusco. At the designated time, the children and their attendants would begin the journey to the sacred places of sacrifice, sometimes hundreds of miles away, dressed in fine clothes and with the various precious offerings to the *huaca* (sacred entity). Their physical cause of death may have been exposure in the cold mountain air, a blow to the head as they sat in their tomb, strangulation, or intoxication to the point of death. In all cases, the integrity of the body was critical to the ritual.

The examples of *capac hucha* told in early historical accounts illustrate diverse origins and interment locales for these children. A young girl named Tanta Carhua was buried alive at a *huaca* in her homeland in the central highlands of Peru after returning from the ceremonies held in Cusco. Another, named Cauri Pacssa, from the northern highlands of Peru, was sacrificed in Chile (Hernández Príncipe in Bray et al. 2005). Archaeological research on the bodies of children from the Llullaillaco *capac hucha* burial in Argentina show they consumed coca and large amounts of alcohol in the month before their interment; intoxication may have opened paths to the spiritual realm in Inca beliefs (Wilson et al. 2013).

The *capac hucha* demonstrates that death is not a single moment in Inca conception. The moment the children are chosen for the *capac hucha*, they begin a process of transformation. The Jesuit priest Bernabe Cobo indicates that parents obliged to give up their children were not allowed to express any sadness, but rather gestures of happiness that the honor was a great reward were required (Wilson et al. 2013). The moment of transfer from their previous social existence to an Inca offering represented a fundamental transformation in their being. As they left their village, never to return again, they left their social world forever. Their social death preceded by months their physical interment on a mountain summit or in an island tomb.

The days or weeks of ceremonies in Cusco represented the transformation of the children from earthly beings to offerings to the sacred. The moment of biological death, be it through physical violence at the site of their interment, or intoxication and hypothermia that led to the ceasing of their heart and brain to function, was not a clear break either. In fact, the physical preservation of their bodies, surrounded by the precious offerings that made them sacred, was likely intended for them to serve as conduits to the *apu* and the sacred realm. In a spiritual sense, it is unclear if they may continue to exist in a spiritual cognizance with the *huaca* in which they were interred.

We cannot know how these children felt about their sacrifice on the mountain summits and in the island grave.

Figure 3.10. Inca *capac hucha* assemblage from Isla de la Plata, Ecuador: miniature ceramic jar (FM 4459); ceramic pedestal-base pot (FM 4460); miniature ceramic plate (FM 4367); gold figurine (FM 4450); and silver figurine (FM 4354).

That they went in altered states under the coercion of powerful political leaders at such a young age belies any choice they had in the matter. But it does call us to examine the questions: what is death and when does it occur? Death is not purely a biological process, but a transformation from one state to another, and one that depends on social roles, physical processes, and spiritual presence in defining how that process occurs.

References

Bray, T. L., Minc, L. D., Ceruti, M. C., Chávez, J. A., Perea, R., and Reinhard, J. 2005. "A Compositional Analysis of Pottery Vessels Associated with the Inca Ritual of Capacoch." *Journal of Anthropological Archaeology* 24, no. **1:** 82–100.

Dorsey, G. A. 1901. *Archaeological Investigations on the Island of La Plata, Ecuador* (Vol. 2, No. 5). Chicago: Field Columbian Museum.

McEwan, C., and Silva, M. I. 2000. "La presencia Inca en la costa central de Ecuador y en la Isla de la Plata." In *Compendio de investigaciones en el Parque Nacional Machalilla*, edited by M. Iturralde and C. Josse, 71–102. Quito, Ecuador: Centro de Datos para la Conservación, Fundación Natura.

McEwan, C., and Van de Guchte, M. 1992. "Ancestral Time and Sacred Space in Inca State Ritual." In *The Ancient Americas: Art from Sacred Landscapes*, edited by R. F. Townsend, 359–71. Chicago: Art Institute of Chicago.

Wilson, A. S., Brown, E. L., Villa, C., Lynnerup, N., Healey, A., Ceruti, M. C., Reinhard, J., Previgliano, C. H., Arias Araoz, F., Gonzalez Diez, J., and Taylor, T. 2013. "Archaeological, Radiological, and Biological Evidence Offer Insight into Inca Child Sacrifice." *PNAS Proceedings of the National Academy of Sciences* 110, no. 33: 13322–27.

In the African Diaspora, sacred vessels house various aspects of the soul, and can liberate these souls upon an initiate's death. Haitians refer to the physical body as the *kò kadav*, and within the body, seven "soul-selves" reside: the *gwo bon anj* (personality soul), the *ti bon anj* (morality soul), the *zetwal* (astral soul), the *lwa rasin/lwa eritaj* (root or inherited soul spirits), *lwa mèt tèt* (master of the head soul spirit), *wonsiyon* (collective of soul spirits that accompany the *mèt tèt*), and *nanm* (the full self in totality) (Beauvoir 2006). In Vodou cosmology, mystic clay pots serve an essential role during major life changes, as these various vessels each claim responsibility for distinct souls. Haiti boasts several mystic pots: *plat marasa* (ceramic pots sacred to Marasa, the divine twins akin to the Yorùbá *ibeji*), *krich* (clay drinking vessels), *pòt tèt* (ceramic initiation soul chambers), *zen* (clay or iron ceremonial pots for initiation and mortuary rites), *govi* (spirit residences, divination implements, and funerary vessels), and *kanari* (large clay mortuary vessels). Several of these Haitian mystic clay pots associated with the souls are featured in this exhibition, including two *govi* and one *kanari* (see for example Figure 3.4).

When a Vodou initiate dies, a primary mortuary rite known as *desounen* takes place, during which the deceased's body is prepared for burial, various pots are nourished and destroyed, and several souls (the *gwo bon anj, ti bon anj,* and *lwa mèt tèt*) are removed from a person. *Desounen* literally translates as "an uprooting of sound" or removal of life from a person's body. In essence, the ritual of *desounen* "desacralizes the body, extricating it from all divine manifestations, and at the same time freeing the *gwo bon anj* and the *mèt tèt* to be initiated among the community of the dead" (Desmangles 1992, 69). To ensure a person's many souls make safe passage to the spirit realm, biological and spiritual family members gather together to perform *bohoun*, special funerary songs and drumming. The devotee's physical body (*kò kadav*) is publicly released from its mortal duties and sent to a subterranean spiritual realm to be refired for the entrance of a new soul (Daniels 2023). Enormous mystic pots known as *kanari* (Figure 3.4) play a central role here, even in their humble state as unadorned clay vessels. They are ceremonially broken during *desounen* in a rite called *kase kanari*, which liberates the deceased person's souls and head-spirit so that they may join their unique spirit realms.

If *desounen* "uproots sound" to release the body's souls, *kase kanari* shatters a small portion of the universe to embody the deceased's final act as a physical person. At this time, three of the devotee's souls—the *gwo bon anj*, the *ti bon anj*, and *lwa mèt tèt*—are all liberated to pursue their respective paths: the *ti bon anj* journeys to heaven, the *gwo bon anj* goes underwater to the ancestral realm of Afrik-Ginen, and the *lwa mèt tèt* is released into the ether to rejoin the other cosmic spirits. *Kase kanari* is conducted by both the biological and spiritual family, signifying the rupture of the initiate's passing and also embodying the liberation of multiple souls and spirits who have animated the initiate. Inducted into ceremony by the community, the purchase and subsequent shattering of the mystic pot *kanari* embodies a family's commitment to honor the deceased's many souls and continue the family legacy of spirit worship in the next generation.

The smaller Haitian clay pots known as *govi* (Figure 3.4) serve three principal roles in Vodou divination rites: as residences for the spirits, as divination implements, and as mortuary vessels for the ancestors. During rites of initiation in southern variants of Haitian Vodou, each devotee receives seven *govi* in honor of seven principal *lwa* or spirits of the temple. These Haitian *govi*—a Fongbe word from ancient Dahomey/Benin, *vi* meaning small or child and *go* meaning gourd or bottle (Blier 1995)—are blessed, fed, and become dwellings for an initiate's spirits on her personal altar. The mystic pots are dressed in colored satin or silk robes that honor the spirits whom they embody: white for the elder serpent spirits Danbala and Ayida Wèdo, red for the warrior spirit Ogou, and blue for the mother warrior spirit Èzili Dantò. In their second role, *govi* are also used as traditional divination implements, as priests and priestesses (*houngan* and *manbo*) invoke the *lwa* using the clay pot as a channel to directly contact the spirit realm.

In secondary mortuary rites of Haiti, the same earthenware *govi* appear again in their third role as mortuary vessels. As previously mentioned, *desounen* is performed when a devotee transitions to release several of her souls. At this juncture, her *gwo bon anj* or personality soul travels under the water (*anba dlo*) to the divine realm of Afrik-Ginen, where the spirits and ancestors all reside. One year and one day after a person has been buried, another ceremony occurs known as *wete mò nan dlo* (or *retire mò nan dlo*)—literally, to call or pull the dead from the water. In this secondary mortuary rite, the buried person remains undisturbed in her tomb, but the deceased's soul undergoes a transition of residence. Devotees invoke the names of the dead in ritual song to call forth the *gwo bon anj* of various loved ones who have been stationed in Afrik-Ginen (Deren 1953; Métraux 1959). Each deceased ancestor's *gwo bon anj* soul is ritually prepared for a return to the mortal world, this time not in a human vessel but in a mystic clay pot. At the right moment in the ceremony, the *gwo bon anj* souls of the dead being called forth are ritually "captured" in their respective *govi*, and the ancestors regain their ability to speak through the clay vessel. The *govi* thus become funerary pots as well as "homing" receptacles for the ancestors. From then onward, the ancestral *govi* will be preciously kept on a family altar or in the community temple, and can be accessed through divination rites for counsel and advice regarding illness, misfortune, or family difficulties. The mystic pots featured here in this exhibition—*kanari* and *govi*—ultimately represent the distinct journeys of a Haitian Vodouizan's souls after death. While certain souls are released into cosmic realms, others will be recalled in a new manifestation of ancestral presence on the earthly altars of their devotee descendants.

Twin Souls and Double Deaths

Twins present a fascinating case of plural soul-selves in Africana cosmologies, which explains their complex relationship to death and the invisible realm. While the rates of identical twins appear roughly the same across the world, BaKongo societies of Central Africa (Angola, Congo-Brazzaville, and Congo-Kinshasa) and Yorùbá societies of West Africa (southwestern Nigeria and southern Benin) produce some of the highest rates of fraternal and sororal twins in the world (Bandama in this volume; MacGaffey 1986). Twins are regarded in both regions as possessing divine qualities, and must be propitiated while living on earth and afterwards in death. Mapasa, as they are known in Kongo regions, historically followed certain ritual taboos, such as refraining from eating leopards and certain big cats, sacred animals whose spotted or striated coats signal their ability to communicate with the spirit realm (MacGaffey 1986; Fu-Kiau Kia Bunseki-Lumanisa 2001). Traditionally regarded as mediators between worlds, as were Inca noble children (see Williams on the Inca *capac hucha* ritual in this volume), Kongo twins were instructed neither to kill nor consume the flesh of these revered forest creatures who lived between realms, for to do so would be akin to taking one's own life.

In Yorùbáland, Nigeria, ìbejì or twins similarly express otherworldly qualities as part human and part spirit. Sacred wooden statues of Yorùbá twins called *ere* ìbejì may be carved at different points in the twins' lives. In this volume, Foreman Bandama helpfully explains how "twins have the same combined soul, whose stability needs to be maintained if one dies." Indeed, in the Yorùbá universe, each person possesses a divine double (*enìkejì*) in the spirit realm who walks alongside one during the entirety of one's life. When twins are born, it is said that the *enìkejì* has come along with the mortal person as a newly incarnated spirit (Olúpọ̀nà 2022). Because no distinction can be made between the mortal-twin and spirit-twin, ìbejì must be treated exactly the same. In Yorùbá and Kongo communities alike, twins are showered with loving care and attention, for any angered twin can bring strife to the family, and orchestrate great chaos in the community.

Vibrant twin traditions persist in the African Diaspora, with elaborate ceremonies to honor twins known as *gemelos* in Cuban Spanish and *jimo* in Haitian Kreyòl (from the French *jumeaux*). Tellingly, while twins possess these secular titles in both Caribbean nations, they are revered as both mortal and divine, and thus also carry mystic monikers: *ibeji* in the Cuban Lucumí/Regla de Ocha/Santería religion and in Haiti, the more commonly used term is *marasa* (a clear derivation of the KiKongo *mapasa*), especially among the Vodou communities. Such twin devotion appears on altars, as with the *ibeij* statues of Cuban Lucumí/Regla de Ocha/Santería traditions. Here the wooden-carved twins likely imported from Nigeria are paired with two porcelain ceramic vessels with different colored beads. The male twin (left) stands behind a pot with a red-and-white necklace for the *orichá* (spirit) of thunder and lightning Changó, while the female twin (right) faces a pot with mostly clear and blue beads for Yemayá, *orichá* of the sea and mother of fish and all humankind. These vessels are periodically fed as divine nourishment for the doubled spirits of *ibeji*.

Figure 3.11. Yorùbá *ere ibeji*: twin figures in wood (FM 303438, 9-A114395d).

3C The Yorùbá *Ere Ibeji*: Reincarnation of Twins

Foreman Bandama
Field Museum

Life and death are powerful forces whose balance, or lack thereof, cannot be left to chance or nature. But what happens when they are doubled, literally, through the birth or death of twins? Traditionally, the birth and/or death of twins always swings the pendulum of these forces rather violently amongst many African communities (Mobolade 1997). For much of Africa, twins are feared and considered a bad sign of impending danger that can be averted by the elimination of one or both of the newborn children. However, historical shifts amongst the Yorùbá people led to the current patterns in which twins are revered and celebrated both in life and in death (Leroy 1995).

The Yorùbá people are concentrated in southwestern Nigeria, but they are also found in neighboring Togo and Ghana. They are one of Africa's largest ethnic groups, with over 25 million members (Leroy et al. 2002). One of their most peculiar features is a genetic disposition that has given the Yorùbá people the highest recorded rate of twin births in the world. Their dizygotic twinning rate is 4.4 percent of all maternities, or about 45 sets of twins in every 1000 births. This, coupled with other historical challenges, often led to high infant deaths. In ancient times, the Yorùbá people, just like most of the African ethnic groups, used to reject and even sacrifice newborn twins. This is now all but forgotten and twins are welcomed and celebrated in grand style, both at their birth and after death. Anthropologists posit that the shift into the *ere ibeji* system was a copying mechanism for an ethnic group that witnesses more twin birth/death than others.

In the Yorùbá language, twins are called "*ibeji*," which is a compound name; "*ibi*" (which means born) and "*eji*" (which means two/twice) (Mobolade 1997, 14). The first-born twin is usually named "Taiyewo" or "Taiwo," meaning to have the first taste of the world, and the second is named "Kehinde," which means arriving after the other (Figure 3.11). *Ere* then refers to a sacred statue/carving commissioned and created to symbolically perpetuate the life of the departed, when one or both twins die (Leroy et al. 2002).

To the Yorùbá people, twins have the same combined soul, whose stability needs to be maintained if one dies. Accordingly, most twins' activities and appearances are also matched. For instance, they wear the same clothing, eat the same food, and even share in all services (Idowu 1962). The celebration of the twins begins immediately after birth with elaborate feasts that may even involve neighboring villages, depending on the status of the parents. Soon after birth, a divining priest is consulted to find out about the future of the twins and to obtain specific instructions on how to care for the newborns. A major component of this consultation includes finding out whether carved figures (*ibeji*) should be commissioned immediately or not. In the latter case (*ibeji* not decreed at birth), the carved figure(s) will be required when one or both die. When one twin dies, an *ibeji* image is fashioned and kept to house the soul of the departed, thereby maintaining balance in the soul of the surviving twin. The death of both twins is followed by the commissioning of two *ibeji* statues that are treated with reverence as if the twins were still alive. The pampering of the *ibeji* includes occasional feeding (food touching the mouths), facial markings, bathing, singing, clothing, elaborated ornamentation such as beads and painting, as well as soaking in magic potions (Johnson 1921). It is the primary responsibility of the parents to treat these statues as if they were the living children because failing to do so is believed to lead to negative consequences such as poverty and illness (Mobolade 1997). This responsibility is then passed on to the surviving twin when he/she is older.

The manufacture of the *ibeji* statues among the Yorùbá people was done by skilled carvers because they are made from wood. The wooden figures are always carved in an erect adult posture with hands on the hips and are fixed to a round or rectangular baseplate. Often, the associated adornment included non-wooden materials such as bracelets, waistbands, and necklaces made from terracotta clay, cowrie shells, or valuable metals like copper, bronze, or silver. The statues are generally small and never life-size (about ten inches tall), but carved in unmistakable human likenesses. These sizes have to do with how they are used at special occasions, because the mothers of the deceased twins are expected to dance with these *ibeji*s tightly held in their palms or tucked in the wrappers on their waist at annual occasions (Leroy et al. 2002). The general workmanship of the *ibeji* statues speaks to the long artistic traditions expressed in ancient kingdoms such as Benin and Ife. Marked stylistic differences do occur according to the region and artists, and these differences can be noticed in facial expressions, hairdos, tribal scarring heads, and head covers.

Yorùbá's *ere ibeji* tradition has since spread to several parts of the world, mainly to the West Indies and the eastern coast of South America (the "slave coast") because of the transatlantic slave trade. Accordingly, the transposing of the Yorùbá twin belief system into African Diaspora religions Candoble and Macumba (Salvador de Bahia region) and Umbanda (Rio de Janeiro and Sao Paulo regions) in Brazil is not surprising (Leroy et al. 2002).

References

Idowu, E. B. 1962. *Olodumare, God in Yoruba Belief.* London: Longmans, Green & Co.

Johnson, S. 1921. *The History of the Yorubas*. London: Lowe & Brydone.

Leroy, F. 1995. *Les jumeaux dans tous leurs* états [Twins in every state]. Brussels: Deboeck Université.

Leroy, F., Olaleye-Oruene, T., Koeppen-Schomerus, G., and Bryan, E. 2002. "Yoruba Customs and Beliefs Pertaining to Twins." *Twin Research* 5, no. 2: 132–36.

Mobolade, T. 1997. "Ibeji Custom in Yorubaland." *African Arts* 4, no. 3: 14–15.

Pauline, V., and Sealey, R. N. 1973. "Ibeji: The Deity of Twins among the Yoruba." *Journal of National Medical Association* 65, no. 5: 443.

Marasa in Haiti refers to mortal twins as well as the sacred twins who represent the spirit of children. Traditionally, the term *marasa* also refers to "uncanny children" with mystic qualities, those born with a caul, with teeth, with hair, or those of breech birth (McGee 2022). Though in recent decades, the carved tradition of wooden statues has not been maintained in Haiti as in West Africa, twins are honored with *plat marasa*, ceramic vessels that hold offerings for a family's mortal twins and the sacred spirit duo. *Plat marasa* comes either as a tripartite ceramic set with three removable pots in three conjoined bowls or as two conjoined bowls with pots and one ancillary bowl and pot that can be added or removed. It may appear peculiar that mystic pots honoring the sacred twins include *three* mystic pots, but this embodies the principle of *marasa twa* (literally, "twins of three"). *Marasa twa* honor either triplets or the child who follows twins—*dosu* if a boy, *dosa* if a girl. It also recalls the Vodou adage that 1+1=3, a philosophy that highlights the mystic power of exponentiality, in which twins manifest a divine energy more powerful than the sum of their combined parts. More studies should be conducted on the intriguing parallels between the practice of twins veneration among African societies and that of noble children, particularly with physical malformations, leading to their sacrifice among the Indigenous communities of pre-Hispanic Peru, such as Chimú, Moche, and Inca (*capac hucha*) groups.

As divine mortal beings, twins' mortuary rites often blend worship traditions for revered ancestors and spirits. Following a twin's end of life (or the tragic death of both twins) in Yorùbá communities, the *ere* ìbejì play an essential role as an embodied manifestation of the lost twin, ensuring that parents and relatives can continue to care for the deceased twin's spirit. These *ere* ìbejì may be adorned with beaded necklaces and intricate regalia, including cloaks of cowrie shells or colorful seed beads in more affluent families to signal a family's devotion in honoring the legacy of their departed twin(s). In Haiti when a family experiences great strife, especially with (twin) children who persistently fall ill, people may identify this misfortune as a result of displeasure of the *Marasa*, referring either to the spirit twins or a deceased pair of twins in the family lineage. To appease the divine duo, Vodouizan will host a ceremony called *manje marasa*, a sacred feeding of the twins. As mortal manifestations of the *lwa Marasa*, neighborhood children are invited to partake in a spiritual feast, and offered *mayi moulin* (cornmeal porridge) on traditional "plates" of banana leaves, along with sweet treats and *kola kouronne* (Haitian cola). In this way, the *lwa Marasa* (twin spirits) as well as the family's *zansèt marasa* (deceased twin ancestors) may be satiated, and can restore harmony and wellness to the living family.

Disruptive Death: COVID-19 and the Haitian Earthquakes

Cosmologically speaking, Vodouizan do not pray for immortality, as only the *lwa*—the divine energies who orchestrate order in the universe—live forever. But like so many religious devotees around the world, a common Haitian prayer for elders and juniors alike is the blessing of a long and productive life. The most devastating deaths are those that occur traumatically and unexpectedly: the deaths of children, road accidents, deadly illnesses with no treatment, natural disasters, and pandemics. Haiti has experienced its own share of catastrophic deaths en masse, including two seizable earthquakes in the past 12 years: the 7.2 magnitude earthquake of Port-au-Prince on January 12, 2010, and the recent 7.0 magnitude earthquake of Les Cayes on August 14, 2021. The 2010 earthquake killed approximately 250,000 people, injured 300,000, and left millions of people displaced (Germain 2011); the 2021 earthquake killed approximately 2250 people, injured 12,765, and left at least 330 missing (International Medical Corps 2021). These earthquakes are the result of Haiti being situated between two geographic fault lines: the Septentrional Fault and the Enriquillo-Plantain Garden Fault. Such scientific explanations must be underscored as missionaries and televangelists such as Pat Robertson asserted that Haitians were killed during the 2010 earthquake and other historical atrocities due to a supposed "pact with the devil" made in 1791 to defeat the French colonizers (Stewart [Diakité] 2010). The truth is that Haitian maroon soldiers and enslaved citizens held a revolutionary congress at a northern site called Bwa Kayiman, and in a Vodou ceremony honoring the spirits on August 14, 1791, they pledged their allegiance to the *lwa* to build a free Black republic and the world's first anti-imperial nation-state.

While the nation's physical damage proved calamitous in both Haitian earthquakes of 2010 and 2021, the most harrowing reality involved the tragic loss of so many lives, and people's inability to bury their loved ones. Aid workers and healthcare providers worked to dig mass graves for the dead and the dismembered, but hundreds of thousands of missing-person reports seemed to flow in an endless stream of grief. In Vodou as in Christianity, being unable to find loved ones and inter the dead can have disastrous spiritual consequences for the soul, which caused tremendous upheaval in a nation beset by mass mourning. More recently, Haiti has been reeling from the effects of the coronavirus pandemic. And while COVID-19 has had far more devastating consequences in North America than in Haiti, concerns surrounding such a dangerous virus in a nation already struggling with public health infrastructure problems have alarmed healthcare workers about the possibilities of a full-blown outbreak.

Haitian artists, similarly to other artists all around the world (see Wali on responses to the pandemic in this volume), have responded to these recent natural disasters and the pandemic with portraits of earthquake victims and survivors; divinely inspired artists have also portrayed the spirits' interventions in human affairs to save their devotees from COVID-19. Remarkable *drapo* depictions of the 2010 earthquake have been produced in exquisite beaded detail by Myrlande Constant (Ulysse 2022), Evelyn Alcide (Daniels 2021), Roudy Azor, and most recently, ritual flag and mixed media artist Ronald Edmond. Edmond founded the artisanal Port-au-Prince workshop *Atelye Deliverans* (Artistic Workshop of Deliverance), and as a skilled ritual flag designer and maker, he and his team of artisans typically complete flags within several weeks or months depending on their size and intricacy. However, as a survivor of the earthquake himself, Edmond reflects that it took him over a decade to actualize a ritual flag portrayal of the 2010 earthquake as he experienced and envisioned it. Haiti's most recent major earthquake of 2021 encouraged him to return to this earlier work with intentions to manifest the flag fully.

Completed in 2022, Ronald Edmond's *Le Sèisime du 12 Janvier 2010*/The Earthquake of January 12, 2010 (Figure 3.1) depicts a harrowing scene of chaos and destruction in the capital city, despite the fact that the earthquake's epicenter was in Léogâne, roughly 16 miles from Port-au-Prince. Concrete buildings are cracked and splayed, foundations unearthed, houses toppled over. Victims have been crushed beneath edifices, and severed limbs haunt the lower corner of the tapestry. While certain figures appear faceless, standing in for all unnamed victims of the earthquake, several other peoples' eyes capture our attention, either calling for help in the wreckage or assertively fixed on the mission to save any possible survivors. A telephone pole has fallen over next to a stalled yellow car. A cinder block, disengaged tire, and red tool box all litter the ground in various corners, and a pool of blood seeps from victims' bodies onto toppled concrete walls. And while foreign aid intervention is visible from the United Nations helicopter overhead (noticeably absent from both Alcide and Azor's earthquake depictions), on the ground, Edmond renders the real front-line workers of 2010: Haitian civilians and local aid workers, including a pair of civilians who transport an injured woman to safety (see also Mutcherson in this volume, on other front-line workers disproportionately affected by the pandemic in the US). The flag also renders a sophisticated *trompe l'œil* effect, with a skewed perspectival landscape of the Earth. Along with overturned houses and shattered concrete buildings, the Earth is unevenly rendered, and appears menacing as it threatens to swallow the city and its inhabitants whole.

Before our eyes, the metropolis of Port-au-Prince has become a necropolis, but the Vodou spirits have not forgotten their children. In the upper left corner, the mother warrior spirit Èzili Dantò wears her signature crown and a pair of orange wings to rescue a woman from her home; the woman wears dark blue, Dantò's signature color, perhaps signaling her devotion to the Black Madonna. Above in the top right, the mermaid queen of the seas LaSirènn swims through the sky with a tail of multi-colored scales and pulls another survivor from the ruins. Poised with the ritual rattle (*ason*) in her right hand that marks her priesthood, she may be preparing a ritual healing ceremony for the injured mortal. Alternatively, this same spirit could also be interpreted as the rainbow serpent spirit Ayida Wèdo with her brightly colored serpent tail. Finally, the *lwa* Brav Gede (at times also known as Gede Nibo) appears in the top right corner with a dark-colored suit and top hat. Golden speckled angel wings may allow him to rise more swiftly from his subterranean domain of the afterworld Afrik-Ginen. In his left hand (the spiritual side), he carries a calabash bowl of food offerings to nourish the human child he has rescued from below. LaSirènn and Brav Gede hover over a partially crushed long white building. Two of the building's doors are open, one orange and the other red, and they resemble the intricate iron doors of urban Vodou temples. This may signal that while largely accosted by Pentecostals who accused Vodou devotees of having caused the earthquake (Payton 2019), Vodouizan kept their temple doors open, and often held mass funerals to pray for the unburied dead, regardless of their religious orientation. A large mystic eye likely inspired from Freemason iconography (Kali 2019) emerges next to cumulus clouds, perhaps a signal that *BonDyè* (the creator God) bears witness to all devastation.

3D Sex, Death, and Life Regeneration in the Moche World, 200–900 CE

Luis Muro Ynoñán
Field Museum

Between the third and tenth centuries CE, in one of the driest deserts of the Western Hemisphere, the Moche society thrived. Considered by many as one of the first state-level entities from the pre-Hispanic Andes (cf. Quilter and Koons 2012), the Moche were organized into diverse political confederations governed by elite family clans, who controlled large portions of the valleys of the north coast of Peru (Quilter and Castillo 2010).

The Moche are particularly recognized, among many aspects, by the level of complexity of their elite burials. Discovered within large adobe pyramids or *huacas* (e.g., Sipán, Úcupe, El Brujo, and Huaca de la Luna), the Moche elite burials are composed of underground quadrangular-shaped adobe chambers often decorated with niches, platforms, and mural painting. The chambers contain the remains of high-status Moche lords and ladies accompanied by dozens of luxury items, including silvered and gilded copper crowns, nose ornaments, and headdresses, as well as warfare and ritual paraphernalia of various materials decorated with the most intricate designs and motifs.

Something particularly intriguing about these contexts is the striking similarity between the funerary ornaments that accompany the individuals and those with which mythological beings are depicted in Moche narrative art while performing ceremonial activities. For many, this is an indicator not only of the religious nature of the funerary items, but also their powerful transformative agency (Kaulicke 2000), suggesting that high-status individuals were interred as personifying gods and goddesses from the Moche pantheon. Whereas discussions about whether these divine identities were gained (and performed) in life or ascribed during funerary rituals have remained unresolved, it is undeniable that, in Moche society, immense power, prestige, and wealth was held in the hands of a few families in the region, who were likely related one to each other by kinship and hereditary rights.

But, as many have claimed, the Moche cannot be reduced to the sophistication and material richness of their grave goods, despite their exuberance. Death in the Moche world was particularly conceived in relationship to a specific understanding of environment, landscape, ancestors, and life regeneration. The Moche are considered both a cause and consequence of a long process of adaptation to an unpredictable environment, process that initiated around 14,000 BP with the first human groups arriving and settling down on the north coast of Peru. Impacted by heavy rainfalls and subsequent droughts caused by ENSO (El Niño Southern Oscillation) events, this region has been the backdrop of long-term cultural resilience, where the populations turned the threats imposed by nature into true opportunities to thrive. But, the unpredictable natural world of the Moche was not only "domesticated" through successful socioecological strategies, but also religion, mythology, and ritual practice. Through religious narratives, the Moche turned the wild landscape of the region into an animated world inhabited by devouring mountain-gods, gigantic killing spiders, dangerous maritime creatures, and even animated objects that could dangerously rise up in rebellion against humans (Quilter 1990). Risk and danger were always present in the Moche world, and Moche groups were constantly confronting the destabilizing forces around them.

But, as suggested by some Moche iconographers (Donnan and McClelland 1999), the chaos produced by natural forces and nonhuman agents was always brought into order by the intervention of the "mythological hero." The so-called hero (Ai-Apaec or Wrinkle Face) travels to the ends of the known world—from the mountains to the ocean, from the forest to the desert—fighting the monstrous creatures he encounters on his way toward the sun (Rucabado Yong 2021). After defeating these creatures, the hero acquires parts of their physical attributes, enabling him to remain victorious in his feat, which culminates in a copulation act with the moon goddess, from which emerges the so-called "tree of life." Some iconographers have suggested that the "tree of life" emerged, too, by the intervention of ancestors, who needed to be sexually stimulated for such an endeavor. The ancestors were thus mediators for the reestablishment of the much-desired order.

Although perhaps disturbing for modern eyes, graphic and vivid representations of sexual acts, possibly mimicking the deeds of the Moche mythological hero, are ubiquitous in Moche art. Humans, nonhumans, and hybrid beings are represented as actively engaged in sexual practices that involve masturbation, fellatio, and coitus. But not all entities had the same privilege to be represented, and Moche sex cannot be equated with erotism or pornography. Elite individuals seem to be preferred in these type of depictions and it is very likely that sexual acts were ritually performed, too, as part of larger performances of death in Moche religious centers (Muro Ynoñán 2019). The prominence of the sex organs (both male and female) in the artistic representations emphasizes the relevance of the *stimulus*, as well as the acceptable limits of the interaction between bodies.

So, it is not the sexual act in itself that is central in these representations. Instead, it is the capacity of given individuals to serve as a receptacle and means for the transmission of the *vital fluids*: those that guarantee the continuity of life and the maintenance of the social and natural order.

Figure 3.12. Moche vessel featuring ancestor-like figures engaged in an activity of sexual stimulation (FM 288074).

The Moche people conceptualized the elements of reality as made of, and linked through, fluids and substances (Weismantel and Meskell 2014). Landscapes, bodies, and things were perceived as containing an animated force (*camaquen*), which could flow from one entity to another, as well as transmute and transfigure. Both human blood and semen were interpreted as tangible expressions of such vital forces and, as such, were highly valued. In the sacrificial performances orchestrated in large-scale Moche temples (Uceda, Morales, and Mujica 2016), human blood and semen were obtained from the defeated warriors in ritual combats, after they had been stripped of their garments, paraded naked through the public plazas, and violenty dispatched. In fact, bio-archaeological data suggest that the corpses of the sacrificial victims might have also been involved in *postmortem* rites, where they were manipulated theatrically and sexually (Bourget 2001) (Figure 3.12).

The relationship between sex and death was thus present in the religious narratives, practices, and mythology of the Moche world. It is believed that while victims' bodies were ritually "consumed" under the eyes of spectators at the large temples, in the underworld, or *uku pacha*, the dead and the ancestors celebrated the reestablishment of the social and natural order. They did so dancing along with living women and children around the "tree of life." Only then was the process of life regeneration and reestablishment of order guaranteed.

Moche vital fluids were imbued with deep political symbolism. Their materialization in the form of erotic vessels, or sex-pots (Weismantel 2021), made for easier circulation and distribution, although their archaeological occurrence, mostly in high-rankling burials, suggests that this circulation was tightly controlled by elite families. Some have suggested that the possession of these items, along with other ornaments of metal and semi-precious stones, in the hands of given elite families provided the means for them to claim rights of ancestrality over lands, water, and resources and, thus, legitimize their political and economic power over local populations. As represented in the art, the multi-generational transmission of the vital fluids, from ancestors to parents and from parents to their descendants (Figure 3.13), seems aimed to guarantee the perpetuation of power of given lineages. In this sense, the reproduction and nourishment of new members of these lineages were also seen as repetitive reproductive cycles that involved the participation of multiple agents, living and nonliving, in a process where time and space, life and death, power and memory, were perpetually unified.

References

Bourget, S. 2001. "Rituals of Sacrifice: Its Practice at Huaca de La Luna and Its Representation in Moche Iconography." In *Moche Art and Archaeology in Ancient Peru*, edited by J. Pillsbury, 88–109. Washington, DC: National Galery of Art and Yale University Press.

Donnan, C., and McClelland, D. 1999. *Moche Fineline Painting: Its Evolution and Its Artists*. Los Angeles: UCLA Fowler Museum of Cultural History.

Kaulicke, P. 2000. *Memoria y Muerte En El Perú Antiguo*. Lima: Fondo Editorial de la Pontificia Universidad del Perú.

Muro Ynoñán, L. A. 2019. "Tracing the Moche Spectacles of Death: Performance, Ancestrality, and Political Power in Ancient Peru: A View from Huaca La Capilla-San José de Moro (ad 650–740)." Doctoral dissertation, Department of Anthropology, Stanford University.

Quilter, J. 1990. "The Moche Revolt of the Objects." *Latin American Antiquity* 1, no. 1: 42–65.

Quilter, J., and Castillo, L. J. 2010. *New Perspectives on Moche Political Organization*. Washington, DC: Dumbarton Oaks Research Library and Collection.

Quilter, J., and Koons, M. 2012. "The Fall of the Moche: A Critique of Claims for South America's First State." *Latin American Antiquity* 23, no. 2: 127–43.

Rucabado Yong, J. 2021. "Los Otros, los 'No-Moche': Reflexiones en Torno a la Formacion y Representacion de Identidades Colectivas." In *El Arte Antes de la Historia: Para una Historia del Arte Andino Antiguo*, edited by M. Curatola Petrocchi, C. Michaud, J. Pillsbury, and L. Trever, 259–90. Lima: Fondo Editorial de la Pontifica Universidad Catolica del Peru.

Uceda, S., Morales, R., and Mujica, E. 2016. *Huaca de la Luna: Templos y Dioses Moche*. Lima: Fundación Backus & World Monument Fund.

Weismantel, M. 2021. *Playing with Things: Engaging the Moche Sex Pots*. Austin: University of Texas Press.

Weismantel, M., and Meskell, L. 2014. "Substances: 'Following the Material' through Two Prehistoric Cases." *Journal of Material Culture* 19, no. 3: 233–51.

Edmond has also created a magnificent collection of ritual flags depicting the spirits valiantly fighting *Kowona* (the coronavirus), the most deadly infectious disease to affect Haiti since the cholera epidemic of the 2010s. In these *drapo*, the spirits of the dead combat larger-than-life representations of the coronavirus, entering a martial dance of epic proportions. The healer-warriors portrayed include both the Gede pantheon as well as their sibling spirits of life and death, the *lwa Bawon*. In Edmond's 2020 *Bawon le Médcin du Covid-19*/Bawon the Doctor of Covid-19 (Figure 3.3), *Bawon* appears in a grey fedora, black pants, and a white suit jacket long enough to recall a doctor's authoritative white coat. In his right hand, he holds a tall baton, which simultaneously symbolizes his status as an elder and also the virility of his phallus. Bawon's eyes are concealed behind a pair of sunglasses which allow him to see in both visible and invisible realms, and he judiciously wears a face mask to protect himself (and his loved ones) from the virus. A white candle in his left hand hints that he is saluting the ancestral bones over which he dances. Night appears to have fallen from the chrome-colored beaded background, and the coronaviruses glow blue and red as they illuminate the tombstone behind him,

Figure 3.13. Moche vessel depicting a simultaneous scene of breastfeeding and coitus (FM 100140).

one of so many which has claimed the lives of his mortal children. To be clear, Bawon the COVID-19 Doctor is a new spirit of the Vodou pantheon. In the same way that the Dahomean-Benin spirit Sakpata of disease developed the powers to cure his devotees of smallpox, a contagious virus which devastated global communities between the 1600s and the 1800s, a new Haitian *lwa* was needed in the face of the coronavirus pandemic of the twenty-first century. And who else could battle the virus with as much grace as the great healers and arbiters of life, death, and rebirth—the Gede and Bawon spirits? In these Kowona flags, the spirits of death reveal themselves as healer-warriors, combatting mortal diseases with mystic powers and great aplomb. Haiti's Gede and Bawon spirits thus emerge not as fearsome grim reapers but rather as fearless protectors of their human children.

Vital Force: Livity and Longevity

Across the Black Atlantic world, religious devotees work to restore cosmic harmony through the active maintenance of vital force, especially in the face of death. Vital force refers to the divine source of energy that resides in every single entity—animal, vegetal, and mineral. In Yorùbá traditions of southwestern Nigeria, this principle is called *àse* and in Fon regions of southern Benin *se* identifies the same concept. Each being possesses *àse* or *se* that is fortified through righteous living and ritual practice. This notion of vital force has persisted in the African Diaspora as well. Haitian Vodouizan use the term *fòs* to discuss physical strength and spiritual power, while *nanm* refers to the soul or cosmic energy of a person or sanctified object. In Jamaican Rastafari, *livity* identifies righteous living and the concept that Jah or God has imbued an energy or life force in all living beings (Edmonds 2003).

Immortality is neither sought nor desired among most Africana religious communities. Indeed, the life expectancy of Black people in Africa as well as the African Diaspora remains decidedly lower due to heavy histories of colonialism, neocolonialism, and more contemporary ramifications of racial injustice. However, prayers abound for Black Atlantic devotees to live full, purposeful, and intentional lives. A life of longevity, vibrancy, and integrity honors the destiny linked with one's unique soul collective. Righteous living in African-derived traditions includes worship and care for guiding ancestors and spirits, the utmost respect for elders, the maintenance of harmonious relationships and vital force, and leaving a meaningful legacy for the next generations to come. These concepts resonate with the ideologies of life and death still present among many other Indigenous groups all around the world. When death occurs, a ripple emerges in the cosmic pool of the universe. In addition to the physical acts of care that prepare a deceased person for rest and burial, death must be addressed on a spiritual level to restore harmony to the community and assist newly initiated ancestors in their transition to the ancestral realm. It is through the cultivation of a vibrant life and divine fortification of the soul(s), the creation of mortuary arts and rituals of balance, that death can be recognized not as enemy of humankind but as one of many cosmic energies to be propitiated in the restoration of harmonious communal living.

References

Beauvoir, M. G. 2006. "Herbs and Energy: The Holistic Medical System of the Haitian People." In *Haitian Vodou: Spirit, Myth, and Reality*, edited by P. Bellegarde-Smith and C. Michel, 122–33. Indianapolis: Indiana University Press.

Beier, U. 1966. *The Origin of Life and Death: African Creation Myths.* London: Heinemann.

Blier, S. P. 1995. *African Vodun: Art, Psychology, and Power.* Chicago: University of Chicago Press.

Daniels, K. M. 2021. "Art of the Earthquake: A 2021 Reflection on Haiti." *VÈVÈ Haitian Art Society* 4: 6–7.

Daniels, K. M. 2022. "Vodou Harmonizes the Head-Pot, or, Haiti's Multi-Soul Complex." *Religion* 52, no. 3: 359–83.

Daniels, K. M. 2023. "Vodou's Private Soul Pots and Public Mortuary Vessels, or, Haiti's Multi-Soul Complex Revisited" (forthcoming).

Deren, M. 1953. *Divine Horsemen: The Living Gods of Haiti.* London: McPherson & Co.

Desmangles, L. G. 1992. *The Faces of the Gods: Vodou and Roman Catholicism in Haiti.* Chapel Hill: University of North Carolina Press.

Edmonds, E. B. 2003. *Rastafari: From Outcasts to Culture Bearers.* Oxford: Oxford University Press.

Germain, F. 2011. "The Earthquake, the Missionaries, and the Future of Vodou." *Journal of Black Studies* 42, no. 2: 247–63.

Girouard, T. 1995. "Sequin Artists of Vodou." In *Sacred Arts of Haitian Vodou*, edited by D. Cosentino, 357–77. Los Angeles: UCLA Fowler Museum of Cultural History.

Fromont, C. 2014. *The Art of Conversion: Christian Visual Culture in the Kingdom of Kongo.* Chapel Hill: University of North Carolina Press.

Fu-Kiau Kia Bunseki-Lumanisa, A. 2001. *African Cosmology of the Bāntu-Kōngo: Tying the Spiritual Knot: Principles of Life and Living.* New York: Athelia Henrietta Press.

Hackett, R. 1988. *Religion in Calabar: The Religious Life and History of a Nigerian Town.* Berlin: Mouton de Gruyter.

Hackett, R. 1998. *Art and Religion in Africa.* London: A&C Black.

International Medical Corps. 2021. "Haiti Earthquake Situation Report #3, September 20, 2021." https://reliefweb.int/attachments/6d1263c5-260c-3040-9cda-6045d6a102fd/IntlMedCorps-HaitiEarthquake2021_SitRep03.pdf.

Kali, T. 2019. "Masonic Symbolism in Haitian Vodou." Memphis Hoodoo, Medium (website), December 1, 2019. https://memphishoodoo.medium.com/ masonic-symbolism-in-haitian-vodou-70faa1a9ee40.

MacGaffey, W. 1986. *Religion and Society in Central Africa: The BaKongo of Lower Zaire.* Chicago: University of Chicago Press.

Mafundikwa, S. 2007. *AfrikAlphabets: The Story of Writing in Africa.* Brooklyn: Mark Batty Publisher.

Martínez-Ruiz, B. 2013. *Kongo Graphic Writing and Other Narratives of the Sign.* Philadelphia: Temple University Press.

McGee, A. M. 2022. "Marasa Elou: Twins and Uncanny Children in Haitian Vodou." In *Gemini and the Sacred: Twins and Twinship in Religion and Mythology: A Very Short Introduction*, edited by K. C. Patton. London: Bloomsbury Academic.

Métraux, A. 1959. *Voodoo in Haiti.* Translated by H. Carteris. New York City: Schocken Books.

Ogunnaike, O. 2012. "Myth and the Secret of Destiny: Mircea Eliade's Creative Hermeneutics and the Yorùbá Concept of Orí." *Journal of Comparative Theology* 3, no. 1: 4–42.

Olúpọ̀nà, J. K. 2014. *African Religions: A Very Short Introduction.* Oxford: Oxford University Press.

Olúpọ̀nà, J. K. 2022. "The Code of Twins: Ìbejì in Yorùbá Cosmology, Ritual, and Iconography." In *Gemini and the Sacred: Twins and Twinship in Religion and Mythology: A Very Short Introduction*, edited by K. C. Patton. London: Bloomsbury Academic.

Payton, C. 2019. "Vodou and Protestantism, Faith and Survival: The Contest over the Spiritual Meaning of the 2010 Earthquake in Haiti." *The Oral History Review* 2: 231–50.

Polk, P. 1997. *Haitian Vodou Flags.* Jackson: University Press of Mississippi.

Ross, D. H., ed. 1998. *Wrapped in Pride: Ghanaian Kente and African American Identity.* Los Angeles: UCLA Fowler Museum of Cultural History.

Scheub, H. 2000. *A Dictionary of African Mythology: The Mythmaker as Storyteller.* Oxford and New York: Oxford University Press.

Stewart [Diakité], D. M. 2010. "The Myth of 'Voodoo': A Caribbean American Response to Representations of Haiti." Religion Dispatches (website), January 21. https://religiondispatches.org/the-myth-of-voodoo-a-caribbean-american-response-to-representations-of-haiti.

Thompson, R. F., and Cornet, J. 1981. *The Four Moments of the Sun: Kongo Art in Two Worlds.* Washington, DC: National Gallery of Art.

Thornton, J. K. (1992) 1998. *Africa and Africans in the Making of the Atlantic World, 1400–1800.* Cambridge: Cambridge University Press.

Ulysse, G. A. 2022. "Constant's Consort and Marvelous Work." In *Myrlande Constant: The Work of Radiance*, edited by K. Smith and J. Philogene. Los Angeles: UCLA Fowler Museum.

World Health Organization. https://covid19.who.int/region/amro/country/ht.

4

Performing Death

Luis Muro Ynoñán

Field Museum

Abstract: Death affects the living in multiple and complex ways. Social groups across time and space have designed diverse coping strategies to deal with the pain, frustration, and anger that the loss of a loved one produces on the living. Mortuary rituals play a critical role in how humans deal with emotions associated to death. Rituals are important in processes of remembering and forgetting. They also offer the possibility to reconfigure and restitute the social relationship of the living: forging, challenging, and reinforcing (new) social orders. When we die, we continue influencing the relationships between others long beyond our physical presence. This chapter offers perspectives about the performance of death, the agency of the dead, and how our existence transcends and continuously gives shape to the memories, actions, and hopes of the living. Case studies present examples of non-Western practices orchestrated around the preparation, both physical and symbolical, of the body before its eternal journey to the afterlife.

Resumen: La muerte afecta a los vivos de formas múltiples y complejas. Los grupos sociales a lo largo del tiempo y el espacio han diseñado diversas estrategias para afrontar y lidiar con el dolor, la frustración y la ira que produce en los vivos la pérdida de un ser querido. Los rituales mortuorios juegan un papel fundamental en la forma en que los humanos lidiamos con las emociones asociadas con la muerte. Los rituales son importantes en los procesos de memoria, pero también de olvido. Ellos ofrecen la posibilidad de reconfigurar y restituir las relaciones sociales entre los vivos: forjando, desafiando, y/o reforzando (nuevos) órdenes sociales. Cuando morimos, seguimos influyendo en las relaciones entre otros, aún mucho más allá de nuestra presencia física. Este capítulo ofrece perspectivas sobre la escenificación de la muerte, la agencia de los muertos, y cómo nuestra existencia trasciende y continuamente da forma a los recuerdos, acciones, y esperanzas de los vivos. Los artículos que este ensayo contiene exploran ejemplos no Occidentales de la ritualización y la escenificación alrededor de la muerte.

"Death may be the greatest of all human blessings."

—Socrates

"Our dead are never dead to us, until we have forgotten them."

—George Eliot

Epicurus once said that death should not worry us, because as long as we exist, death is not here, and when it comes for us, we no longer exist. Through death, we become aware of our finitude. However, whereas for many of us death might be imperceptible and perhaps sudden, for those that we leave behind, death is a deeply affective experience producing feelings and emotions from which they can hardly escape. Death affects us in multiple and complex ways, and, as Damien Hirst reminds us, it is perhaps the impossibility of comprehending it that that causes us the most anxiety, terror, and fear.

Throughout time and space, humans have created diverse ways to cope with the pain, frustration, and anger produced by the loss of a loved one. Rituals have played a critical role in how humans deal socially with the sensations of emptiness, chaos, and crisis that death creates. Rituals are important in the processes of remembering, as well as forgetting. They also offer the possibility to reconfigure or restitute the social order of the living: forging, reinforcing, and challenging (new) social relationships and meanings.

But social relationships and meanings are not just cognitively constructed. They are forged through actions and experience. Unlike ritual—often framed within religious structures and liturgies—performances are actions that, because of their aesthetic, theatrical, and dramatic nature, forge meanings through the body, movement, and nonverbal language. Whereas all rituals are performances, not all performances are rituals. Yet, they both constitute means of expressing emotions in moments of crises and disruption: from the large-scale funerary spectacles celebrated by the Inca of Cusco to the small-scale Japanese household commemoration rituals. Social actions orchestrated around death, whether collective or individual, ritual or not ritual, forge potent meanings that enable us to reconfigure our position in the world. We could say, then, that human beings face the tragedy of death through actions, and that the human experience with death is, above all, performative.

Both rituals and performances around death have been critical in the social evolution of human groups, and have contributed to the formation of communities, identities, social hierarchies, and religious beliefs. Such rituals and performances, with a special emphasis on those from the pre-Hispanic Andes, my own area of expertise, occupy a central theme of this chapter (Figures 4.1–4.7). The power of action, perhaps even more than thought, lies in its capacity to activate emotions, memories, and experiences, and thus constitutes a powerful tool to heal

Figure 4.1. Nasca bird whistle, which produces a high-pitched sound reminiscent of the sounds made by native desert hummingbirds (FM 171064).

Figure 4.2. Nasca ceramic *antara* (panpipes) created haunting melodies when played (FM 170214).

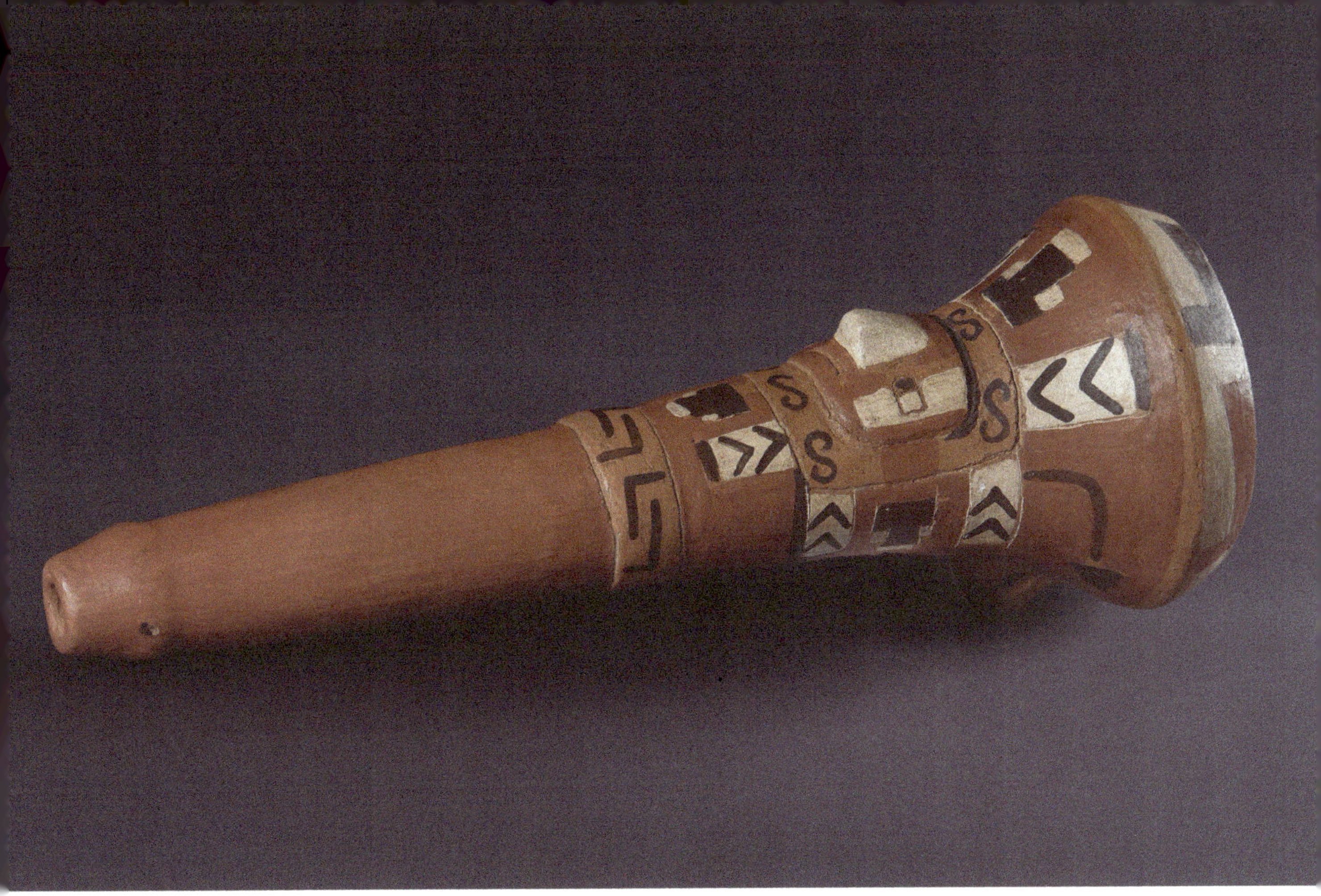

Figure 4.3. Wari/Tiwanaku replica ceramic trumpet from Moquegua, Peru. Original dates to ca. 800–1000 ce and was from a cist burial (FM 359535).

Figure 4.4. Lambayeque whistling vessel, where a whistling sound is created as liquid moving from one chamber to the other forces air to pass through the tube (FM 169918).

Figure 4.5. Moche drummer representation with a deformity which may have made them a ritual mediator between the living and the dead (FM 100153).

the emotional and affective disruption produced by the loss. I focus, then, on the importance of the actions, which, when orchestrated around both death and the dead, become important forces for both life and the living.

Funerary Behaviors in Evolutionary Perspective

Discussions about when humans began to grieve and mourn have usually been framed within evolutionary models of behavior. These models indicate that social behaviors were acquired as cognitive capacities of humans developed. However, responses to death do not seem to be exclusive to the human species. As this exhibit shows, animals also appear to grieve. Mammals and primates, among other animal species, produce sounds and gestures, and make use of their body as a whole, to signal frustration, irritation, and being upset, when encountering the dead body of one conspecific. In spite of that, evolutionary scientists do no necessarily grant these responses the status of "behaviors," but mere reactions.

Although with skepticism, the idea that early hominids could have developed a certain type of funerary behavior, understood as conscious acts to revere the dead, is becoming further accepted by specialists (see Feinman and Williams in this volume). Nonetheless, some have argued that the formulation of the category "dead"—as something other than a "sleeping individual" who refuses to wake up—could only have occurred when spoken language was fully developed (Renfrew 2016, 4). Modern *Homo sapiens*, with their advanced linguistic capacities, would be the only hominid species that produced a conceptual differentiation and, thus, a verbalization, of the term "death." This could have ultimately led to the distinction between those with life and those without. Once this process was achieved, it is believed that a self-awareness could have emerged, and with that a notion of identity and *otherness* (Pettitt 2018). The inclusion of personal adornments and ornamentation in early burials would have been a manifestation of the process of the formation of individuality. Therefore, the funerary behavior could, in fact, be a distinctive feature of the human beings through evolutionarily acquired capabilities.

But these early funerary behaviors might have been deprived of religious meanings. Although performative and highly symbolical, the act of burying the dead by early humans did not necessarily imply a belief in a deity or deities. Religion entails action and conduct designed to please the divine forces that rule us (Insoll 2004). While many have held that religion first emerged among human groups settling down and experimenting with plants and animals in the Late Paleolithic period, evidence actually seems to suggest that religion was the factor that triggered the first processes of sedentism and domestication in the Old World (Thomas 2011), and that death and the dead might have had a key role in that process. It is very likely that the necessity of returning to the grave sites to honor the dead planted the seed for the emergence of a mystic religious belief that fueled, in turn and along with other factors, the permanence of the human groups in specific places in the landscape.

This process could have been first seen in sites such as Çatalhöyük (7100 BCE) in southern Anatolia, and was intimately linked to the construction of spatial identity and social memory (Hodder 2010; 2014). At this site, early houses also became sites of burial. Multiple bodies were placed beneath the floors of the houses, which were cyclically replastered as new architectural elements were added. What is interesting at this site is that the houses were spatially and consciously organized, transformed, and ornamented around the dead, who were revered through symbolic art on the house's walls. Moreover, the documentation of bodies lacking skulls suggests, for example, that the skulls were intentionally removed and circulated among diverse household units, where special spots were reserved for their placement. There is even evidence that the skulls, and other body parts, were theatrically manipulated in household ritual performances. Therefore, it is generally through repetitive, cyclical, and conscious actions in the domestic space that the dead (as an inert body) became a deceased (an esteemed and revered dead), and that performances around death acquired a much deeper religious meaning.

Inscribing Meanings on the Bodies: Personhood, Identity, and Status

Identity and Personhood

The notion of inscribing (and imposing) a particular identity on the dead seems to have had a much later manifestation within human history. Both funerary identity and personhood are idealized notions of one individual that are culturally constructed. They often respond to the community's necessities, aspirations, and hopes, and they are ritually "inscribed" on the dead through funerary performances. Whereas "identity" is related to the individual's age, sex, class, race, group affiliations, and so on, "personhood" "refers to the state or condition of being a person" (Cerezo-Román 2015, 354), and as such, it is constructed across life through social relationships and interactions with the material world (Fowler 2004; Gillespie 2001). During the funerary performances, multiple identities and personhoods can be constructed and inscribed on both the living (mourners) and the dead. The progressive stages of the mortuary rituals, as suggested by van Gennep (1960)— separation, liminality (transition), and (re)incorporation—enable the deceased to pass "from being biologically dead into a transitional stage, and [the deceased] only later becomes socially dead"

(Cerezo-Román 2015, 354). During this transformative process, the personhood of the participants (living and dead) is reconfigured through processes of dissolution, creation, negotiation, and transformation of their social identities, and, only in a few cases, the deceased also becomes an ancestor: a named and esteemed deceased who is revered through long-term ritual service and tendance (Hill 2016).

The body of the dead plays a special role during this process, as the inscription of a funerary identity and personhood is ultimately achieved through actions that involve its direct modification, both physically and symbolically. The Chinchorro mummies (5000 BCE) discovered in the Atacama Desert, in modern-day Chile, could be considered the earliest expression of this practice and its complexity, with processes that enabled the preservation of the body through mummification. After literally skinning the dead and removing their muscles and organs, the Chinchorro reshaped (or rehumanized) the corpses using sticks, reeds, clay, and sea-lion skin. Wigs made of human and animal hairs were also attached to the bodies, which were then decorated with black and red pigments, indicating a particular sense of the aesthetic and beauty (Arriaza 1995). In a mortuary practice that long pre-dated the ancient Egyptians, the Chinchorro mortuary practices provide critical information about the emergence of the concepts of the self and soul in semi-nomadic groups of hunters and gatherers in South America. It is perhaps the intention of preserving the human qualities of the body that suggests the emergence of a much more articulated notion of an afterlife, as well deities, among early groups in the Americas.

In cultures with more complex religious systems there existed a belief that changes on the body mirrored changes in the soul (Kus 1992). Therefore, the preservation of the material dimension of the body guaranteed, in some ways, the preservation of its immaterial dimension. In this sense, the successful construction of the "new persona" (new personhood) is subject to processes that unfold both in the world of the living and the dead—the latter being governed by mythological gods. For example, for the ancient Egyptians the body had to be as carefully cared for as the soul, and the correct realization of the rituals of mummification accompanied by magical recitations and spells, as described in the Book of the Dead (see Teeter in this volume), paralleled the progressive advancement of the soul of the person toward the afterlife.

But for the ancient Egyptians, the body was perceived as something more than a surface of inscription or canvas for identity. It was considered a plane of convergence between the self, experience, and subjectivity. Death, then, brings together the *lived experience* of the individual that is molded through gender, sexuality, identity, power relationships, and so forth (Meskell 2004).

Ranking, Hierarchy, and Status

But we cannot deny that, through death, the body also becomes a means to construct and display hierarchy, ranking, and status—notions that are also ritually built. In many cases, and particularly in premodern societies, the dead body was treated in ways analogous to how the individual was treated in life, with important individuals buried lavishly and eloquently. Luxury costumes and body ornaments were distinctive markers of identity and class and, as such, were carefully placed within burials as a way to display (and fossilize) the status that prestigious individuals acquired in life.

In non-Western premodern societies, mortuary rituals were particularly centered on the body: its embellishment, ornamentation, and use to inscribe desired notions of beauty, power, and status. Whether socially acquired or familiarly inherited, status was expressed through the quality and complexity of grave goods. Grave goods were either exclusively manufactured to accompany the dead or also passed on, by the dead's family, from generation to generation, as relics. This usually reinforced the ancestral ties of the dead and allowed them to legitimate their position in the society: in the world of the living and of the dead.

For example, pre-Columbian cultures that thrived on the desert coast of Peru invested a great deal of energy, labor, and resources to guarantee such an outcome. In many cases, the sophistication of the burials was an expression of the wealth and power of the family or community to which the individual belonged. Whereas archaeologists have traditionally linked economic wealth with the level of complexity of the society, it is now commonly accepted that the investments seen in ancient burials show, instead, preoccupations of a religious, ideological, and eschatological nature. Societies such as the Moche, Nasca, and Chancay of ancient Peru constructed complex underground chamber tombs made of adobe bricks or mud and, many times, decorated with mural paintings and niches. Whereas the Moche invested significant labor and resources for the production of ceramic and metal objects to be placed within the tombs, the Nasca and Chancay did so for the production of refined textiles and other items (see Slovak in this volume). High-quality decorated textiles were used to wrap the bodies of important individuals, and their level of decoration and complexity was an indicator of the status of the person as well as his or her power as an ancestor.

Figure 4.6. Chancay *chicha* vessels with paired figures holding cups (FM 1416, 5802).

4A Chancay Burials

Nicole M. Slovak
Santa Rosa Junior College

Famed for their sophisticated textiles, black-on-white painted pottery, and human clay figurines known as *cuchimilcos*, the Chancay culture flourished during the Andean Late Intermediate Period (LIP) (1000–1470 CE). Chancay sites were concentrated in the Chancay and Chillón valleys on Peru's arid central coast, with Chancay cultural influence extending northward and southward into the Huara and Rimac Valleys, respectively (Lumbreras 1974; Stone-Miller 2002). Despite more than a century of research, surprisingly little is known about Chancay's sociopolitical structure (Krzanowski 1991). Instead, most scholarship has focused on Chancay art and mortuary practices. Indeed, the majority of excavated Chancay materials derive from funerary contexts, including those on display in the Field Museum's *Death: Life's Greatest Mystery* exhibition. Although associated with death, these objects tell us much about the then-living Chancay community.

Thousands of Chancay burials have been discovered at various sites throughout the central coast (Dorsey 1894; Horkheimer 1963; Kaulicke 1997; Kroeber and Uhle 1926; Lothrop and Mahler 1957; Reiss and Stübel 1880–87; Watson Jiménez 2019). Tomb forms range from deep circular, rectangular, or L-shaped pits to more shallow rectangular structures. Tomb chambers were dug directly into hard gravel or sand or otherwise lined with rectangular adobes or *tapia* (Lothrop and Mahler 1957). Many burial chambers were capped with cane rooves (Ravines 1981). Tombs contained either single individuals or multiple interments (Kaulicke 1997), with the deceased most often interred as mummy bundles, or *fardo funerarios*—a tradition that flourished on the central coast during the preceding Middle Horizon Period (550 CE–1000 CE) and continued throughout the LIP.

Fardos were elaborate constructions in which the deceased's body was enshrouded and enveloped in multiple layers of textiles and vegetation, forming a large rectangular or ovular mummy bale. At the center of the *fardo* was the body of the deceased, often bound by ropes in a seated, flexed position, although variation in the position of the body has been observed (Watson Jiménez 2019). Immediately surrounding the body, wads of cotton, grass, and other absorbent organic materials often were placed (Lothrop and Mahler 1957; Watson Jiménez 2019). The bundle was covered with either a plain or decorative cotton or wool textile and, especially in the early half of the LIP, capped with a false head or mummy mask. Mummy masks were square or rectangular in shape, often small cotton sacks, stuffed with leaves and embellished with shell or wooden eyes, a wooden nose, and a cotton-thread mouth (Menzel 1977). Sometimes the mummy masks would be capped by a wig of hair or topped with a woven straw headband. Rarely, mummy masks were decorated with silver or copper objects (Horkheimer 1963; Menzel 1977). Often the mummy mask was obscured by an additional layer of textile (Reiss and Stübel 1880–87). The outer bundle was then bounded by a series of corded, knotted ropes and placed at the base of the tomb. The continuity and consistency of Chancay *fardos* across multiple sites indicates that funerary rituals were widely shared and largely consistent among members of Chancay society.

On the other hand, the envelopment of the body was almost certainly an intimate, individualized activity between the deceased and the living community. We have no way of knowing who or how many people participated in preparing the body for interment, although there likely were at least two to three individuals owing to the complexity of the process (Cornejo Guerrero 1991). The inclusion of small ceramic vessels, gourd bowls, coca leaves, weaving needles, metal bracelets, and other small objects embedded and enfolded within the layers of the bundle (Slovak 2020; Watson Jiménez 2019) suggests a highly personalized component to death and burial among the Chancay. It is possible that these objects were personal keepsakes of the individual or mementos that belonged to family, friends, or community members that were then gifted to the individual at death (Figures 4.6–4.7). The proximity of these objects to the body itself suggests that these items were essential to the deceased's identity and/or well-being. That they were incorporated into the final physical embodiment of an individual's existence renders them powerful, meaningful symbols of personhood.

In addition to grave goods placed within the *fardo*, objects such as pottery, gourd bowls filled with maize, cotton, and other vegetation, weaving baskets replete with spindles and spindle whorls, fishing implements, and so-called "God's eyes," or woven designs made out of yarn or fiber upon a wooden cross, were included in graves alongside individuals. Many of the aforementioned objects appear to have been placed in specific tombs because of their association with the deceased, likely because these things belonged to, or were used by, the interred individuals in life. Grave 121, a Chancay-period tomb excavated by George Dorsey (Dorsey 1894) at the archaeological site of Ancón, Peru, in 1891 and currently housed at the Field Museum, beautifully illustrates this point. Containing the remains of three *fardos*—Mummies 170, 171, and 172 (identified by Dorsey as an adult female, adolescent female, and child, respectively)—Grave 121 included a number of artifacts of an intimate nature, such as an intricately constructed weaving basket containing the sticks of a loom and several spindles still wound with thread. Near to the smallest mummy, Dorsey (1893) encountered 70 spindles, all of which were painted and incised with geometric and zoomorphic imagery. Also accompanying the deceased were a pair of remarkably preserved hair combs—small

Figure 4.7. *Cuchimilco* figurine, perhaps representing an ancestor, that accompanied the Chancay dead to the grave (FM 5803).

rectangular objects that fit in the palm of one's hand. When observing these objects, it is easy to imagine the human fingers that held the spindles, or the hair that would have been held back by the exquisite cotton and wooden hair combs. Based on the personal nature of these objects, it is likely that they belonged to one or more of the individuals found in the tomb.

Importantly, mortuary ritual did not end with an individual's interment. Instead, among the Chancay, as was true for many other ancient Andean cultures, funerary rites continued to be performed after an individual's death. Evidence for bundles being opened and reconstituted (Reiss and Stübel 1880–87), additional individuals being placed in burial chambers at later dates, and ritual feasting occurring near to tombs (Uhle [1912] 1968) suggest that the dead were continually remembered, grieved, honored, and celebrated. The Chancay tomb, therefore, appears to have been at once a formal commemoration of death and a dynamic component of Chancay life.

References

Cornejo Guerrero, M. A. 1991. "Patrones Funerarios y Discusión Cronológica en Lauri, Valle de Chancay." In *Estudios Sobre la Cultura Chancay, Perú*, edited by A. Krzanowski, 19–36. Krakow: Universidad Jaguelona.

Dorsey, G. 1893. *The G. A. Dorsey Papers—WCE Expedition 1893: Folder 1*. Chicago: Field Museum.

Dorsey, G. 1894. "An Archaeological Study Based on Personal Exploration of Over One Hundred Graves of the Necropolis of Ancón." Doctoral dissertation, Harvard University.

Horkheimer, H. 1963. "Chancay Prehispanico: Diversidad y Belleza." *Cultura Peruana* 23 nos. 175–78: 62–69.

Kaulicke, P. 1997. *Contextos Funerarios de Ancón: Esbozo de una Síntesis Analítica*. Lima: Pontificia Universidad Catolica del Peru.

Kroeber, A. L., and Uhle, M. 1926. *The Uhle Pottery Collections from Chancay*. Berkeley: University of California Press.

Krzanowski, A. 1991. "Chancay: Una Cultura Desconocida." In *Estudios sobre la cultura Chancay, Perú*, edited by A. Krzanowski, 19–36. Krakow: Universidad Jaguelona.

Lothrop, S. K., and Mahler, J. 1957. *A Chancay-Style Grave at Zapallan, Peru: An Analysis of Its Textiles, Pottery, and Other Furnishings*. New Haven, CT: Peabody Museum.

Lumbreras, L. G. 1974. *The Peoples and Cultures of Ancient Peru*. Translated by B. J. Meggers. Washington, DC: Smithsonian Institution Press.

Menzel, D. 1977. *The Archaeology of Ancient Peru and the Work of Max Uhle*. Berkeley: R. H. Lowie Museum of Anthropology Univeristy of California.

Ravines, R. 1981. "Practicas Funerarios en Ancón (Segunda Parte)." *Revisita del Museo Nacional* 45: 89–166.

Reiss, J. W., and Stübel, M. A. 1880–87. *The Necropolis of Ancon in Peru: A Contribution of Our Knowledge of the Culture and Industries of the Empire of the Incas, Being the Results of Excavations Made on the Spot*. Translated by A. H. Keane. Berlin: A. Asher & Co.

Slovak, N. M. 2020. "Reassembling the Mortuary Assemblage: New Investigations into the Field Museum's Osteological and Artifact Collections from Ancón, Peru." *Ñawpa pacha*, 40. no. 1: 81–99. https://doi.org/10.1080/00776297.2019.1710365.

Stone-Miller, R. 2002. *Art of the Ancient Andes*, 2nd ed. London: Thames & Hudson.

Uhle, M. (1912) 1968. "Die muschelhügel von Ancón, Peru: International Congress of Americanists." Proceedings of the XVIII Session, London.

Watson Jiménez, L. 2019. *Los fardos de Ancón-Perú (800d.c–1532d.c): Una Perspectiva Bioarqueológica de los Cambios Sociales en la Costa Central del Perú*. Oxford: BAR Publishing.

But it is not only the objects themselves and how they were potentially used that is relevant, but also how and when they were placed in the funerary contexts. The action of placing, arranging, and rearranging the grave goods, occurring before, during, and after the burial act itself, is also charged with potent symbolism for the dead, and slight variations in the spatial patterns of the objects within the context might indicate relevant aspects of the personhood of the individual and his or her social and political ties. For example, many Moche elite burials present evidence of multiple reopenings and reenterings; in each, new elements of non-Moche affiliation were added. Wari objects placed near the head of individuals could have indicated a new political affiliation of the individual and his or her community at large.

Coffins are also particularly relevant items within the burials, as they constitute potent conveyers of status and hierarchy. They not only served as the first receptacle of the body of the individual, but also embodied his or her essence, as well as capabilities. The capacity for acquiring these items, especially the most refined, could have been fairly limited by the common people, as described, for example, in the historical texts recovered from the Egyptian community of workmen at Deir el-Medina. Overall, decoration, iconography, and symbolic codes depicted on them could have aimed at boosting the capacities of the deceased, both in the realm of the living and the dead. For example, in many cases, the Moche coffins, made of wood or canes, were usually decorated with metal plaquettes representing parts of the human body, namely, legs, arms, and masks mimicking human faces, with the intention of humanizing the coffin, giving the coffin its own agency. One particular Moche coffin from the Late Moche cemetery of San Jose de Moro, Jequetepeque Valley, was also decorated with metallic plaques similar to fishnets and wave designs, mimicking a reed boat navigating and giving the coffin a capacity of movement and transportation (Muro Ynoñán 2010). A similar metaphor can also be found in modern coffins of traditional societies in northwestern Africa (see Bandana in this volume, on Ghanaian fantasy coffins).

The Powerful Dead: Commemoration, Affect, and Memory

As pointed out above, not all the dead had the same importance or were equally esteemed by society. Individuals converted into ancestors were particularly revered for long periods of time after their death and their influence on the society determined the renovation of new social and political ties among the living (Hill and Hageman 2016). Remembering some ancestors in particular could imply forgetting others. As Borić (2010, 65) reminds us, through practices of construction of social memory "the memory of the dead might be both recollected and then collaterally lost."

In the past, the conversion of specific individuals into ancestors sought to promote the transcendence of the remembrance of such individuals both in memory and history, and this allowed the living to engage in new forms of rituality and sociality. For instance, as described in many colonial documents, ancestors played a key and active role in the social, economic, and political life of the communities of ancient Peru. The ancestors (and their representations) were often consulted, even about domestic decisions, and in both elite and non-elite residences, spaces were delimited exclusively for such consultative practices. Performances of ancestor commemoration in ancient Peru were complex and, in many cases, constituted long and large-scale events. Communities gathered in public plazas at times likely defined by ritual calendars. Remarkably, in the cemetery of San Jose de Moro, evidence of large-scale feasting has been documented around the tombs of elite members, who were transformed into powerful ancestors through lavish mortuary spectacles (Muro Ynoñán 2019). Here, feasting events entailed the preparation and consumption of abundant amounts of foodstuff and maize-based beer (*chicha*), which were stored in ceramic containers near elite mortuary structures for months, if not years. Similar to pre-Hispanic Mesoamerica, in the Andes there was a metaphoric relationship between the maize's lifecycle and the life/death cycles of the people; once the maize was converted into beer, and then stored for commemoration rites, its aging paralleled the aging of the ancestors and, thus, therefore, their empowerment (Lau 2013).

The consumption of alcohol, in particular, during feasting and banquets of ancestor commemoration, seems to have been a means, and not an end in itself. Chicha beer prompted a specific form of sacrality, which was facilitated through intoxication and drunkenness. The ingestion of hallucinogenic substances during these events could have also promoted heightened states of consciousness through which communication with the ancestors was facilitated and benefited. Contemporary Peruvian shamans, for example, still make use of psychotropic substances to increase the sensorial experiences during divination and propitiatory performances that involve the participation of ancestral and natural spiritual forces (*apus*).

But commemorative performances required, in many cases, the real and physical presence of the body of the ancestor. A common practice, seen in pre-Hispanic societies across America and elsewhere, involved the reopening of tombs and the removal of the all or parts of the body of the dead. Heads, hands, and limbs of prestigious individuals, once removed from the burial, became true relics and were passed on from family to family (within the same lineage) as a way to solidify the ties of family members with powerful ancestors, who were sometimes considered the founders of given lineages. For many, the body and its parts were not a mere *representation* of ancestral power, but were the *true* source of political and religious power.

The Incas from Cusco took this notion further. The *mallqui*, the royal mummy of the Inca emperor, whose remains were preserved in sacred chambers at the temple of Coricancha in Cusco, was taken in a procession to the public plaza of imperial Cusco, Huacaypata. Here, the *mallquis* of all the emperors, spatially arranged based on their importance and "age," were revered and consulted. Commemoration rituals involved offerings of food and drink to the *mallquis*, as well as the celebration (and reenactment) of their achievements during their reign. For the Incas, the *mallquis* were more than ancestors participating in the political life of the community; they were the source of political and religious power in the empire and, as D'Altroy (2016, 404) puts it, "were considered as the point of convergence between a dualistic view of the reality: between life and death, time and space, past and present, vitality and causality, knowledge and epistemology." They were so venerated by the Incas that the Spanish *conquistadores* sought their capture and destruction, which they eventually accomplished.

Experimenting with the body of the ancestors in real life was, therefore, critical for the commemoration and production of affect in relation to them. This notion has parallels in other cultural realities. For example, in modern Indonesia, the real presence of the body of the deceased and its movement around the house or houses of the family defines the social interactions of relatives whose actions are centered on continuing to please the deceased. The body of the dead remains at home for a very long time, months and even years, while the mortuary rituals are prepared. The deceased is dressed, re-dressed, perfumed, and fed properly, and also participates in social and family events. For Indonesians, the loved one is not dead, but only "sick" until finally buried.

Figure 4.8. Canopic jars used to contain and preserve the viscera of the mummified individual (FM 31380, 81, 82, 83-A115240d_001A), and embalming hook used to remove the brain from the nose (FM 30368).

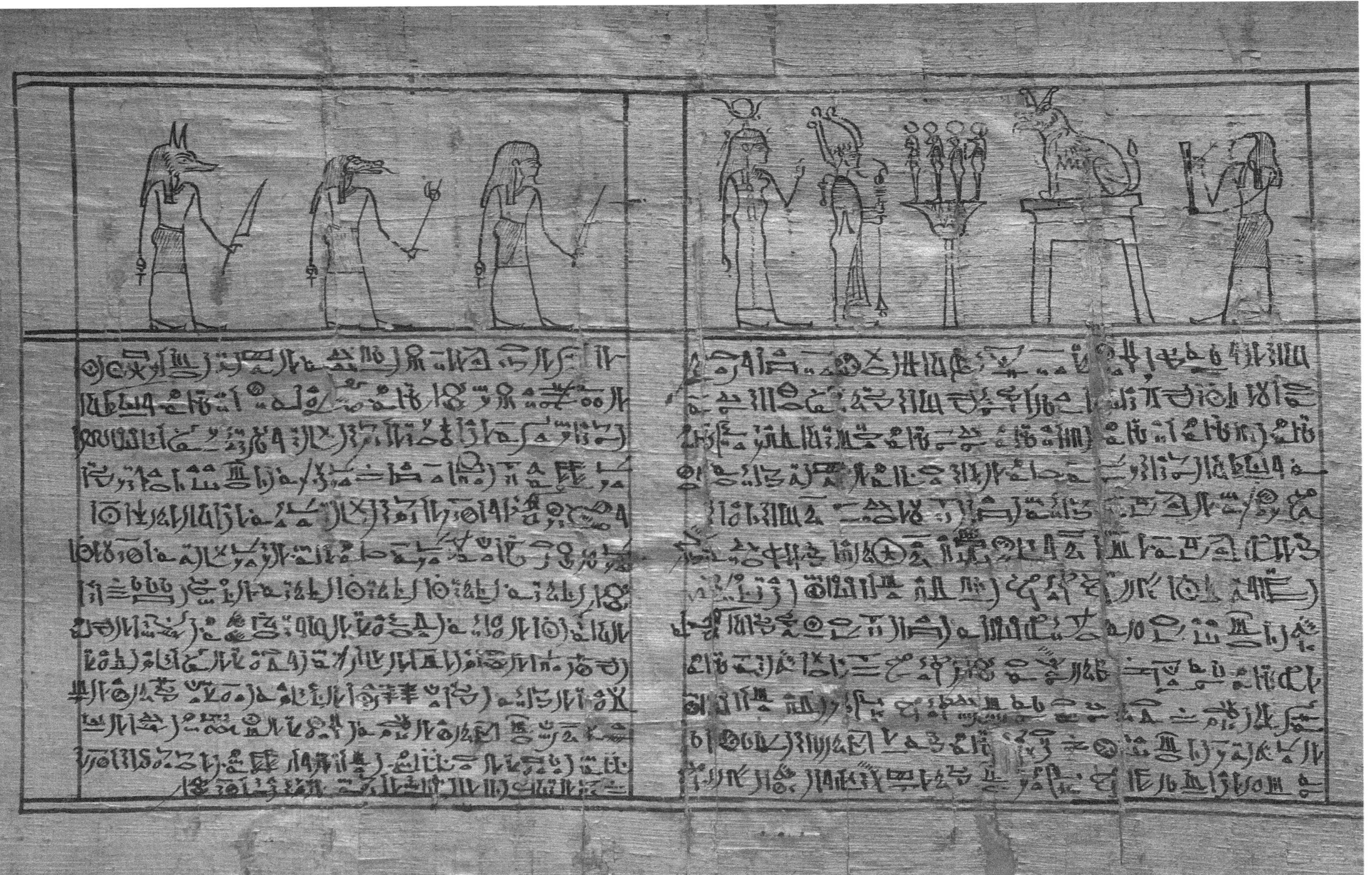

Figure 4.9. Egyptian Book of the Dead, detailing how the heart of the dead will be weighed against the feather of truth in view of the gods (FM 3132-A115261d_027d).

4B Egyptian Mummification

Emily Teeter
University of Chicago

The ancient Egyptians believed that following the successful judgment of their moral worth, the deceased became an imperishable god who dwelled forever in the afterlife. The preservation of the body was thought to be essential to this eternal life because the spirit (the *ka* and *ba*) needed an earthly home.

The key to Egyptian mummification was the removal of moisture. Until about 2900 BCE, bodies were buried in direct contact with the desert sand that acted as a natural desiccant. As burials became more elaborate and the deceased was placed in mats or coffins, new techniques of artificial preservation were developed and, by at least 2560 BCE, desiccation was aided by the removal of the internal organs.

By about 2450 BCE, after their death both men and women were thought to become Osiris, the god of the dead. Legends relate that Osiris was murdered and dismembered, and that his wife Isis gathered the pieces of his body and bound them together with linen, allowing for his revivification. This was the mythical basis for human mummification and renewed life—the linen wrappings of a mummy imitated the bindings of Osiris and promised eternal life among the gods.

Although mummification was the ideal, it was not always practiced. Throughout ancient Egyptian history, members of the non-elite were still buried in desert graves where they were naturally preserved, and there are examples of affluent individuals who were not artificially mummified (Toivari-Viitala 2001, 223; Cooney 2011, 36).

In the fullest form, mummification was an elaborate and expensive process that ideally took 70 days, an interval based on observations of the decans—stars that rose above the horizon every 70 days, an appearance equated with rebirth (Hornung 1990, 136). The corpse was taken to the embalming workshop, called a *wabet*, the "pure place," where it was cleaned, and the stomach, liver, lungs, and intestines removed through an incision made on the left side of the abdomen. The kidneys and reproductive organs were usually not removed, and there is inconsistency whether the heart was left in place. The brain was usually removed through the nose. From about 500 BCE, quicker and less expensive methods of injecting caustic solutions into the body and skull could be employed (Figures 4.8–4.13).

The body was then packed with natron (sodium carbonate or bicarbonate), a salt that occurs in the Wadi Natron northwest of modern Cairo (whence "Na" for sodium on the periodic table). Once dry, a process that took about 40 days, the body was wrapped in meters of linen, often with layers of resin, or later bitumen (a petroleum product), that acted as an adhesive and waterproofing. Stone or faience amulets might be positioned on or between the wrappings. Depending upon the family's budget, the bandaging could be extremely elaborate, with each finger and toe being individual wrapped. Usually, a large linen shroud was wrapped over the mummy and tied with linen strips.

The four internal organs were separately dried and placed in canopic jars (Figure 4.8). The Four Sons of Horus—the gods Duamutef, Qebehsenuef, Imseti, and Hapi—protected the organs (stomach, intestines, liver, and lungs, respectively). Until about 1200 BCE, all four gods shown on the lids of the jars had human heads; thereafter they were shown as a jackal, falcon, human, and ape. The brain was discarded. In many cases, a large stone scarab, usually inscribed with Book of the Dead Spell 30, was placed on the chest as a substitute or spokesman for the heart (Figure 4.9).

Once finished, the mummy was released to the family for burial. In some eras, a wood or stone tag with the name and age of the deceased was hung around the neck to ensure that the finished mummy was delivered to the correct family.

Animal Mummies

Animals were also mummified. Some dog, cat, and gazelle mummies were once beloved pets. Some bulls, crocodiles, and falcons that dwelled in temples were considered to be the earthy incarnation of a god, and they were mummified and buried in elaborate coffins. A much larger number were "victual mummies," fowl or choice pieces of bovines that were preserved and placed in the tomb as food for the mummy.

By about 600 BCE, the majority of animal mummies were produced as offerings to the gods. They included dogs, cats, birds, monkeys, mongooses, shrews, crocodiles, bovines, fish, and other animals. They were associated with a specific god through shared traits. For example, the shrew's keen eyesight was equated with that of the falcon who represented the gods Horus and Re, and the cat with the fierce lioness Sekhmet. These animals were raised commercially by temple staff, then killed, mummified, and sold to pilgrims who offered them to the god in hope of the deity interceding on their behalf, as related by inscriptions that ask the god to grant "life and prosperity," to the donor. Once a year, amidst processions and rituals, the priests would transfer the mummies to the temple catacombs.

Figure 4.10. Egyptian model house, also called "soul house" (FM 31594), and leather sandals belonging to an elite Egyptian individual (FM 110847).

Donation of animal mummies was not only a common practice but a big business, and it has been estimated that four million mummified birds were deposited in the ibis catacombs at Saqqara alone (Ikram 2005, 11).

The majority of animal mummies were not eviscerated, but rather dried with natron, or dipped in a preservative and aromatic like turpentine. In contrast, the linen wrappings could be very elaborate, with different colored linen strips creating herringbone or diamond patterns, and the exterior painted with the animal's features. Some animal mummies were placed in coffins, others in clay pots, and yet others were simply stacked in the chambers of the catacomb.

The Embalmers

Our fullest documentation about embalmers dates to the seventh–first centuries BCE and consists of contracts, receipts, and letters. As a result, the written sources relate more about the administrative side of mummification than the processes involved. Embalming was a male-dominated profession, but a few women also functioned in that role (Cannata 2020, 118, 495–96, 574). Embalmers (*kes* or *cheryw-heb*) and the ranks of funerary priests were professionals organized into associations with rules about their behavior and mutual support (Reymond 1973, 23–29; Cannata 2020; Donker van Heel 2021). They were assisted by funerary priests ("lectors") who recited the protective spells and sequence of actions.

References

Cannata, M. 2020. *Three Hundred Years of Death: The Egyptian Funerary Industry in the Ptolemaic Period.* Leiden and Boston: Brill.

Cooney, K. 2011. "Changing Burial Practices at the End of the New Kingdom: Defensive Adaptations in Tomb Commissions, Coffin Commissions, Coffin Decoration, and Mummification." *Journal of the American Research Center in Egypt* 47: 3–44.

Donker van Heel, K. 2021. *Dealing with the Dead in Ancient Egypt: The Funerary Business of Pedubast.* Cairo and New York: American University of Cairo Press.

Hornung, E. 1990. *The Valley of the Kings.* New York: Timken.

Ikram, S., ed. 2005. *Divine Creatures: Animal Mummies in Ancient Egypt.* Cairo: American University in Cairo Press.

Reymond, E. A. E. 1973. *Catalog of Demotic Papyri in the Ashmolean Museum,* Vol. 1, *Embalmers' Archives from Hawara.* Oxford: Griffith Institute.

Toivari-Viitala, J. 2001. *Women at Deir el Medina.* Leiden: NINO.

Ancestor Simulacra

But when the real body is absent, societies make great efforts to produce representations, or even simulacra, of ancestors. Simulacra were the exact representation or imitation of an ancestor. For some societies, simulacra were more than representations, they were the embodied personification of the deceased and, as such, an ancestor in his or her own right (Alberti and Bray 2009). The physical manipulation of images, symbols, objects, figurines, or simulacra of ancestors gave the living a sense of "control" of the dead, propelling the dead's conversion into a tangible expression for easy experimentation: an object amenable to worship.

Many times, the placement of these simulacra in specific spaces of the household or the community bestowed sacrality on such spaces, as ancestors were seen as "inhabiting" those spaces through their physical presence. These spaces become, too, loci of encounter and interaction, ornamented with elements that reinforce their sacrality. Ancestor simulacra were the center of symbolic actions and performances that were orchestrated both on ordinary and extraordinary occasions. At home, these spaces were constantly revered, offered, and evoked during domestic tasks.

Pre-Hispanic cultures of the Andes such as Recuay, Pucará, and Chiripa produced real-size ancestor imagery in the form of lithic sculptures, and the people's engagement with this imagery was active and deeply emotive. Ancestor imagery was placed in patios and plazas in an upright position, as if standing, and it was impossible to pass by without giving them "recognition" and "acceptance." Despite their recurrence, representations of ancestors showed differences between one another, suggesting a desire to display a particular individuality. The face, for instance, was an important locus of recognition and was a means for the adscription and recognition of individual and group identity (e.g., through facial markers and paints). Likewise, different types of facial and ear ornaments, headdresses, and other bodily ornaments could have indicated an identity, affiliation, or rank among the ancestral entities themselves (Lau 2013). In addition, the head was an essential locus of interaction and was considered the prime vehicle of communication and direct mediator between the social actors and ancestors. As Lau (2013, 64) states: "the physical interaction was directed to the ancestor's ears (songs), nose (aromas), and mouth (feeding). The eyes were an important means for co-presence and ubiquity. The always oversized and wide-open eyes marked the ancestor's capacity to witness, observe, and give acquiescence of living people's action."

Figure 4.11. Shabti figure of individual placed in burial (FM 31605.A and .B), and scarab amulet (FM 238009), symbolizing immortality and resurrection, top and bottom.

Figure 4.12. Mummified remains of an Egyptian cat (late first millennium BCE), perhaps an offering to the cat-headed goddess Bast or a revered pet (FM 111505).

Figure 4.13. Shabtis: figures of individuals placed in the burials to act as servants for the deceased in the afterlife (FM 31024, 31029, 24423.1, 31031).

In general, the inability to interact with ancestors, either in their real or representational form, could have been seen as a critical rupture with the divine forces, and the physical absence of the ancestor as something tragically irremediable. If the capacity to materialize the presence of the ancestor into something tangible was absent, then that could have symbolized the oblivion of, and disaffect by, that powerful ancestor (see Kusimba in this volume).

Sensoriality and Experience

Sensorial perceptions are important aspects of death-related rituals and performances. Although many have argued that senses must be understood as culturally constructed, linguistically determined, and essentially arbitrary and unfettered by the external world, we cannot deny that memory is "put to work" when senses are properly stimulated (Connerton 1989). Yannis Hamilakis (2013) argues that sensorial experiences from the past are not ephemeral but, rather, material phenomena, as they require contact with the material in order to be activated. However, performance scholars argue that the body does not need the material to activate its own stimuli, as the body remembers through its own corporeal and kinetic memory (Giannachi, Kaye, and Shanks 2012). During death-related rituals and performances, sight, sound, touch, hearing, and smell, and other senses, either working independently or synesthetically (all together), are, ultimately, the means through which we connect with emotions and activate memory. We can safely say that the effectiveness of the production of meanings, emotions, and memory during funerary performances is highly reliant on the level of stimulus of our senses.

Music and auditive sensations are key in the ritual experience of the death, and it is particularly the control and the manipulation of sound, in its various manifestations, that were sought in the past (and even in the present) to create augmented sensorial experiences. Wind instruments (and their potent vibratory amplitude), such as the ones documented in archaeological contexts from the Andean region (Figures 4.1–4.3), were likely used as means of overture of mortuary performances, as well as of invocation of the ancestral presence. In the ancient Andes, flutes, panpipes, *pututo* conch trumpets, and whistles—as well as the still poorly studied whistling bottles that produced sound through an interplay of water, air, and matter within the ceramic bodies (Figure 4.4)—were played in performance settings, such as the circular sunken plaza of Caral (3000 BCE) or the underground galleries of Chavín de Huantar (1200 BCE). In general, music set the mood and enabled the initiation of an extraordinary time, of liminality, when the participant begins a process of social reconfiguration.

Wind instruments as the ones displayed in this exhibit were manufactured using materials such as bone, ceramic, and reed, and it is believed that the zoomorphic depictions rendered on some of them had a relationship with the type of sound the instrument could reproduce—and even instruments generating meaningless or clangorous (to modern ears) sounds could have been highly desired in ritual settings. Nasca whistles with bird representations, for example, produced sounds as high-pitched as the ones produced by desert hummingbirds from the south coast of Peru, and the connection between these particular animals and the Nasca ancestors seems to have been manifested through their representation in gigantic geoglyphs drawn on the desert, which can only be seen from the sky and mountains.

Although still poorly studied, musicians in Andean funerary rituals could have fulfilled particularly important roles, not only through their performative skills, but also their capacity to create sounds and vibrations that were considered "stabilizing" of the chaos (La Chioma 2018). Cosmogonic myths ethnographically collected in the Amazon region, for example, highlight the role of music and musicians in the process of both creation and destruction of the world. As recounted by Eduardo Huárag Álvarez (2018), for the Amazon native people from the Marañón Basin, the world is believed to have been created by a female musician-priestess who, with the help of their ancestors and other divine forces, travels around the woods while playing a flute. This flute was then hidden in her genitals.

The role of musicians was greatly appreciated in the past and, perhaps, was a symbol of status and prestige. In iconographic representations, Moche musicians are depicted lavishly dressed and participating in large-scale funerary performances and processions celebrated in Moche temples, along with ritual officers, dancers, and skeletal figures representing ancestors. Musicians with particular disabilities (e.g., lip and nose deformation) were considered mediators between the world of the living and the dead: they had the capacities to transit between different worlds, linking the mundane and spiritual (Figure 4.5). Moche Musicians typically played percussion instruments (drums and rattles) during the ritual enactments and, sometimes, used their own body to produce sounds. Percussive sounds helped create paused rhythms marking time during rituals and, as Jerry Moore has noted, percussion, and drumming in particular, could have been key in large-scale Chimú funerary spectacles to drive away evil spirits, encourage the soul on its own flight, summon the spirits, and create social solidarity through a shared sensitive experience (Moore 2006). Similarly, for the Moche, it has been proposed that rattles were rhythmically played during funerary spectacles in order to "awaken" the ancient ancestors (Bourget 2006) and help reopen the underworld, so the newly converted ancestor could emerge victoriously from it.

4C The Ghanaian Fantasy Canoe Coffin: A Box with Proverbs

Foreman Bandama
Field Museum

When unmitigated against, death may mark the end of many people's dreams, but throughout the world many families use burials and associated grave goods to ensure that the wishes of the dead are met. Beyond wishes, funerary objects are used to communicate and celebrate deceased's occupation, familial identity, and social position (Otto 2019). In Ghana in West Africa, a combination of chance and curiosity in the face of the changing colonial and postcolonial dynamics surrounding death, leadership, and community relationships led to a twentieth-century tradition of elaborate fantasy coffins.

Under the British colonial law dating back to 1888, Ghanaians were forced to use public cemeteries, as opposed to the traditional, relatively private, burial under house floors. By the 1930s, the people of Ghana were already warming up to the idea of abandoning basket- and mat-wrappings in favor of coffins (Gundlach 2017). The transition to fantasy coffins was spurred by the Ga people's long tradition of figurative palanquins that were used exclusively by the chiefs (Secretan 1995; Bonetti 2010). A palanquin is a one-passenger box or seat carried on two horizontal poles by four or six bearers. Both figurative palanquins and fantasy coffins relied on a deeply rooted practice of commissioning crafts, but skewed access to wealth and power meant that the elites were the ones who had the luxury and political muscle to commission the best works.

For a long time, Ghanaians and their neighboring communities used palanquins (also commonly known as sedan chairs) as figurative royal coffins. In the 1950s, among the Ga people, the dominant ethnic group of the region of Accra in Ghana, what started off as a routine figurative royal palanquin for a local chief turned into reality when a cocoa-pod-shaped palanquin was used as the actual coffin of the commissioning chief, who died unexpectedly before the festival (Kreamer 1994). The unique coffin drew many admirers beyond royalty. Inspired by the enthusiasm of the crowds at the chief's funeral, Seth Kane Kwei (1925–92), one of the cocoa-pod-coffin carpenters made an airplane-shaped coffin for his grandmother who died not long after the first palanquin coffin event. His grandmother grew up in Teshie, a coastal suburb near Accra's airport and was fascinated by the idea of planes, but she never got the chance to fly. By burying her in an airplane-shaped coffin, Kane Kwei ensured that his grandmother would fly into eternity but, more importantly, this seeded the idea that even commoners can choose to celebrate death in palanquin coffins.

Several local people began to request customized fantasy coffins soon after the airplane coffin event (Figure 4.14). As the practice became widespread, the Ga people gave these coffins a new name: *Abebuu adekai* meaning boxes with proverbs. The motifs of the coffins revealed a number of things: (1) the message for perpetuity of one's profession (for instance, a fisherman would be buried in a boat-shaped coffin); (2) the dreams and aspirations of the deceased, such as a plane or a luxurious car; (3) character or temperament, such as a coffin in the shape of a red-hot chili pepper for an assertive person; or (4) status (for instance, certain animal shapes such as the elephant were reserved for high-ranking officials) (Van Der Geest 2000; Otto 2019; Gundlach 2017).

The tradition never lacked admirers and soon its popularity spread beyond the borders of the Ga people of the Accra region, to the Ashanti region (Kumasi), the Ewé region, and even as far as parts of Togo. It also did not take long for the fantasy coffins to catch the attention of Western museums which began collecting and commissioning several examples for their own museum displays in the 1970s. Seth Kane Kwei remained one of the household names, together with a few others, such as Joseph Ashong, popularly known as Paa Joe (Otto 2019). Kane Kwei and Paa Joe have since been featured in several art festivals, shows, and galleries around the world because of these fantasy coffins. It was within this context that the canoe-shaped Ghanaian Fantasy Coffin which appears in this exhibition was produced by Seth Kane Kwei himself in 1989. The shape is consistent with the motifs of Ga fishermen, who used to carve and place a little dummy-canoe on the graves of their deceased, long before fantasy coffins were introduced (Potocnik 2018). The canoe-shaped coffin was on display at a gallery in Los Angeles, and was produced just three years before the death of Kane Kwei. His family continued the workshop and its tradition, and the workshop is now managed by his grandson, Eric Adjetey Anang, an artist and master coffin maker himself (http://www.kanekwei.com/past-events). The business is generally a high earner, with a typical fantasy coffin costing nearly as much as an average Ghanaian earns in a year.

The commissioning and acquisition of fantasy coffins for museum and art gallery displays necessitated additional changes. For instance, coffins destined for burial were typically made from light wood such as *Altonia boonei* but those manufactured for Western museum displays are now made from hard wood such as *Terminalia superba* or African mahogany (*Khaya ivorensis*; http://www.kanekwei.com/past-events).

References

Bonetti, R. 2010. "Alternate Histories of the Abebuu Adekai." *African Arts* 43, no. 3: 14– 33. https://doi.org/10.1162/afar.2010.43.3.14.

Gundlach, C. 2017. *Art and the Afterlife: Fantasy Coffins by Eric Adjetey Anang*. Exhibition at UIMA.

Kane Kwei Carpentry Workshop website. n.d. http://www.kanekwei.com/past-events.

Kreamer, C. M. 1994. *A Life Well Lived: Fantasy Coffins of Kane Quaye*. Kansas City: University of Missouri-Kansas City Gallery of Art.

Otto, K. 2019. "Shapes of the Ancestors: Bodies, Animals, Art, and Ghanaian Fantasy Coffins." *Museum Anthropology Review* 13, no. 1: 58.

Potocnik, M. 2018. "A History of Death and Funeral Rites: A Case Study of the Ga in Jamestown (Ghana)." MPhil dissertation, University of Ghana.

Secretan, T. 1995. *Going into Darkness: Fantastic Coffins from Africa*. London: Thames & Hudson.

Van Der Geest, S. 2000. "Funerals for the Living: Conversations with Elderly People in Kwahu, Ghana." *African Studies Review* 43, no. 3: 103–29.

Death as Politics and Politics as Spectacle

For some societies, life goes with death in such an important way that life cannot go on if death is not "performed" first. The spectacularity and exuberance of some mortuary performances, and the great investment of labor, time, and energy put into them, make these enactments arenas for political consolidation and negotiation, as well as subversion. Clifford Geertz (1980), for example, notes that the poetics and aesthetics of funerary spectacles were indispensable for constructing institutionalized power in nineteenth-century Balinese Negara. The tangible images of the ruler's body and state buildings and the collective acts of their public display were critical to what many individuals consciously recognized as the established social order. The dramatic displays of state symbols not only constituted a political strategy of governance, but were the state in their own right: "theatre-states" (Geertz 1980, 93). In this sense, the state was (re)created insofar as death was celebrated under public scrutiny as the corpse of the ruler personified statehood.

But the power of death and its deep influence on politics and governance have clear correlates even in our day. The large and spectacular funerary processions that preceded the burial, for example, of the US former president John F. Kennedy, the Argentinian first lady Eva Peron, and Pope John Paul II are eloquent displays of the potent symbolism of the dead body, as well as the real power that is inscribed in it while seen by, and moved through, thousand if not millions of spectators. The funerals of these important individuals produced profound impacts on the societies to which they belonged, and time and space were particularly reconfigured while their deaths were "performed." The deaths of these charismatic leaders shocked people at first, but then people collectively participated in their funerals, while witnessing an exuberant display of state paraphernalia and religious emblems that visually reinforced political discourses of domination and hierarchical power structures. Walking through their tombs, visiting their memorial monuments, whether collectively or individually, and living through their predicaments are clear signs of how death, power, and politics are particularly intertwined with each other.

This has important parallels in both the past and present. In fact, Foucault (1977) argued that, in premodern times, power was exercised through spectacle, and that institutionalized discipline in particular was manifested through "was what was seen, what was shown, and what was manifested" (quoted in Inomata and Coben 2006, 26). Namely, power was body-centered and exercised through control of the body's freedom and of its emotions and perceptions. The conversion of ancient political and religious leaders into gods or goddesses through complex rituals of deification had potent effects on the viewers and the ways they perceived political and social reality. As happened in ancient Rome and Angkor, the "god-king after corporeal demise went on to a condition of immortality" (Renfrew 2016, 9), and this immortality and divinity of the sovereign constituted the basis of the political articulation and legitimacy of the system as a whole. From the deceased buried beneath the house floors of Çatalhöyük to the Incan mummies paraded through the Coricancha plaza, it was the power of what was seen and shown through such spaces that sedimented, in the witnesses' minds, a perception, as well as justification, of a given political and social order. And this happens even in our times.

Now, death continues to be intimately linked to politics and power along with inequality and inequity. While death is a universal phenomenon, it is not experienced in the same way by groups across the globe. As this exhibit also shows, economic, social, racial, and ethnic differences also determine the ways in which people suffer, and display their suffering, when facing death. In Latin America, my own home region, experiences around death are tragically disproportionate. While some bury their deceased with great pomp, others, from historically marginalized groups, cannot even find the bodies of their loved ones, because they were victims of armed conflict, forced migrations, institutionalized violence, or gender-based crimes, among other causes. Whereas in developed nations, to not bury your loved one with the deserved love and affection might often seem unthinkable, in developing nations some people have been deprived of their right to know what has happened to their missing relatives.

Figure 4.14. Ghanaian wood coffin of a canoe with rowers by Seth Kane Kwei, ca. 1981 (FM 361842.1-.12).

Figure 4.15. Ancestral shrine at Bungule, Kasigau, Taita-Taveta County, Kenya.

4D Tsavo Shrines

Chapurukha M. Kusimba
University of South Florida

Throughout our history, humankind has developed myriad ways to remember the dead, from leaving them in their homes to burying them at sea. Many of these ways leave no trace, so we may never fully appreciate how some communities memorialized the dead. We can, however, understand the pain they endured and continue to endure when we lose loved ones. Still, there remains a considerable bias in how the dead were remembered. Today's archaeological record mostly recounts the narratives of the elite, whose relatives could afford to inter the remains of their loved ones. For the most part, the remains of commoners were often discarded in the wilderness. However, archaeologists utilize the few memorials available to determine how each society viewed and dealt with death.

A Field Museum anthropological archaeology expedition in the Tsavo National Park in southeast Kenya recovered several hundred graves, cemeteries, cairns, and skull interment sites (Kusimba and Kusimba 2000). These memorial sites belonged to ancestors of Kenyan people who inhabited the Tsavo plains until they were designated a national park in 1948. These memorial sites provided the most substantial evidence of identities, mortuary behavior, and the people's belief systems during the precolonial period before many converted to Christianity and Islam. The cairns housed the remains of the pastoral Oromo; the graves were variously attributed to the agropastoral Wambisha and Wataita, who inhabited the Tsavo plains before warfare instigated by drought, disease, and the slave trade forced them to migrate to the Taita, Saghala, and Kasigau Hills. These migrants were to eke out a living on the congested hill for the next four centuries, after which peaceful coexistence was reestablished following the abolition of the slave trade and the advent of European colonial rule in the late nineteenth century. How did the people of southeast Kenya maintain relationships with the ancestral shrines which they abruptly abandoned in the Tsavo plains? How and in what ways did their new refuge residences influence their mortuary behavior and practices?

The Field Museum expedition recovered evidence indicating that as they moved to new, more congested hills, these refugees radically changed how they memorialized their ancestors. Slavery, famine, disease, and other crises had forced them to adopt a nomadic lifestyle which involved them regularly moving with little warning. Many adopted a mortuary behavior pattern of migrating with their ancestors. Beginning from the sixteenth century, instead of burying the dead in graves, they began to disinter their ancestors' skulls and built shrines for them wherever they settled. To maintain strong bonds between ancestors and their descendants, the ancestors were regularly propitiated with gifts of food and drink. They reciprocated by protecting their descendants from calamities and crises like drought, diseases, sterility, and witchcraft. Large partially broken pots and gourds found at interment sites were used in the ceremonial feasting that occurred at these sites.

Our team recovered four such shrine sites in the Tsavo region. One was located in a deep ravine in Sungululu village near Wundanyi town. This one contained 26 skulls, including one of a sheep. The second was found in Kajire, a rocky promontory above the central zone of habitation on Saghala Hills, which included more than 300 cranial remains arranged in different areas of a composite of rocky outcrops. The third was found in Bungule in the Kasigau Hills (Figure 4.15). The Bungule shrine bore 45 individuals. The fourth was the shrine in Makwasinyi, Kasigau Hills, which contained 25 individual skulls.

Elders from the Sungululu community related that the skull of sheep stood in for an ancestor who was lost to the community in a slaving raid. His body was never interred with the ancestors and his mortal remains never returned to his community after his disappearance. Yet he is remembered by those he left behind, and the skull of an animal fulfills his place in the relocated shrine in the Tsavo Hills. Sometimes, an individual's removal from his community marks his social death, as his physical death and mortal remains are never seen by those family members who were ripped from his existence.

Informants confirmed that the groups of cranial remains represented their patrilineage of ancestors. Individuals would be buried in graves for two years, following which the deceased's skull would be disinterred and placed in a cranial display niche. Only married individuals with children were disinterred. Although the practice of disinterring ancestral skulls declined in the 1920s following conversion to Christianity and the colonial decree which discouraged the practice, informants argued that the skulls' rituals continued into the 1950s. The shrines of Tsavo remind us that physical death does not mean an end to familial relationship. Shrines ensure continuity and permanence between the dead, the living, and the unborn.

Reference

Kusimba, C. M., and Kusimba, S. B. 2000. "Hinterlands and Cities: Archaeological Investigations of Economy and Trade in Tsavo, South-Eastern Kenya." *Nyame Akuma* 54: 13–24.

Death and performances around it are continuously used to model experiences in the world. Don Handelman (1990) introduces the term "technology of events" to indicate how the logic of design of public spectacles dictates the way in which one perceives social and political reality. His proposed typology of events—"events that present," "events that model," and "events that re-present"—makes explicit reference to the constant manipulation of the design, as well as the internal setting, of the events in order to project and impose on participants desired notions of society, performances of death being an advantageous opportunity for such a process.

As I stated at the beginning of this essay, death should not worry us to the extent that we will not really face the aftermath of our own death. But perhaps this is an unfair characterization and death should worry us, after all, as this will be a continuous arena of dispute for justice and dignity for those that we leave behind. And although death always finds its own ways to make us face the imbalance of power present in our society, death also presents us with the opportunity to reinterpret, subvert, and openly criticize the preexisting social orders, fighting through the power of our actions and performances.

References

Alberti, B., and Bray, T. 2009. "Special Section: Animating Archaeology. Of Subjects, Objects and Alternative Ontologies." *Cambridge Archaeological Journal* 19, no. 3: 337–43.

Arriaza, B. 1995. *Beyond Death: The Chinchorro Mummies of Ancient Chile*. Washington, DC: Smithsonian Institution Press.

Borić, D. 2010. "Introduction: Memory, Archaeology and the Historical Condition." In *Archaeology and Memory*, edited by D. Borić, 1–34. Oxford: Oxbow Books.

Bourget, S. 2006. *Sex, Death, and Sacrifice in Moche Religion and Visual Culture*. Austin: University of Texas Press.

Cerezo-Román, J. 2015. "Unpacking Personhood and Funerary Customs in the Hohokam Area of Southern Arizona." *American Antiquity* 80, no. 2: 353–75.

Connerton, P. 1989. *How Societies Remember*. Cambridge: Cambridge University Press.

D'Altroy, T. 2016. "Killing Mummies: On Inka Epistemology and Imperial Power." In *Death Rituals, Social Order and the Archaeology of Immortality in the Ancient World*, edited by C. Renfrew, M. Boyd, and I. Morley, 404–22. Cambridge and New York: Cambridge University Press.

Foucault, M. 1977. *Discipline and Punish: The Birth of the Prison*. London: Penguin.

Fowler, C. 2004. *The Archaeology of Personhood: An Anthropological Approach*. London: Routledge.

Geertz, C. 1980. *Negara: The Theatre State in Nineteenth-Century Bali*. Princeton, NJ: Princeton University Press.

Giannachi, G., Kaye, N., and Shanks, M. 2012. *Archaeologies of Presence: Art, Performance and the Persistence of Being*. New York: Routledge.

Gillespie, S. 2001. "Personhood, Agency, and Mortuary Ritual: A Case Study from the Ancient Maya." *Journal of Anthropological Archaeology* 20, no. 1: 73–112.

Hamilakis, Y. 2013. *Archaeology of the Senses: Human Experience, Memory, and Affect*. Cambridge: Cambridge University Press.

Handelman, D. 1990. *Models and Mirrors: Toward an Anthropology of Public Events*. Cambridge: Cambridge University Press.

Hill, E. 2016. "Images of Ancestor: Identifying the Revered Dead in Moche Iconography." In *The Archaeology of Ancestors: Death, Memory, and Veneration*, edited by E. Hill and J. Hageman, 189–212. Gainesville: University Press of Florida.

Hill, E., and Hageman, J. B. 2016. *The Archaeology of Ancestors: Death, Memory, and Veneration*. Gainsville: University Press of Florida.

Hodder, I. 2010. *Religion in the Emergence of Civilization: Catalhoyuk as a Case Study*. Cambridge: Cambridge University Press.

Hodder, I. 2014. "The Entanglements of Humans and Things: A Long-Term View." *New Literary History* 45, no. 1. https://doi.org/10.1353/nlh.2014.0005.

Huárag Álvarez, E. 2018. *Mitos de La Creación Del Mundo: Mitopoéticas Amazónicas*. Lima: Universidad Ricardo Palma, Editorial Universitaria.

Inomata, T., and Coben, L. 2006. *Archaeology of Performance: Theaters of Power, Community, and Politics*. Oxford: Altamira Press.

Insoll, T. 2004. *Archaeology, Ritual, Religion*. Oxford and New York: Routledge.

Kus, S. 1992. "Toward an Archaeology of Body and Soul." In *Representations in Archaeology*, edited by J. C. Gardin and C. Peebles, 168–77. Bloomington: Indiana University Press.

LaChioma, D. 2018. "La Antara en el Arte Moche: Performance y Simbolismo." In *Música y Sonidos en el Mundo Andino: Flautas de Pan, Zampoñas, Sikus y Ayarachis*, edited by C. Huaringa, 37–74. Lima: Fondo Editorial de Universidad Nacional Mayor de San Marcos.

Lau, G. 2013. *Ancient Alterity in the Andes: A Recognition of Others*. London and New York: Routledge.

Meskell, L. 2004. *Object Worlds from Ancient Egypt: Material Biographies Past and Present*. London: Berg.

Moore, J. 2006. "The Indians Were Much Given to Their Taquis: Drumming and Generative Categories in Ancient Andes." In *Archaeology of Performance: Theaters of Power, Community, and Politics*, edited by T. Innomata and L. Coben, 47–80. Lanham: Altamira Press.

Muro Ynoñán, L. A. 2010. "La Tumba del Sacerdote de San José de Moro." In *Programa Arqueológico San José de Moro: Informe Ejecutivo de la Temporada 2009*, edited by Luis Jaime Castillo, 280–397. Lima: Pontificia Universidad Católica del Perú.

Muro Ynoñán, L. A. 2019. "Tracing the Moche Spectacles of Death: Performance, Ancestrality, and Political Power in Ancient Peru. A View from Huaca La Capilla-San José de Moro (AD 650–740)." Doctoral dissertation, Department of Anthropology, Stanford University.

Pettitt, P. 2018. "Hominin Evolutionary Thanatology from the Mortuary to Funerary Realm: The Palaeoanthropological Bridge between Chemistry and Culture." *Philosophical Transactions of the Royal Society B: Biological Sciences* 373, no. 1754. http://dx.doi.org/10.1098/rstb.2018.0212.

Renfrew, C. 2016. "'The Unanswered Question': Investigating Early Conceptualisations of Death." In *Death Rituals, Social Order and the Archaeology of Immortality in the Ancient World: "Death Shall Have No Dominion,"* edited by C. Renfrew, M. Boyd, and I. Morley, 1–14. New York: Cambridge University Press.

Thomas, J. 2011. "Ritual and Religion in the Neolithic." In *The Oxford Handbook of the Archaeology of Ritual and Religion*, edited by T. Insoll, 371–86. Oxford: Oxford University Press.

Van Gennep, A. 1960. *The Rites of Passage*. Chicago: University of Chicago Press.

5

Jewish and Christian Perspectives on Death

William Schweiker
University of Chicago

Abstract: Jewish and Christian perspectives on death are examined in this thematic essay, and emphasis is given to Christianity, the area of the author's expertise, with comparisons to Judaism within each of the topics to be explored. The essay examines the origin of death, living while dying, dying and the dead, and, finally, what is thought to be beyond death. Importantly, Judaism and Christianity look forward to the coming of the Messiah, the anointed one (Judaism) or his return. This messianic outlook means that what is beyond death is not only personal or communal eternal life, but, more centrally, the reign of God throughout the whole of reality. The case studies explore examples of Christian and Jewish traditions, including syncretism with Indigenous religions and perspectives from other world religions.

Resumen: En este capitulo se examinan las perspectivas judías y cristianas sobre la muerte. Se da énfasis al cristianismo, el área de especialización del autor, con comparaciones con el judaísmo dentro de cada uno de los temas a explorar. El ensayo examina el origen de la muerte, el "vivir muriendo," el morir y los muertos y, finalmente, lo que se piensa que hay más allá de la muerte. Es importante destacar que el judaísmo y el cristianismo esperan la llegada del Mesías, el ungido (judaísmo) o su regreso. Esta perspectiva mesiánica significa que lo que está más allá de la muerte no es sólo la vida eterna personal o comunitaria, sino, más centralmente, el reino de Dios en toda su extensión. Los artículos aquí contenidos exploran ejemplos de tradiciones cristianas y judías, incluyendo el sincretismo con las religiones indígenas y las perspectivas de otras religiones del mundo.

Religion and Death

It is often argued that the origin of religion is fear, especially fear of forces beyond human control and particularly death. From ancient thinkers, like the Greek philosopher Epicurus (341–270 BCE), to Enlightenment thinkers such as Scottish philosophers David Hume (1711–1776) and Sigmund Freud (1856–1939), and Bertrand Russell (1872–1970), the origin of religion and ideas about the gods and an afterlife originate in the fear and wish-fulfillment of death. God is to be worshipped and obeyed in order to diminish fear and relieve guilt, or rituals and practices are meant to provide relief from fear and its causes. Whether or not that is a sufficient explanation of the origin of religion, there are good reasons to doubt it. The fact remains that the world's religions do provide realistic responses to the fact of human death. However, it is also true that the religions insist that death is not the final word or the meaning of finite reality. Whether in Hindu ideas of rebirth (Figures 5.1–5.3), Buddhist ideas about Nirvana as extinguishing the fire of desire and releasing the person from the cycle of suffering, Christian conceptions of Heaven as union with or vision of the Divine, or belief among Indigenous religions in the power of ancestors to aid one in the present life, religions hold that death is not the ultimate horizon of human existence. This double perspective must be kept in mind as this essay explores death in Judaism and Christianity. That is, religions realistically face the fact of death and yet also insist that it is not the ultimate truth of human existence. It is this double perspective on death that allows one to compare and contrast religious traditions.

I emphasize Christian perspectives on death, the area of the my expertise, and compare to Judaism within each of the topics to be explored. Of course, every religious tradition is exceedingly complex, with many different beliefs and practices internal to and shared between religions. Given that reality, a comprehensive treatment of Judaism or Christianity, much less their comparison, is impossible. Accordingly, I will examine the origin of death, living while dying, dying and the dead, and, finally, what is thought to be beyond death. Importantly, Judaism and Christianity look forward to the coming of the Messiah, the anointed one (Judaism) or Christ's return (Christianity). This messianic outlook means that what is beyond death is not only eternal life, but, more centrally, the reign of God throughout the whole of reality.

The Origin of Death

Judaism is more a religion of practice, unlike Christianity with its many creeds and doctrines. Life is valued by Jews almost above all else. The Talmud, the basic compendium of Jewish *Torah* (law or teaching), even states that, since all people are descendants of one man (Adam), to take a life is like destroying the world. To save a life is to save the world. Death as a

150384

Figure 5.2. Devotion to a Hindu deity is one way to travel the path to *moksha*. Deities Shiva and Parvati (FM 89225).

←

Figure 5.1. Hinduism teaches that each living thing goes through a cycle of birth, life, death, and rebirth until one attains enlightenment (*moksha*). Hindu goddess, Shiva (FM 150384).

natural process has meaning, then, in the context of a profound affirmation of life within God's plan for the Jewish people. *Chevra kadisha* (Jewish burial societies) are associated with synagogues and both ritually clean and dress deceased Jews for traditional burial customs and to protect bodies from desecration (see Zoloth in this volume). Not all Jews believe in life after death. Here complexity is found in the tradition. Orthodox Jews do affirm life after death, while Reform Jews may not. Conservative Jews hold both views on life after death. These differences reach back in time to the clash between the Sadducees and Pharisees during the Second Temple period (second century BCE–70 CE) with the destruction of the Temple. Sadducees denied the resurrection of the body and so denied an afterlife, while the Pharisees affirmed the resurrection of the body. For Jews who do believe in an afterlife, one gains such life through doing good works for others (*mitzvah*), as taught in the *Torah*. Those that deny an afterlife believe that one continues in the memory of the people. In the Hebrew biblical texts, there is no mention of heaven or hell but rather She'ol, a dark underworld where all of the dead go.

In Christianity the origin of death is due to the sin of Adam and Eve, eating from the forbidden fruit of the tree of the knowledge of good and evil (see Wali in this volume, on Guna *Molas*). Adam and Eve are exiled from Paradise (the Garden of Eden) to live and die in a world marred by sin, that is, disobedience and separation from God. Death enters the world through sin. This is decisively different than Judaism and is why Christians believe in a savior, Jesus Christ, who redeems people from sin and reconciles them to God and one another. Western Christianity, decisively influenced by the thought of St. Augustine of Hippo (396–430 CE) holds that because of Adam's and Eve's first "Original Sin," every human being inherits the guilt of that sin and its consequences. Orthodox Christians also believe in Original Sin, but people only bear its consequences, foremost death, and not Adam's and Eve's guilt. Nevertheless, Christians do not believe that death was part of God's creation but enters the world through sin, that is, disobedience and unbelief in God. However defined, "original sin" is passed on from generation to generation in the reality of death and for the Christian in guilt. In either case, no human being is born without original sin and thus the fact and reality of death. In this way, death is seen as the "final enemy" that will, in the end, be destroyed by Christ, as St. Paul put it in 1 Corinthians 15:25–26. Christ atones for sin and with his resurrection from the dead is the victory of God over death for the sake of humanity. Baptism and entrance to the Church and a life of love is how one participates in Christ's atonement for sin. Christianity also has a conception of a "second death," that will be explored later in this essay.

Living While Dying

In human life, living and dying are intimately related even as people have various ways of existence. A person dying from cancer might be vibrantly alive intellectually or spiritually. Someone dying from a disease that has robbed them of their mental capacities, might, nonetheless, be physically sound. This means that living while dying, which people are always doing, is not just a physical process but, much more, a deeply moral and spiritual one. Given that Christianity and Judaism acknowledge and insist on the reality of death in human life, they also necessarily provide ways to live even as people are aging and dying. For Christians, this means "walking in the ways that lead to life," which include adhering to the Ten Commandments, doing works of love, participating in church life and the sacraments, and having an abiding faith in God through Christ and the Holy Spirit. In this way, a Christian's living toward death is enfolded within the life of the Church, the body of Christ in the world. Albeit in different ways, Jews and Christians link the challenges of living a mortal life to the importance of the moral life. Both value membership in a community, the Church, or the Jewish people.

For Christians this membership begins with the sacrament of baptism, a ritualized death when one is then raised into new life in the body of Christ as the Church. Christians may differ on the forms of baptism and whether it is for infants or adults, but all Christians affirm baptism because Jesus Christ himself was baptized. The Christian life is then sustained by the worship and sacraments of the Church, although Christians differ on the number of sacraments. Protestants typically celebrate baptism and the Lord's Supper or the *eucharist*. Catholic and Orthodox Christians celebrate as sacraments: baptism, confirmation or chrismation, penance, marriage, the *eucharist*, ordination, extreme unction (anointing of the sick and dying), and last rites shortly before death.

Figure 5.3. The Hindu deity Vishnu (FM 150432).

קנקן חדש
דקברנים יצ״ו
מכיסם בשנת
לקידושא

5A The *Chevra Kadisha*

Laurie Zoloth
University of Chicago

Of all the ritual acts that are a part of the community life of a commanded faith tradition, none is as little known as the work of the *chevra kadisha*, or the Jewish ritual burial society. Operating in every Jewish community, the *chevra* is a selected group of women and men who prepare the body of the dead according to rabbinic tradition with a liturgy based in the Song of Songs and a practice that forces the abstract discourse of death and the afterlife into intimate, tangible detail of embodiment (Madsen 1998). The laws of ritual burial are straightforward: every Jewish person is to complete his or her life in the same way: washed clean, with a specified amount of running water poured from the hands of her *chevra*, gently patted dry, dressed in simple unbleached linen shrouds, sewn by hand, *tachrehin* (Lamm 2000). The same for all, the rich, poor, powerful, and powerless: unembalmed, unadorned. Each is wrapped in linen with small handfuls of dirt from Mt. Scopus in Jerusalem, placed at their heart, eyes, and womb, lifted into a pine box made without nails, the lid closed and a candle lit on the top, and watched until carried to the grave (Epstein 1995). Women prepare women, men prepare men, all in silence, never turning their backs to the body of the dead (Diamant 2001; Epstein 1995). The term *chevra kadisha* is an Ashkenazi one (Sephardic Jews refer to this as the *lavadores*, those who wash). The concept of a separate grouping that is assigned to this tradition is referred to in the Babylonian Talmud.

Participation in the *chevra kadisha* is a "hard mitzvah" that is "not for everyone," noted one participant from a small community (Zoloth 1998). Yet it this very secrecy and sense of utter responsibility that makes the act obligatory, and in the framing of the performance as chosen, ritualized and mandatory, a social contract is created in which role-specific duties emerge. It is a feature of the act itself that makes these role-specific duties an ethical gesture and not merely an act of faithfulness (Light 2013). The people who perform the act must not be related to the dead person, nor can they be *students* of the deceased. They must be strangers, yet they must enact the most primal of interactions: the primate bonding rituals that mark the beginning of the first human relationships at birth. These include skin-to-skin touch (or, since the AIDS epidemic, skin-to-glove), grooming, and the face-to-face gaze. It is precisely these behaviors that are initiated at birth by all of humanity, and it is these acts that are re-created by the strangers toward the *metah*, the dead one, at the moment of transition from death to burial, light to darkness, being to unbeing.

The act of the creation of the *chevra kadisha* represents a critical moment in how a community relates to the divine (Epstein 1995). Note that the mediation of the death process is simple, and in the hands of the laity (Abeles and Katz 2010). Unlike Egyptian religions, which in important respects centered around the ritual preparation and celebration of death, Jewish law ensures that all will be afforded a burial and that the act of burial is linked to the larger notion of a human order. Priests (*cohenim*) are forbidden to touch the dead, further ensuring the democratizing thrust of the practice. In most communities, members are secret, known only to one another. Yet it is clear that, at least in some historical periods, the society consisted of a rotational membership, affording each with the opportunity to confront death (Ochs 2017)

As one community participant noted: "It is true that is it is hard work. It means dealing with blood, lifting the body, twice, once onto special boards to be washed, once into a coffin. 'How can we go on?' I sometimes think, in the middle. But this is a task that we must complete, and when we are done, she is pure, the body of the dead one, transformed. After we close the lid, we take our gloves off, and we ask forgiveness, in silence, from her. We are sorry, our human selves, we are tired, we are clumsy, we drop things, we are sorry beloved stranger, please forgive us" (Greenhough 2002; Ochs 2017; Zoloth 1998).

The act of the *taharah* is the taking of the body of the dead and returning it ritually to a human and particular self (Mitntz 1999). Let us reflect on what precedes this. In many cases, death in modernity is a battle lost. Death is seen as the problem, the structural enemy that is engaged by the moral gesture of medicine itself. But medicine is both a moral gesture and an act in the marketplace economy. Hence, when the body is no longer a patient, with all that status entails, it is discarded by a certain prestigious sector, whose attention no longer is repaid. The body then is treated as though it has returned to an animal state. It is wrapped, refrigerated, and handled in this way.

It is at precisely this moment, the moment one would turn from in the secular word, the *chevra* are reminded that each person is made in the image of God—and then they recite verses of love and praise of the beautiful, sensual body: hair, eyes, breasts, thigh, verses from Shir haShirim (Madsen 1998). A stunning moment: the poem of desire at the moment of distance. These are the only words spoken aloud during the *taharah*.

> Oh, your hair is like the most fine gold, black and curling, oh heaps of dark curls are as black as a raven.
> Eyes like doves beside the waterbrook, bathing in milk and fitly set.
> Cheeks like a bed of spices, towers of sweet herbs
> Lips are roses dripping flowing myrrh.
> Arms are golden cylinders set with beryl

Figure 5.4. *Chevra kadisha* silver ritual ewer, for water to clean the body of the deceased (TJM-f3589_1).

Body as polished ivory overlaid with sapphires
Legs are pillars of marble, set upon foundations of fine gold
You are like Lebanon, as rare as her cedars
Your mouth is most sweet, and you are altogether precious
This is my beloved, and this is my friend, daughters of Jerusalem.

The first gesture of the *taharah* ritual is the creation of a different tangible relationship, a ritual and temporal space in which the body is named, with the Hebrew name of her child-self, and invited to the act of care by the community (Figures 5.4–5.5). Her utter inability to respond means that the act will have no direct benefit to the participants. In fact, it is given as an example of working beyond the line of the law. She will be washed of all the last indignities of dying, and she will be re-dressed in the stylized garments unchanged in shape or construction since the first century: a tunic and a shirt, a bonnet for her hair. The *metah* is turned gently to dry her back, her belly, her legs, the childbirth marks, her scarred knee. She is dressed in the simple clothes, twisted bows and knots of cloth shaped so they will look like the letters of God's name *shin*, four turns of the knot, *dalet*. And the still body stands as the *yod*. She is lifted in the arms, placed in the coffin, her blue hands in the plain white muslin.

The body of the dead one, the *metah* is a body that is as much as can be possible, pure, irreducible body. Because we only know the Hebrew name of the *metah*, and because she is a total stranger to us, naked, without title, clothes, or history, we receive her without the trappings or illusions of power, or linkages to politics, rationality of history. Hence, she will be reconstituted by the ritual itself. Because this act is done in silence, and its perimeters are not subject to negotiation, it is an example of what Pierre Bourdieu (1977) describes as "a dialectic of objectification and embodiment" that make it the locus for the coordination of all levels of bodily, social, and cosmological experience. She may have died as a body, ravaged by the travails at the nexus of modernity, medicine, and illness, but she will be buried as a Jew, in exactly the ritualized body of the Jew thousands of years previous to her particular story, thus relinking her, and the ones who prepare her, with the mirrored, replicated selves.

But the body of the *metah* is not the only ritualized body—the bodies of the *chevra* become ritualized by the process of *taharah* as well. It is the series of physical movements, ritual practices that spatially and temporally construct an environment organized according to schemes of privileged opposition. The construction of this environment and the activities within it simultaneously work to impress these schemes upon the participants. For example, there is tension between pollution and purity, death and love, blood and water, nakedness and clothing, the poetry of the liturgy and the starkness of the directions (place the feet toward the door); all of which potentiates the essential contradiction: the *chevra*, alive and the *metah*, dead (Friedman 2013). In asking the question about whose obligation it is to care for the bodies of the dead, we begin to understand why the act of caring for the dead one transforms us. Rather than reifying the horror of death, the work ritually prepares us to face death nobly—one of the key tasks of a human life. It is one of the tragedies of modernity, that in our eagerness for the triumphs of medical science, we no longer witness birth and death first hand, so live as if the great mess and tumult of endings and beginnings of life are subjects best handled in a separate, clinical arena. But the concept of the *chevra* as one in which each is obligated to participate deconstructs such a distance. The vulnerable nakedness of the *metah* imposes a great lesson of death—that possessions are, in the deepest sense, pointless, and that what is left to you is literally the company of community, the last hand that will touch you will be empty of all but the moral gesture of *chesed*.

The *taharah* offers an extreme and final comment on the oddity of the American culture of the body. The members recite the Song of Songs over their work, a passionate liturgy of love as they clean a dead, often aged, broken body, and come to see it as beautiful and pure by virtue of their account and attention. Every beautiful body will lie at some point as this body lies, naked, dependent on our love. The *chevra* are the last ones to see the vulnerability of the breasts, the belly-house of the children. Their task is to remake this body one last time, to one last time create human order over the chaos of death, without obscuring it. This is what love does, allows for the essential core self to be intimately and nakedly gazed upon, and seen in all of its vulnerability, and found utterly and completely beautiful (Ochs 2017). The *chevra* see, when they see the *metah*, a double visage, themselves in the darkest mirror, their own death.

It is at the *taharah* that the sense of the utter otherness of the stranger is most strongly felt. The gaze toward the beloved stranger cannot be returned (Lamm 2000). Silence surrounds her narrative, and it is at that moment, in the fictive, imagined, and internalized conversation that one is unable to remain entirely discreet. For the power of the work of the *taharah* is that the participants must touch the person and make her the center of intense and highly detailed activity. The act is not over when one is bored, or tired, it is only over when all details are perfectly complete (Marwell 2001). And this intense focus on the utterly other reveals in the encounter that a moment of radical recognition—this one will be you. Otherness is both total, and as vanished, because while I may never really be the other that I meet, the powerful one or the vulnerable one, except in my moral imagination, I will in fact be exactly this other at some point. And the one who is other-than-self is not faceless. Each by each by each, the dead will be carefully dressed, and the encounter will underscore the uniqueness of each. The other is irreversibly herself and irretrievably gone, but is incontestably you, as well, because you, too, will be certainly dead as she is (Friedman 2013). What the actions of the *chevra kadisha* offers is the inescapability of the recognition that this is the road for all of us.

The quiet act interrupts the social order. It is the unchosen nature of the event, the torn fabric in the middle of our lives, that is then repaired by faith and by solidarity alone, stitched together by hand like the shrouds of the burial *tachrehin*, that makes a human life possible again (Bar-Levav 2003). The *chevra kadisha* leave the stranger and go back into the night and their lives knowing the *metah* is accompanied by their mundane, commanded, moral gestures, a small good act, knowing she is illuminated by a small candle and that a witnessing member of the community will stay by her side all until the morning, and her burial. Death is transformed by the smallest acts, and by the lifting of the body into the air, the tying of her bonnet just so, the buckets, and the wood.

Acknowledgment

Special thanks to Kavod b' Nichum, and the *chevra kadisha* of Berkeley, California. Kavod b' Nichum has worked since 2000 to create, support, and sustain traditional and nontraditional *chevra kadishas* in Jewish communities to ensure that all Jews have access to respect and care at the end of life, regardless of status, affiliation, or ability to pay. For many resources and further reading: https://kavodvnichum.org/category/chevra-kadisha.

References

Abeles, M., and Katz, J. S. 2010. "A Time to Mourn: Reflections on Jewish Bereavement Practices." *Bereavement Care* 29, no. 1: 19–22.

Bar-Levav, A. 2003. "Jewish Rituals for the Sick and Dying." *Sh'ma* 34, no. 603: 11.

Bourdieu, P. 1977. *Outline of a Theory of Practice*. Translated by Richard Nice. Cambridge: Cambridge University Press.

Diamant, A. 2001. *Saying Kaddish: How to Comfort the Dying, Bury the Dead and Mourn as a Jew*. New York: Schocken Books.

Epstein, M. 1995. *Tahara Manual of Practices: Including Halacha Decisions of Hagaon Harav Moshe Feinstein, Zt'l*. Bridgeport: Chevra Kadisha Zichron Shabtai Leib of Greater Bridgeport.

Friedman, H. H. 2013. "And to Dust You Shall Return': The Jewish Approach to Funerals and Burial." *SSRN*, 2329558. https://dx.doi.org/10.2139/ssrn.2319558.

Greenhough, L. 2002. "We Do the Best We Can: Jewish Burial Societies in Small Communities in North America." PhD dissertation, Royal Roads University, Canada.

Lamm, M. 2000. *The Jewish Way in Death and Mourning*. Middle Village: Jonathan David Publishers.

Light, R. 2013. *Final Kindness: Honoring K'rovei Yisrael. Guidelines for Burial Preparation of Non-Jews Who Are Part of the Jewish Community*. Self-published.

Madsen, C. 1998. "Love Songs to the Dead: The Liturgical Voice as Mentor and Reminder." *CrossCurrents* Winter: 458–70. http://www.crosscurrents.org/madsen.htm.

Marwell, N. K. 2001. "A Feminist Perspective on Jewish Death Rituals." In *Considering Religious Traditions in Bioethics: Christian and Jewish Voices*, edited by M. J. Iozzio, 129. Scranton: University of Scranton Press.

Mitntz, B. W. 1999. "Religious Approaches to Death and Dying: The Jewish Approach." *Jurist* 59: 161.

Ochs, V. L. 2017. "Jewish Funeral and Mourning Practices." In *The Routledge Companion to Death and Dying*, edited by C. Moreman, 55–65. Abingdon: Routledge.

Zoloth, L. 1998. "Doubled in the Darkest Mirror: The Ritual and Practices of the Chevra Kadisha." Paper presented at American Academy of Religion Annual Meeting, Orlando, November.

While there are some differences between Orthodox Christians and Western forms of Christianity, the point is that life is to be lived within the embrace of these communal forms of grace; that is, divine forgiveness and empowerment through the Holy Spirit. This is why all Christians celebrate the two "dominical sacraments," baptism and *eucharist*. Just like baptism, Christians differ on how to understand Christ's presences in the *eucharist*. Some hold that it is a commemorative meal, while others, like Catholics, believe in the real presence of Christ's body and blood in the elements of the sacrament (bread and wine). But, again, all Christians celebrate the Lord's Supper or *eucharist* because it was instituted by Christ in his last meal with his first disciples before his crucifixion. In fact, many Christians hold that the sacrament is a "foretaste" of the heavenly banquet that will be enjoyed in the afterlife (Heaven).

Christianity has been known, but has not always been lived, as a religion of love. One is to love God and one's neighbor as oneself. Jesus even taught to love one's enemy, and so, *in extremis*, to love the threat of death itself (see, Matt. 5:43–48). As Martin Luther taught, in his treatise, *The Freedom of a Christian*, one is caught up in union with Christ through faith and poured out in love for the neighbor. Rightly conceived, the Christian has their life in Christ, who conquers death, and the neighbor who lives while dying. To love thy neighbor as oneself (see Mark 12:30–31 and Matt. 7:12) means to love and do for others in their living as you would want to be loved and treated, a principle taught in some form by virtually every world religion. Salvation, or overcoming the breech with God and thus hope for eternal life, is keyed, in different ways, to the life of faith, hope, and love (I Cor. 13:13). Differences arise among Christians on two points. First, Protestants believe that one is justified, made right by God, through faith in Christ, while one is still a sinner (Rom. 5:8) in this life. This faith is then to flow forth in love and the hope and trust of eternal life. One can grow in holiness, sanctification, but one is nevertheless justified as a sinner. In Catholicism and

Figure 5.5. ***Chevra kadisha*** **silver ritual comb and nail pick, used to groom the deceased individual (TJM 2012-91_1-2).**

Orthodoxy, the process of salvation includes doing good works, taking the sacraments, and through God's grace eventually being given the Vision of God, the Beatific Vision in Catholicism or divinization (*Theosis*) among Orthodox Christians. Despite these differences, and others, all Christians believe that divine forgiveness and empowerment for life is a gift from God; it is grace through Jesus Christ.

Jewish practices take place within the community, its rites, laws, traditions, and holy days. The Jews are called by God to help mend the world and be a light to the world about the Lordship of God. In this way, *Torah* and its laws are a gracious teaching of how to live up to dying and to do so in freedom amid an often hostile world. For the practicing Jew, this means following the 613 commandments of the Law (*Torah*). *Mitzvah* refers to these commands to be performed as a religious duty. They too include alms giving, aiding the poor, the outcast, and the widow, and following the Ten Words or Ten Commandments. In this way, the moral life of a Jew is seamed into the religious practice of the community. Following the Law is to choose life and not death. As it is put in Deuteronomy 30:19–20:

> I call heaven and earth to witness against you today that I have set before you life and death, blessings and curses. Choose life so that you and your descendants may live, [20] loving the Lord your God, obeying him, and holding fast to him; for that means life to you and length of days, so that you may live in the land that the Lord swore to give to your ancestors, to Abraham, to Isaac, and to Jacob.

5B The Guna, *Molas*, and Religious Syncretism

Alaka Wali
Field Museum

The Guna people of Panama are renowned for their determination to remain autonomous in the governance of their homeland, for their art as manifest in the *mola* textiles used to make women's blouses, and for their creative blend of spiritual practices meshing their preconquest beliefs with Christianity. The Guna (a population of over 50,000) live principally on islands off Panama's Caribbean Coast and on the mainland in the Darién region. These regions are demarcated as *comarcas*—territories governed by the Guna under their own system of political leadership. The largest *comarca* is today called GunaYala, and comprises the San Blas Islands and a strip of land on the Caribbean coast. Many Guna also live in Panama's cities, but often travel back to home villages. A smaller group lives on two different *comarcas* in the interior of Darién province (cf. Wali 1989 for details on these communities). Their economic system is a mix of self-subsistence through cultivation of small plots on the mainland strip and fishing, and income generation through the sale of handcrafts and coconuts, tourism, and wage labor. The system of government has been well documented in the ethnographic literature (Howe 1986; 1998). Each village has hereditary chiefs and attendant officials who enforce decisions and norms developed in consensus at nightly gatherings of all the villagers in a special lodge. Guna Yala is governed by an overarching body—the Guna General Congress—comprised of all the leaders of the villages, who elect three chiefs to represent the whole *comarca*. Although Panama's government imposes some laws on the *comarca*, most of the laws and norms are determined at the local level and by the Guna General Congress.

Women are not usually in positions of political power, but exert influence in both daily life and in village-level decision-making through their economic contributions and participation in the village gatherings. Guna women's commercialization of the *mola* textile has been a significant aspect of Guna Yala's economy since at least the mid-twentieth century. In 1964, women across several island villages formed a cooperative to sell their textiles and, at its peak, about 2000 women were members (Tice 1995). The trade in *molas* spread into the international market, and the *mola* became iconic of Guna artisanry.

The *mola* is a component of the traditional women's blouse. Typically, two *mola* panels are sewn together and attached to a yoke at the top and a ruff at the bottom. For commercial purposes, many *mola* textiles are sold as individual panels. The technique of making *molas* is sometimes referred to as "reverse appliqué" and involves layering cloth, cutting out patterns, and embroidery. The earliest designs were geometric patterns, probably reflecting body-art designs that preceded access to cloth in the nineteenth century. Women then started to innovate, making patterns that reflect local flora and fauna (Ventocilla, Herrera, and Nuñez 1995), local events, and noted figures. Eventually, as Guna gained access to magazines and other visual media, women drew inspiration from pictures, copying images or improvising to meld together older designs with new themes and motifs. The textiles are recognized for their brilliant use of color combinations, their often symmetrical designs, and for elements of whimsy and humor that are infused into the clothes. Guna women are proud of their craftsmanship, and critique each other frequently on the quality of the embroidery and the freshness of the design. Although there are no rigid rules for the creation of patterns, *molas* often have a symmetrical design, reflecting an aesthetic that strives for balance as well as expressions of the relation between person, nature, and the cosmos (Fortis 2010; Salvador 1997).

Museums in Europe and the Americas started collecting *molas* in the late nineteenth century. An early collection was made for the Göteborgs Etnografiska Museum in Sweden by Erland Nordenskiold, one of the first ethnographers of the Guna. Other collections can be found at the National Museum of Natural History of the Smithsonian and the National Museum of the American Indian. The Field Museum's collection ranks among the most significant both because of its time depth (from 1919 to 2017) and because of its size and variety. The collection has both full blouses and separated *mola* panels. It also contains patches and other objects that have *mola* designs. In total the Field Museum's collection contains 513 *mola* textiles—81 full garments and 437 blouse panels. *Molas* comprise about half of the total collections from Panama (ethnographic and archeological). The earliest materials were collected by Mr. G. L. Fitz-William, a chemical and mining engineer from Hammond, Indiana, sometime in the early 1900s and accessioned into the museum collection in 1919. The next large accession came from the purchase at a railway auction and was accessioned in 1965. In the late 2000s Field Museum staff brought in another substantial number of contemporary *molas*. Thus, the collection represents an opportunity to understand how design motifs and styles have changed over time.

The diversity of designs and motifs in *molas* makes it difficult to discern any overarching themes (Marks 2014). However, religious motifs are popular subjects for Guna women. *Molas* with churches, religious figures, and scenes can be found in museum collections. As with other Indigenous people who have been subject to missionization in the aftermath of the Spanish conquest, the Guna accepted Christianity but retained their own cosmology and belief systems. Christianity took hold systemically among the Guna in the early twentieth century when one of the chiefs on the island of Nargana invited a Jesuit priest to start a school for boys. Later, a Protestant missionary also came to the island. As Christianity spread, it was not universally embraced, but tolerated. More often than not, women probably included religious themes in the *molas*, not out of religious dedication but because they liked the story or because it conformed to their aesthetic principles (Figure 5.6). This is manifest in the *mola* depicting Adam and Eve displayed in the exhibition. The *mola* embodies the symmetric principle, balancing Adam and Eve. Note that the tree is more palm tree than the conventional apple tree of biblical lore. Except for the most religious among the Guna, the concept of "original sin" and the expelling of Adam and Eve from the Garden of Eden was probably not taken seriously or treated as a reason to be "reborn" in Christ (for the Guna creation story, see Chapin 1997).

Guna death rituals are elaborate rites of passage through which the dead continue to an afterlife attended by food and belongings needed in everyday life. Guna women designated as specialists lead the mourning, chanting and keening over the dead wrapped in a shroud and placed in a hammock usually well into the night. The deceased is then carried to the mainland cemetery and placed in the ground in the hammock. Sometimes a hut is erected over the grave and food is left there. In sum, the Guna have maintained a strong sense of identity and retained cultural practices that allow them to maintain pride in their art and belief systems. They continue to defend their autonomy in the face of pressures to accept national norms and practices.

References

Chapin, M. 1997. "The World of Spirit, Disease, and Curing." In *The Art of Being Kuna: Layers of Meaning among the Kuna of Panama*, edited by M. L. Salvador, 219–44. Los Angeles: UCLA Fowler Museum of Cultural History.

Fortis, P. 2010. "The Birth of Design: A Kuna Theory of Body and Personhood." *Journal of the Royal Anthropological Institute* 16, no. 3: 480–95. https://doi.org/10.1111/j.1467-9655.2010.01635.x.

Howe, J. 1986. *The Kuna Gathering: Contemporary Village Politics in Panama*. Austin: University of Texas Press.

Howe, J. 1998. *A People Who Would Not Kneel: Panama, the United States and the San Blas Kuna*. Washington, DC: Smithsonian Institution.

Marks, D. 2014. "The Kuna Mola, Dress, Politics and Cultural Survival." *The Journal of the Costume Society of America* 40, no. 1: 17–30. https://doi.org/10.1179/0361211214Z.00000000021.

Salvador, M. L. 1997. *The Art of Being Kuna: Layers of Meaning among the Kuna of Panama*. Edited by Mari Lyn Salvador. Los Angeles: UCLA Fowler Museum of Cultural History.

Tice, K. E. 1995. *Kuna Crafts, Gender, and the Global Economy*. Austin: University of Texas Press.

Ventocilla, J., Herrera, H., and Nuñez, V. 1995. *Plants and Animals in the Life of the Kuna*. Austin: University of Texas Press.

Wali, A. 1989. "In Eastern Panama, Land Is the Key to Survival." *Cultural Survival Quarterly* 13, no. 3: 3.

Rabbi Hillel (ca. 110 BCE–10 CE), one of the founders of the *Mishnah*, is noted for saying, "If I am not for myself, who will be? And being only for myself, what am I? And if not now, when?" That is, one has duties to self, and our humanity is expressed in how we treat others. Further, one should not delay in these duties. This teaching is grounded in the Jewish and Christian conviction that human beings are created in the image of God. As stated in the Talmud (Sanhedrin 37a): "Whoever saves a single life is considered by scripture to have saved the whole world." This shows the great importance of life and death in Judaism, and the reason Jews are called to mend the world. Living while dying has then intertwined religious and moral duties such that living as a faithful Jew is imitating the goodness, justice, and mercy of the divine Creator. Life is not simply preparation for death; it is, as with Christians, a calling to a distinctive way of life within a community.

Judaism and Christianity, like most religions, are intensely aware of human fragility in living while dying, human fault, and propensity to do evil and wrong. Christians explain these negative features of human beings in terms of original sin, variously understood. Many Jews hold that evil started with Adam's and Eve's disobedience to God's will and command. Evil then became a human propensity that does not need an external temptation to sin and can be overcome by following *Torah*. This belief is rooted in scripture. After God destroys all living beings, except Noah, his family, and each type of animal in the Great Flood (Gen. 6:11–9:19) because of human sin and evil in order to begin anew, "the Lord said in his heart, 'I will never again curse the ground because of humankind, for the inclination of the human heart is evil from youth'" (Gen. 8:21). However explained, the propensity for evil and wrongdoing seems to be a human trait found in all times, all places, and all people.

Figure 5.6. Guna *mola* textile of the original sin: Adam and Eve in the Garden of Eden (FM 190472).

Figure 5.7. ***Parinirvana*** **Buddha sculpted in soapstone by students from the Royal University of Fine Arts in Phnom Penh ca. 2015 (courtesy Mitch Hendrickson).**

5C Death and the Reclining Buddha

Mitch Hendrickson
University of Illinois at Chicago

The passing of the world's great religious leaders often becomes a transformative event that galvanizes their ultimate message for future followers. Jesus' death and subsequent resurrection, celebrated today by Christians at Easter, reinforces the nature of his sacrifice to die for others. Over half a millennium earlier, in what is now northern India and Nepal, the death of the Buddha represents an equally important but philosophically different perception of what dying, the "afterlife," and living means.

The Buddha's story describes the transformation of Siddhartha Gauthama, a prince of the Shakya kingdom, who rescinds his elite life to become a wandering ascetic focused on understanding the nature of existence and finding an escape from suffering (*dukkha*) and the cycle of rebirth (*samsara*). His teachings, initially passed on orally by monks and centuries later recorded in Buddhist texts, focus on several key events during the Buddha's life: his enlightenment, where he finally grasped the means to escape *samsara* at Bodhgaya; his first sermon, where he shared his teachings (*dharma*) at Sarnath; and finally, his death (*parinirvana*) at Kushinagar. Unlike Jesus, who died violently on the cross at the hands of the Romans, the Buddha passed peacefully in a cave after eating a meal of tainted pork or mushrooms at the age of 80. The record of his death captured in the *Mahaparinirvana Sutra* explains how the Buddha's enlightenment at Bodhgaya allowed him to follow the Noble Eightfold Path in this last life and escape the cycle of rebirth and suffering (Figure 5.7).

The Buddha's final death addressed a fundamental philosophical issue in ancient South Asia. Unlike reincarnation, Buddhists recognized that there is no individual soul (*atman*) and rebirth is merely a transmission of essences between lives (Becker 1993). An apt analogy is to see life as like passing a flame from one candle to the next. The ultimate goal is to extinguish the flame that connects these essences to the physical world and enter into the state of *nirvana*, or nothingness. While later branches of Buddhism evolving in East Asia focus on entering into "heavens," they are not the same as the Western view where one's "self" ends up after living a good and proper life on Earth.

The Buddha's ultimate passing had spiritual and physical impacts across South Asia. His cremated remains were initially divided into eight parts and interred within stupas, mound-shaped monuments which became important pilgrimage sites for those who wished to be in his "presence." Centuries later these remains were unearthed and divided among thousands of sites throughout India and were ultimately disseminated across Asia. A replica of one of the most famous Buddha relics interred in the Temple of the Tooth at Kandy, Sri Lanka, is still annually paraded on the back of an elephant during the Esala Perahera festival to commemorate the arrival of Buddhism to the island nation. While using his corporeal remains appears to stand in direct contrast to the idea of "nothingness" and lack of self, it shows how the Buddha's death continued to breathe life into his faith and spread the word of the *dharma*.

Images of the Buddha himself did not appear—for philosophical reasons—until several centuries after he walked the earth (DeCaroli 2015). The typical form of Buddha is very familiar to anyone who has visited an Asian art exhibit: meditative, seated figures with hands in various gestures (*mudras*) that represent important events in his journey. While the meaning of each hand position is often lost to the casual observer who lacks a deeper understanding of the religion, the image of his death—known as the reclining Buddha—is much more easily recognizable: a robed man, eyes peacefully closed, lying on his right side with his right arm underneath his head and his left stretched out along the top of his body. Examples of this motif commonly appear in carved reliefs and paintings, but is it the creation of colossal statues that signifies the importance of this event. A 14-meter/46-foot-long image made from brick recently dated to the third century CE at Bhamala in Pakistan represents the earliest known example of such larger-than-life representations (Hameed, Samad, and Kenoyer 2020). Colossal reclining Buddhas literally grew in popularity and size as the religion spread eastward within Asia. *Parinirvana* imagery was widespread in China by the fifth century but reached new artistic heights and meaning in the seventh century at the Mogao Caves near the famous Dunhuang monastery (Lee 2010). The numerous reclining Buddhas were carved directly from the rock inside individual caves—the largest of which spanned 17 meters/56 feet in length—to recreate both the event and the space where the Buddha died. In fifteenth-century Cambodia, the Khmer remodeled the entire western façade of their eleventh-century Hindu Baphuon temple to create a 70-meter/230-foot-long reclining Buddha. This act seems to mark the state's official transition to Theravada Buddhism as its sole religion and shows the relationship with spirituality and politics in the past (Leroy et al. 2015).

Reverence for the *parinirvana* image continues today and is most stunningly found in Jiangxi Province, eastern China. Carved directly into the mountain, this *parinirvana* image measures 416 meters/1365 feet long and 68 meters/223 feet high and represents the single largest image ever created of the Buddha's passing. The reclining Buddha displayed in this exhibit lies in stark contrast to the massive examples created throughout Asia's rich history. Hand-crafted by a local Cambodian artist, this small stone image represents a long tradition of capturing this important moment and, like

Buddhism, is available to anyone who wishes to obtain it. In the home of a Buddhist, it could sit in a small shrine, head oriented to the north, facing the direction of the setting sun. In the home of a tourist it may be placed on a shelf as a souvenir that is enjoyed for its peace and tranquility. In both cases, it acts as a remembrance of an important journey into the unknown. Like the Christian cross, the *parinirvana* image symbolizes both the end of a spiritual leader's path and a reminder of all that was accomplished to reach that point. In this way death is not the end but provides an essential way of understanding how to live.

References

Becker, C. B. 1993. *Death and the Afterlife in Buddhism*. Carbondale: Southern Illinois University Press.

DeCaroli, R. 2015. *Image Problems: The Origin and Development of the Buddha's Image in Early South Asia*. Seattle: University of Washington Press.

Hameed, A., Samad, A., and Kenoyer, J. M. 2020. "Discovery of the Earliest Monumental Parinirvana from Bhamala, Khyber Pakhtunkhwa (Pakistan)." *Journal of Asian Civilization* 43, no. 1: 1–21.

Lee, S. S. 2010. *Surviving Nirvana: Death of the Buddha in Chinese Visual Culture*. Hong Kong: Hong Kong University Press.

Leroy, S., Hendrickson, M., Delqué-Kolic, E., Vega, E., and Dillmann, P. 2015. "First Direct Dating for the Construction and Modification of the Baphuon Temple Mountain in Angkor, Cambodia." *PloS One* 10, no. 11: e0141052. https://doi.org/10.1371/journal.pone.0141052.

However, as adherents of religions of justice and mercy, both Christians and Jews hold that repentance is crucial as people live while dying. This is a time that includes ritual practices, prayers, self-examination, and confession of one's sins. Christians begin the yearly Lenten season of 40 days with the imposition of ashes in the shape of a cross while the priest or pastor says, "Remember you are dust and to dust you will return." One is to live in the Lenten season with a constant sense of one's vulnerability, fault, and mortality. For Jews, God, who is merciful, offers people the chance to consider the wrong they have done and repent. This takes place yearly during the Days of Awe, a ten-day period between the Rosh Hashanah (marking the creation of the world) and Yom Kippur (the Day of Atonement). Again, living while dying is hardly just a physical process; it is a moral and spiritual journey.

Dying and the Dead

To understand human life as a moral and spiritual journey with the reality of death in view means that Jews and Christians also have beliefs and practices about dying and the dead. The mention before of the sacraments of Extreme Union and Last Rites clarifies how Catholic and Orthodox Christians treat the dying. Yet, in fact, funerary customs and commemorations of the dead differ among cultures within the Catholic or any other Christian communion: the Day of the Dead in Mexico (see Amat in this volume), All Hollow's Eve and All Saints Day worldwide. Nevertheless, death is set within the sacramental life of every Christian church because of *eucharistic* celebration of Christ's passion, death, and resurrection and, therefore, new life over the sting of death. So too in most churches, one trusts and believes that believers will be part of the cloud of witnesses in life eternal (Heb. 12:1). As noted before, this takes place through baptism into new life of the Church, participation in worship and the Lord's Supper, faith in Christ as the savior, and a life of love and service. The cloud of witnesses, not only one's loved ones, are to aid the Church in times of travail.

During the late Middle Ages in the West, there appeared two texts called the *Ars Moriendi* (The Art of Dying). These gave practical instruction to people on how rightly to prepare for a good death and the experience of dying, as well as aid for those attending to the dying. This began a series of works by important thinkers, such as Erasmus and Luther, and reached an artistic peak with Jeremy Taylor's two volumes *The Rules and Exercise of Holy Living* (1650) and *The Rules and Instruction for Holy Dying* (1651). This tradition of reflection was meant to guide the dying person, to provide consolation, and to face threats to their conscience because of lack of faith, despair, or spiritual pride. The tradition also details prayers for the dying and other instructions for those helping the dying person. While contemporary society has a highly medicalized view of death and dying and often removes the dying from intimate contact with home and family, this Christian tradition understood dying and death itself as moral and spiritual realities. The tradition of *Ars Moriendi*, in its various forms, was meant to aid the dying in their final journey from this life to the next.

Among Jews, there are also rituals and practices that surround death and support the dying. Most importantly, the dying person should not be left alone but surrounded by family and others. There must be time and support for a confession of sin, and time to reconcile with those from whom the dying person is, for whatever reason, estranged. Since God is merciful, it is never too late to return to God. Further, the last words of the dying persons should be the central statement of Jewish faith, the Shema: Hear, O Israel, the Lord our God, the Lord is One (Deut. 6:4). When death does come, there are practices of mourning that last a year and include *shiva*. "Sitting *shiva*" is a term used to describe the action of Jewish mourners. During the seven-day period of *shiva*, mourners receive condolences and sometimes sit on stools or boxes as a sign that the mourner has been "brought low" at the death of the loved one. With the death of a parent, the "Mourner's Prayer," or Kiddish, is recited collectively so that no mourner is alone, and it is also an affirmation of Jewish life and faith.

Because of the central affirmation of life as well as human dignity by Jews and Christians, it is hardly surprising that each tradition has long, complex debates and competing reflections on many topics related to death: abortion, justified war and killing, suicide (assisted or not), euthanasia (passive and active), and capital punishment. It is not possible to engage all these debates other than to note the basic affirmation of the goodness of life even with the realities of death, sin, and evil and thus a bias against unjustified killing, flowing from the command "Thou shall not kill" (Exod. 20:13) and works of love and good deeds for others.

Mention of the cloud of witnesses identifies a common trait among Jews and Christians, that is, the idea of martyrdom. A martyr is a witness for their religious conviction, the God of the Jews and the Triune God of Christian faith. In Judaism *kaddosh* means "[a] holy [one]," and there are many examples in the Hebrew Scripture as well as throughout Jewish history. The six million Jews who died during the Shoah, the Holocaust, under Nazi terror are the *kedoshim*. Likewise, Christians in the early Church died under the directions of Roman emperors and even now face persecution around the world. Jews have suffered throughout the centuries, from the Spanish Inquisition and other times and places to this day. Each tradition has specific directions for determining martyrdom. More importantly, the reality of martyrdom sheds light on Christian and Jewish ideas about death, namely, the physical death is not the greatest threat a human being faces, but, rather, the betrayal of the religious community and the denial of the God from whom one receives spiritual and physical life. Again, human life is understood to be a spiritual and moral journey in company with and for others to manifest love and, for Jews, to mend the world.

Beyond Death

As previously noted, Jews and Christians believe in a Messiah, albeit differently, and thus the ultimate triumph of God over forces that oppose and thwart the divine rule, including human sin and evil. They also believe in an afterlife, variously conceived. Christians hope for eternal life with God in "Heaven," conceived in different ways. For much of Christian history, the Church taught "extra ecclesia nulla salvus," that is, outside of the Church there is no salvation. Even today some Christian churches around the world engage in missionary work to save the souls of nonbelievers. Conversely, there are many contemporary Christians and churches who believe in universal salvation, holding that God's love is for everyone. St. Augustine, one of the major early Christian thinkers who influenced much of Western Christian thought, taught that God's punishment for sinners was to allow them to continue in what they love, that is, their sin that cuts them off from divine love and others in which true human felicity is to be found.

The idea of the afterlife in traditional Christian and Jewish thought and practice also meant that one could be eternally cut off from the divine, the source and ground of life. Called the Second or Eternal Death, these are "souls" forever separated from the divine and often related to punishment, the Lake of Fire, in the Book of Revelation, or more generally "Hell." In the Jewish Bible there is no mention of Hell, but just *She'ol*, a shadowy place, the Pit, where souls await judgment. Analogous ideas are found in other religions. The Egyptian Book of the Dead details how the heart of the dead will be weighed on a scale against Maat, the personification of truth and world order, by Thoth, the ibis-headed recorder of the gods. If the heart balances with Maat, the person will be admitted to the afterlife, if not it is devoured by a terrifying creature. Hindus hold that until one is enlightened in seeing that *atman* and *brahman* are one a person is condemned to a cycle of rebirths, commensurate with one's spiritual goodness, until enlightenment is achieved. In Buddhism there is no eternal heaven or eternal hell and no God who decides reward and punishment (see Hendrickson in this volume). Nevertheless, they do hold that greed, anger, and ignorance are the causes of human evil that stop people from reaching enlightenment. Beings are thereby born into heaven or hell, as conditions of life, according to their *karma*, that is, the good or evil deeds. Here too one sees, across vastly different religious traditions, that death is not only a physical fact but is linked to the spiritual and moral condition of human beings. In this way, the religions proclaim the victory of good over evil, of enlightenment over illusion and suffering, of heaven over hell.

Figure 5.9. Skeleton figure from Capula, Mexico (FM 343421).

←

Figure 5.8. *Calaca*, or skeleton figure, made of ceramic from Central Mexico (FM 343416).

5D Day of the Dead

Álvaro Amat
Crystal Bridges Museum of American Art

I am a Mexican immigrant and practicing orthodox Catholic. I celebrate many things at the same time on the Day of the Dead (Sayer 1994). But my mom, who was raised in Spain with Cuban ancestry, had her own personal reasons to dislike the Day of the Dead. For her, the Day of the Dead was a dark and disturbing tradition. Therefore, we did not follow any of the practices as a family. In a way, I grew up as an external observer who longed to join those traditions in any meaningful way, happy when any of my friends allowed me to be part of their family celebrations. I remember vividly the sugar skulls, or *calaveras* (Mack and Williams 2015), with my friends' names on them and I remember the hope that one day I would have my own sugar *calavera* with my name on it.

When I was very young, the images of *calaveras* and *calacas* (skeletons) scared me, and during the holidays of Día de Muertos in Mexico, *calaveras* are everywhere. Images in printed and TV advertising appropriating or imitating the art of José Guadalupe Posada, creator of famous images like *La Catrina*, would flood streets and homes. Decorated *calaveras* would emerge, populating the shelves and tables of markets and stores of traditional folk art. I was particularly disturbed by the figures of skeletons or *calacas* performing everyday activities (Figures 5.8–5.12). To cope with my fear, I used to run around the house with my fingers pulling my mouth horizontally to show my teeth like a *calavera*. This scared my younger siblings, and we would all end up running around the house, laughing and scaring each other, playing *calaveras*. In a way, we were doing what Day of the Dead accomplishes: sharing the fear and mocking death to make it part of life. I eventually got used to the *calavera* as ubiquitous in the Mexican cultural and artistic landscape. As a young aspiring artist, I greatly enjoyed visiting archaeological sites and the Museo Nacional de Antropología to appreciate the mastery of the great Mesoamerican artists and their geometrically stylized representations of skeletons, *calacas* and *calaveras*. From my art professors in high school and college, I learned to appreciate the art of José Guadalupe Posada and became an admirer of Mexican and popular graphic arts, appreciating the creative representation of human skeletons and skulls for social critique and dark humor.

Many of my friends had *ofrendas* at home and visited their relatives' graves to clean them, bringing flowers and making *ofrendas*. In school, each year we created big collective *ofrendas* dedicated to some famous person, usually someone who had a big impact in our culture who had died recently. Most of the time this would be a Mexican celebrity or artist, but sometimes the passing of an international figure would take over, for example in the year John Lennon was killed we created Beatles-inspired *ofrenda*. But at home we didn't have *ofrendas*, or at least that's what my mom thought. When my dad passed away, and not knowing that my mom did not follow any of Day of the Dead traditions, some of my dad's friends used to bring home some of his favorite cigarettes, food, and beverages to the house, hoping that we could place them in their name on an *ofrenda* dedicated to him. My siblings and I, in collusion with the maid, secretly placed these items with some of his things (his pen, his watch, his lighter) hidden near his photo on the entrance table, with some flowers placed nearby elegantly, so my mom would not identify this arrangement as an "ofrenda."

For me it is hard to distinguish where the Catholic feast begins and where the pre-Columbian tradition ends. The three-day celebration/veneration of the dead includes prayer, two masses, a visit to the cemetery, *ofrendas*, *calaveritas*, *Pan de muerto* (bread of the dead), *cempasuchil* flowers (Mexican Marigolds), costumes, and *fiestas*. These three days are all enveloped in the unique beauty of the Day of the Dead and the solemnity of the Catholic religion. However, secularized celebrations like Halloween have also jumped into the mix with the intensely spiritual practices of our pre-Columbian and Catholic legacy. For me, it all comes together in a seamless celebration. I saw Halloween invade Mexico as it penetrated our culture. I used to visit rural Estado de México, bordering Morelia, during Halloween and the Day of the Dead holidays, which had become a strange week-long celebration. People would go "trick-or-treating" for three or more consecutive nights, singing "Queremos jalagüí" (We want Halloween) as well as "Me da para mi calaverita?" (Do you give me [something] for my little [sugar] skull?). It was a continuous procession of kids wearing homemade costumes of Superman and Spiderman with rubber masks of the current president on top, escorted by adults wearing traditional Mazahua attire, and carrying large plastic *calaveras* as baskets for candy, money, or used as lanterns.

Now that I live in the USA, Halloween has become more important because of my Americanized children, but also because I am fascinated by cultural cross-pollination. Halloween invaded Mexico, but the Day of the Dead invaded Halloween in return; for example, the way in which *Catrinas* have been integrated into the repertoire of American Halloween costumes, or like that James Bond movie that portrayed a fictional Day the Dead parade with giant *calaveras*. Those parades didn't exist when I was growing up in Mexico, but now they have emerged as part of Day of the Dead celebrations all over Mexico. The invasion goes both ways, back and forth.

As an immigrant and as a father, Day of the Dead has gained significance and meaning. I still celebrate both the religious feasts and the cultural traditions together. I don't see any conflict or separation between them. On All Souls Day (*Día de los fieles difuntos*) on November 2 we commemorate the souls of the departed that are in purgatory for their purification. That night I feel particularly connected to my own departed family members and friends. For me, this is when prayer and celebration is most intertwined with the Mexican traditions, and it is more intimate and personal. Since I cannot visit any of my ancestors' graves because they are all buried far away, I make *ofrendas* to remember them here at home. I started placing a small *ofrenda* on the mantel in my house in Illinois, with photos of my wife's and my own family's *muertitos* (beloved dead ones), some of their possessions, favorite foods, yellow flowers, and candles, all under an image of the Virgin Mary and a crucifix. I taught my children to cherish and celebrate these feasts, trying to keep this tradition alive. As I have become more "at home" with having my own traditions and accepting my own heritage, I have made these *ofrendas* larger and more complex, with levels representing Heaven, Purgatory, and Earth. This year I started incorporating a small skull image, a symbol of *memento mori* and at the same time as a *calavera*. I plan on adding more *calaveras* into my artwork and being more intentional in creating these *ofrendas* through the years, hoping to bring my children and their families into these meaningful and beautiful traditions.

For me, these are days of prayer and remembrance. Many of my Mexican friends believe that their loved ones in some way come to visit and join them to celebrate with their favorite food and drink. I don't personally believe that the souls of the dead physically visit us. During those Days of the Dead, I pray to God that He lets my beloved ones be more present in my heart. The practice of the Day of the Dead and its traditions help me feel closer in spirit with my beloved departed, but also serve as preparation for my own death. I hope this helps those around me to be more prepared as well.

References

Mack, S., and Williams, K. 2015. *Day of the Dead Folk Art*. Layton: Gibbs Smith.

Sayer, C. 1994. *The Mexican Day of the Dead*. Boulder: Shambhala.

Figure 5.10. Skeleton figure of ceramic from Oaxaca, Mexico (FM 343441).

Figure 5.12. Ceramic skeleton figure from Central Mexico (FM 341964).

Figure 5.11. Ceramic skeleton figure from Mexico (FM 355626).

Scriptural texts represent "heaven" in various ways, ranging from something like the Garden of Eden, a Heavenly Court surrounding the divine, or a New City and New Earth (Rev. 21:1). In sum, "heaven" is that condition in which God's will is done, and human fulfilment found. It is for this reason that Christians pray to God in the "Lord's Prayer" that "Thy Kingdom come, thy will be done, on earth as it is in heaven." While physical images may be used to imagine heaven, it is a spiritual reality that exceeds the physical reality that is marked by joy, love, and creativity, but also suffering, sin, and death. Like many contemporary Christians, modern Jewish thinkers often shy away from hard-and-fast conceptions of Heaven, Hell, and judgment and prefer to speak of sin as separation from God and the community. More importantly, Christians and Jews insist on the mercy and love of God such that all human beings have inviolable dignity and may share in the blessing of this life and even the life to come. Given the priority of life found in these religious traditions, it is not surprising that the deepest dread is not physical death, but, rather, to be separated from the divine source of life and goodness that can and does happen to the living and perhaps the dead as well. This is also why, as noted above, these religions face the challenges of living a mortal life by stressing messianic hope, the importance of the moral life (*Mitzvot* or the life of love), and membership in a community, the Church, or the Jewish people.

References

Chinca, M. 2020. *Meditating Death in Medieval and Early Modern Devotional Writing: From Bonaventure to Luther*. Oxford Studies in Medieval Literature and Culture. Oxford: Oxford University Press.

Eliade, M. 1987. *The Encyclopedia of Religion*, Vol. 12, 277–78. New York: Collier Macmillan Publishers.

Fishbane, M. 1994. *The Kiss of God: Spiritual and Mystical Death in Judaism*. The Samuel and Althea Stroum Lectures in Jewish Studies. Seattle: University of Washington Press.

Reinis, A. 2007. *Reforming the Art of Dying: The* Ars Moriendi *in the German Reformation, 1519–1528*. New York: Routledge.

Schweiker, W. 2005. *Blackwell Companion to Religious Ethics*. Edited by William Schweiker. Malden, MA: Blackwell.

Schweiker, W., and Clairmont, D. A. 2020. *Religious Ethics: Meaning and Method*. Chichester: John Wiley & Sons.

Sumegi, A. 2013. *Understanding Death: An Introduction to Ideas of Self and the Afterlife in World Religions*. Chichester: John Wiley & Sons.

6

Social Endurance beyond Human Death

Gary M. Feinman and Patrick Ryan Williams
Field Museum

Abstract: This thematic essay considers how the death of an individual reverberates through human social networks and groups. The authors explore how societies endure in the face of individual mortality and how those challenges vary depending on who specifically died and how the social group is organized. The essay transitions from a consideration of death in mobile, small-scale populations to larger human aggregations that were organized in different ways. For example, the death of a leader has been characterized by markedly different cultural patterns and practices depending on the nature of leadership, legitimation, and succession. The case studies explore examples, from the origins of social memories to the roles of different monuments to the dead that reflected the links between leaders, their forebearers, and their followers.

Resumen: Este artículo explora cómo la muerte de un individuo repercute en las redes sociales y los grupos humanos en que este se insertó. Los autores exploran cómo las sociedades resisten y hacen frente a la mortalidad individual, y cómo los desafíos varían dependiendo de quién específicamente murió y cómo está organizado ese grupo social en particular. Este artículo revisa desde una consideración de la muerte en poblaciones móviles y de pequeña escala hasta las grandes comunidades humanas que se organizaron de maneras diferentes. Por ejemplo, la muerte de un líder se ha caracterizado por ciertos patrones y prácticas culturales marcadamente diferentes según la naturaleza del liderazgo, su legitimación, y su sucesión. Los artículos aquí contenidos exploran múltiples ejemplos, desde los orígenes de las memorias sociales hasta los roles de los diferentes monumentos erigidos en honor a los muertos que reflejaron los vínculos entre estos líderes, sus antepasados, y sus seguidores.

During 2022, the US death toll from COVID-19 passed one million. Of course, global totals and the many additional "excess deaths" tabulated by nations around the world portend a human impact even much more severe (Adam 2022; Schreiber 2022; Yong 2022b). Virtually every death leaves a personal void for some or many survivors, depending on the social networks that the deceased belonged to and the extent of their contacts. The ramifying effects—grief, mourning, ritual enactments—from the death of a military and political leader like General Colin Powell extend much more broadly than for most other citizens. Nevertheless, almost every death ignites a social response among those left behind, although the scale and specifics vary widely. Here, we briefly explore why death for our species has always been such a trigger for social response, albeit taking various forms. We ask why these repetitive practices become so encoded, enduring in human traditions and even materialized monumentally on landscapes? We also focus on underlying factors that underpin how and why these reactions vary depending on particular social contexts and the specific roles of the deceased.

Among the living, funerary rituals and interaction between the dead and their earthly descendants are ubiquitous; some researchers even argue that communication with deceased antecedents is a human universal and a key to understanding the underpinnings of religion more generally (Steadman, Palmer, and Tilley 1996, 63). "Of all sources of religion, the supreme and final crisis of life—death—is of the greatest importance" (Malinowski 1954, 47). Ritualized mortuary activities take a wealth of different forms, and not every death receives an equivalent or as ritually full response. Yet it is worth pondering why funerary rituals and correspondence with the dead are such a fundamental aspect of humanity's cultural practice in the past and present (Jong 2016; Steadman, Palmer, and Tilley 1996)? In the archaeological record, funerary behaviors provide some of the earliest material evidence for human ritual behaviors (Pettitt 2011), as with the tomb of King Tutankhamen, among the most stiring and memorable windows into our species' past (Nilsson Stutz and Tarlow 2013).

Although humans generally have a sizeable capacity for selfishness, they also are exceptionally good cooperators. No other animal cooperates with non-kin at the scales that humans do, and in various global regions people established large-scale cooperative arrangements and dense social networks that extend back more than ten millennia. Death, especially sequential or mass death, leaves holes in human social networks and can undermine interpersonal institutions, creating grief and malaise (Yong 2022a). "For those grieving, even more normal times don't feel like old times" (Lee 2022). In other words, at death, gaps in social networks are opened, and people respond in different ways. Steps may be taken by those who do remain to reestablish and patch ties. Alternatively, the interpersonal networks that were severed and disrupted could easily diffuse, splintering human groupings and institutions that foster cooperation (e.g., Bond 2017; Engelke 2019; Hobbs and Burke 2017; Lannutti and Bevan 2022). In essence, death can create new linkages in human networks or cause them to collapse. It is this particular nature of how death affects our relationships across social networks that has the greatest implications for resilience and continuity in human society.

From a cultural perspective, the dead often leave a pall. Cultural responses to death require "time because it takes time for the rent in the social fabric to be rewoven and for the dead to do their work in creating, recreating, representing, or disrupting the social order of which they had been a part" (Laqueur 2015, 10). The dead have two lives, one in culture and the other in nature. Humans are social beings grafted on a material body, the demise of which often punctures the social order. "The relationship between the two conceptions of the dead—mere matter on the one hand, and beings who have a social existence on the other—is what allows bones, ashes, and names to do their work" (Laqueur 2015, 10). What different "rituals have in common is that they provide a mechanism for people and societies to cope with death—both the loss of a social being, and the emergence of a dead body, which creates a new and practical situation to be dealt with by the survivors" (Nilsson Stutz and Tarlow 2013, 5).

Mortuary rites and ancestor communications are so globally and historically widespread because it is through funerary ritual, initial treatment of the body, interment or final disposition, mourning, and other postmortem observances that the dead are gently passed from this world and securely situated into the next. From there, they are integrated into memories and traditions, often folded into communities (see Muro Ynoñán and Feinman in this volume) and landscapes (see Lepper in this volume) where the remains of deceased (and associated markers and monuments) signal connections between peoples and place, and past with present. At the same time, the burial of the dead serves as an emotionally charged context in which relationships of affiliation, status, power, and inequality among the living are frequently negotiated and structured. The heightened emotional importance of death-related rites and their high potential to spark memories make them a potent arena to forge and reaffirm ties and to contend for equity and/or power (Hayden 2009). These long-term implications of how the death of individuals structures the lives and relationships of their survivors for decades or centuries to come are our primary focus in this essay.

Death and the Scale of Paleolithic Social Networks

Although death-prompted rituals and communications between the living and the dead are extremely widespread in time and space, specific funerary behaviors are incredibly diverse and, to degrees, culturally entrenched. Key axes of that variation rest on different historical worldviews and traditions, far too numerous and diversified (Jong 2016) to review adequately here (see also Muro Ynoñán in this volume). Nevertheless, there are relational patterns and processes between mortuary treatments, social scale, status, and the distribution of political power that eclipse local and cultural traditions, and long have been noted and investigated (e.g., Chapman 2013).

Across human history, societal scale is a key factor that undergirds variability in mortuary ritual and the material imprint of those behaviors. For anatomically modern humans and our immediate sapient ancestors, the earliest funerary rituals extend back to the Paleolithic, roughly 50,000 years ago, possibly somewhat earlier, but still tens of thousands of years after the advent of our species. In that era, global populations tended to be mobile, generally dispersed. Not only our species, but close relative of *Homo sapiens*, the Neanderthals, also practiced intentional burial. Early evidence came from Shanidar Cave in Kurdistan (Pomeroy et al. 2020; Solecki 1975), where 70,000 years ago these hominids were buried along with flowers from outside the cave. At the La Ferrassie site in the French Dordogne, a two-year-old child was intentionally interred more than 40,000 years ago (Balzeau et al. 2020). Modern *Homo sapiens* also practiced individual interments during the Paleolithic, such as the Cap Blanc Magdelanian burial that is now housed at the Field Museum (see Martin et al. in this volume). Such early burials generally were placed in caves, rock shelters, or other locations where people periodically or seasonally aggregated. For the Cap Blanc rock shelter interment, the presence of a long sculptured frieze on the cave wall indicates that this was a place to which the mobile Magdelanians regularly returned. In other similar Paleolithic contexts, the dead were interred, sometimes with artifactual accompaniments, which in certain contexts could be surprisingly ample (e.g., Riel-Salvatore and Gravel-Miguel 2013; Wengrow and Graeber 2015).

Investigators do not know why art, music, funerary behaviors, and other symboling became more prominent in the archaeological record (ca. 50,000 years ago). This shift has been termed the "sapient paradox" as it as yet has not been pinned to a specific biological change or linked to only a specific region (Renfrew 2007). A hypothesis advanced to understand this symbolic florescence ties these changes to increases in regional population densities (Powell, Shennan, and Thomas 2009), which occurred at that time.

6A The Magdalenian Skeleton from Cap Blanc

Robert D. Martin, J. P. Brown, Stacy Drake, William Pestle, and William Parkinson
Field Museum

An almost complete human skeleton from the Cap Blanc site in the Dordogne region of southwestern France has been housed in the anthropological collections of the Field Museum in Chicago since 1927. At the time of its acquisition, it was the only virtually complete European Paleolithic human skeleton in the US, and this remains the case today (Figure 6.1). The Cap Blanc site is a rock shelter that is particularly notable because of a striking sculptured frieze extending some 40 feet along its back wall. The frieze includes exquisitely carved images of horses, bison, and reindeer. In 1911, during construction of a wall to protect the frieze and excavation to lower the floor sediments to increase its visibility, a human skeleton was discovered just a few feet from the base of the frieze (Lalanne and Breuil 1911). Unfortunately, the discovery occurred accidentally, resulting when a workman plunged a pickaxe through the right side of the skull, shattering it into several pieces. The individual was probably deliberately buried, as the legs were flexed into a characteristic "fetal position." No grave goods had been included during burial, although a small artifact identified as an "ivory point" was found near the skeleton.

Following their excavation, the encrusted skeletal remains were transported to Paris for expert removal of the surrounding matrix, consolidation of the bones, and initial study involving some reconstruction. In 1924, some years after the skeleton had been excavated, the Cap Blanc landowner, Monsieur Grimaud, shipped it to New York in hopes of selling it to the American Museum of Natural History at a price of $12,000. When negotiations for the sale eventually came to nothing, Henry Field (nephew of the Field Museum's founding director Stanley Field) quickly intervened and was able to purchase the skeleton for the bargain price of $1,000. He subsequently organized a public display of the individual in a specially constructed case, but the individual was laid out in an extended "anatomical" position rather than the original fetal position. Partly thanks to Henry Field's well-honed public relations skills, on the first day of its display the Cap Blanc skeleton attracted 12,000 eager visitors. Fanciful interpretations that probably drove this record-setting attendance included Field's suggestion that the individual might have been a young maiden who had carved the frieze, accompanied by the speculation that the "ivory point" had played a part in her death.

From the outset, the Cap Blanc individual was enigmatic in several respects. To begin with, the geological age remained somewhat uncertain, although the remains likely date to the Upper Paleolithic. Because of certain characteristic tools recovered from the Cap Blanc site (but not in association with the remains), a Magdalenian age is generally accepted. However, some artifacts from the site indicate an older Solutrean date. Despite initial confusion regarding the sex of the individual, the remains were eventually determined to be female. A major factor here was a detailed anatomical study of the skeleton published by Gerhardt von Bonin in 1935, which convincingly established osteological sex as female. Far greater uncertainty, which has persisted up to the present day, surrounds her age at death. Because the wisdom teeth (third molar teeth) had not fully erupted in upper or lower jaws, von Bonin inferred that the individual was aged about 20 years. Yet the rest of the skeleton—portions of which show a more advanced degree of ossification of growth zones in long bones and some evidence of wear and tear in the vertebral column—indicates that the individual had reached adulthood, with an age at death somewhere between 21 and 35 years.

Since 2004, researchers at the Field Museum in Chicago have been engaged in a detailed reexamination of the Cap Blanc individual, using a range of modern methods. Detailed anatomical investigation of the remains has included digital X-rays, CT-scanning, and virtual 3D reconstructions of the skull and pelvis. Information obtained has confirmed that the individual is female and has shed additional light on her likely age at death. Although there is relatively little wear on the erupted teeth, apart from some abrasion of the tips of the incisors, scanning has revealed that development of the unerupted wisdom teeth was anomalous and hence unreliable for inference of age. Moreover, internal imaging of her bones has indicated that their development was quite close to completion.

Virtual reconstruction of the skull from the CT-scans—including mirror imaging to compensate for the damage to the right side inflicted by that workman's pickaxe—indicated that the 1935 physical reconstruction crafted by von Bonin differed in certain key features. Overall, interpretations at that time were reflected by a general bias toward giving the skull a more "primitive" appearance, especially in the facial region. Using the CT-scans, individual bones—which had been firmly integrated with robust plaster in von Bonin's reconstruction—were painstakingly isolated and then gradually integrated into a corrected reconstruction following established anatomical guidelines. That virtual reconstruction was then used to generate a three-dimensional print of the skull for display. Moreover, a copy of that 3D print was dispatched to the renowned French paleoartist Elisabeth Daynès. She was commissioned to produce a captivating bust of the Cap Blanc individual that is now on public display at the Field Museum alongside the original skeleton and a print of the skull.

In tandem with the anatomical investigation, bone samples from the Cap Blanc remains were subjected to radiometric analyses with the aim of establishing a reliable geological age for the individual. However, two samples submitted for C14 dating at the Oxford University Radiocarbon Accelerator Unit in 2004 yielded distinctly different, non-overlapping calibrated dates of 17000–16400 cal BP and 14900–13800 cal BP, respectively. In an attempt to resolve this problem, two additional samples were sent to the Oxford laboratory in 2006. Unfortunately, the new results were also distinctly different and did not overlap with one another or with either of the two initial dates: 12500–11900 cal BP and 9600–9300 cal BP, respectively. One possible explanation for the discordance between the four C14 dates, which extend over a range of over 7000 years, is that the Cap Blanc skeleton was contaminated with organic carbon-containing materials in preparations used to consolidate the bones. Further work is in progress to test the plausibility of this explanation and to seek additional dates with samples from relatively isolated parts of the skeleton.

In sum, although it seems well-established that the Cap Blanc individual is female, uncertainty about her geological age and the age at death has persisted up to the present day.

References

Carretero, J. M., Quam, R. M., Gómez-Olivencia, A., Castilla, M., Rodríguez, L., and García-González, R. 2015. "The Magdalenian Human Remains from El Mirón Cave, Cantabria (Spain)." *Journal of Anthropological Science* 60: 10–27.

Drucker, D. G., and Henry-Gambier, D. 2005. "Determination of the Dietary Habits of a Magdalenian Woman from Saint-Germain-la-Rivière in Southwestern France Using Stable Isotopes." *Journal of Human Evolution* 49: 19–35.

Field, H. 1927. "The Early History of Man with Special Reference to the Cap-Blanc Skeleton." *Fieldiana Anthropology* 26: 1–14.

Field, H. 1953. *The Track of Man: Adventures of an Anthropologist.* New York: Doubleday.

Heim, J. L. 1991. "L'enfant magdalénien de La Madeleine." *L'Anthropologie* 95: 611–38.

Lalanne, G., and Breuil, H. 1911. "L'Abri sculpté de Cap-Blanc." *L'Anthropologie* 22: 385–402.

Nash, S., and Feinman, G. M. (editors) 2003. "Curators, Collections, and Contexts: Anthropology at the Field Museum, 1893–2002." *Fieldiana* 1525, no. 36: 1–346.

Pestle, W. J., Martin, R. D., and Colvard, M. 2008. "How Old Was Magdalenian Girl at Death? The Field Museum Responds to Dr. Sperber's Comments." *AAOMS Today,* March/April, 6–7.

Robinson, M. 2017. "An Object Lesson from the Field Museum's Cap-Blanc Skeleton." BA thesis, University of Chicago.

von Bonin, G. 1935. "The Magdalenian Skeleton from Cap-Blanc in the Field Museum of Natural History." *University of Illinois Bulletin* 32, no. 34: 9–76.

Although mobility remained a key element of human life during the Paleolithic, there are indications that seasonal camps in certain places were occupied for longer durations and by larger numbers of co-residents (Wengrow and Graeber 2015). As the sizes and durations of aggregations increase, so do interactive densities and scales of cooperation. Humans are simultaneously both selfish and competitive (Carballo, Roscoe, and Feinman 2014), so human cooperation is generally strategically situational and contingent on the nature of social ties (Blanton and Fargher 2016, 31–32). Interpersonal networks and aggregations tend to be fluid (Birch 2013), even when specific settlements are more sedentary and temporally durable (Feinman and Neitzel 2019).

For mobile hunter-gatherers, networks of social relationships generally are dispersed, open, and ephemeral, changing as groups and individuals split apart and nucleate. But the most stable unit is small, made up of close kin (and those who are proximate) who have in-depth knowledge of each other (Apicella et al. 2012). These individual relations tend to be face-to-face, personal, and biographical (Coward and Gamble 2008); biographical in the sense that people have in-depth and specific knowledge of those to whom they have ties of deep personal familiarity and details about one another. As a result, most mobile hunter-gatherer groupings are not purely egalitarian, as inequities are often manifest along the lines of age, sex, and ability (Cashdan 1980). Likewise, especially during aggregational episodes, leaders and specialists may arise, but their roles tend to be situational and ephemeral (Feinman 1995).

In general, prior to 12,000 years ago, most preserved funerary remains reflect these social contexts with mortuary placements made in the vicinity to where seasonal aggregations occurred. Nevertheless, as the size of aggregations tended to be limited to scores of people, the labor investments largely were modest (Magdalenian), simple cists or pits in which one or two individuals were situated (Riel-Salvatore and Gravel-Miguel 2013). Likewise, grave accompaniments generally were neither extremely ample nor costly in regard to either labor allotments or material acquisition. Many small ornaments, like beads, found in burials may be items that adorned the individual during life. Where burial populations are clustered and so a broader sample is comparable, individual differences in burials tended not to be extensive; many appear to reflect key attributes, like distinctions in age and sex. The positioning of mortuary interments in spots where people aggregated repeatedly likely provided incentives for the living to return, remember/honor their ancestors, and thus retain ties to other co-residents even following the deaths of

Figure 6.1. Magdalenian woman, a human skeleton from Dordogne, France, dated to the Upper Paleolithic (FM 42943).

people who may have been former forebearers or social intermediaries.

Although most Paleolithic interments were not particularly elaborate, select ones were, and these have been reported from the Dordogne to the Don (Wengrow and Graeber 2015). Most of these contexts contain at most a few individuals. But the interred in these rare contexts often were flooded with adornments, such as the thousands of mammoth ivory beads and perforated fox canines found in select contexts at the Sungir site in Russia. Although archaeologists do not uniformly agree on the meaning of these elaborate burials, they would seem to mark key individuals of skill or importance who in times of aggregation assumed a key role, which was commemorated at their death. Yet there is no indication that their situational and/or achieved status was necessarily transferred to their descendants. These represent some of the earliest examples of what might constitute wealth being interred with the dead. Earlier interments may have constituted intentional burial, and even included grave offerings. It was these more elaborate burials, however, that may have manifested social differences in life and the input of substantial social resources into the chambers of the deceased.

Death and the Scale of Holocene Social Networks

In certain regions, there is ample evidence that human populations grew to higher densities toward the outset of the Holocene (ca. 12,000 years ago). In some of those places, such as the Levant in Southwest Asia, this led to larger, longer aggregations and eventually transitions from mobile lifeways to more permanent settlements. We know that in and of itself sedentism often fosters episodes of demographic growth (Bandy and Fox 2010), due to transport and child-spacing considerations, as well as the availability of weaning foods. Early weaning may shorten nursing, which may affect female fertility. Nevertheless, the specific suite of causal factors may not be uniform from region to region or case to case.

6B The Mortuary and Commemorative Poles from Skidegate, British Columbia, Canada

Luis Muro Ynoñán and Gary M. Feinman
Field Museum

Located at the southern end of Graham Island, British Columbia, Skidegate is a village belonging to the Haida Gwaii Indigenous nation. According to local beliefs (Swanton 1905), the origin of this Indigenous nation dates back to the arrival of the "primordial ancestresses" belonging to matrilineal groups that settled down on the island some 17,000 years ago. Some of these powerful ancestresses include the Foam Woman, Creek Woman, and Ice Woman, whose spirits inhabit, even to the present, the surrounding glaciers. Centrally located within the Haida Gwaii archipelago, Skidegate was named after the chief who ruled the village in early 1880. Skit-ei-get, means "red paint stone," although European colonizers standardized the name of the village to Skidegate (Horwood 2014).

Skidegate, along with other Haida Gwaii communities, is recognized by its cultural traditions, art, language, and, particularly, totem poles. Monumental, elegant, and stylized, totem poles are made of massive trunks of red cedar that are carved and subsequently painted with intricate designs and motifs. Whereas the practice of creating ceremonial carvings in wood is relatively widespread among North American Indigenous groups, the level of perfection, monumentality, and stylization of the Northwest Coast poles is particularly distinctive. As Edward Malin (1996, 18) reminds us "Haida totem poles achieved an artistic significance without parallel in human experience." But the Haida Gwaii poles are more than visual and spatial markers or ornamented pieces of heraldic art. For the Haida Gwaii people, the poles can be better understood as physical manifestations that embody the histories, desires, and rights of each member of the family that owns it (MacDonald 1983). They are consequently items with a deep historical significance. But it is, perhaps, their relationship with the ancestors and death, as well as their capacity to serve as a bridge with the afterlife, that makes these wooden carved poles particularly important for the Haida Gwaii people (MacDonald and Cybulski 1973). The images often displayed are crest figures, many of which represent supernatural beings or ancestors from whom families obtain hereditary rights and privileges. Poles thus proclaim and validate one person's lineage and importance.

Mortuary Poles

In Skidegate, poles are commonly erected for both remembering the dead and serving them as a means for transcendence (MacDonald and Cybulski 1973) (Figure 6.2). In both cases, poles enable the owners to reinforce their links with their lineages, ancestors, and deep family histories. Poles are thus objects of memory that enable the living both to live and remember. As members of the Haida Gwaii recount, when a high-ranking person passes, the clan goes into mourning for about a year. The members of the clan do not attend festivities; they are completely isolated. During this time, the remains of the person are treated according to each of the family traditions. Furthermore, the clan gathers the necessary resources to hold what is called "an end of mourning ceremony." During all this time the spirit of the dead remains near the living. At the ceremony itself, the remains of the person are put into a box, "a funerary box," which is raised to the top of the pole with a plaque in front of it. Raising the deceased, and placing the body into the box aims to raise his or her spirit up, and shove it into the next realm. The ceremony is considered to be completed when the dead finally comes back, after one generation or two, in the form of a reincarnated entity (Jefferson 2009). The extra height that some of the poles present helps the soul of the individual find its way back to the village, once the process of reincarnation is over.

Commemorative Poles

Memorial poles reflect a similar process (Malin 1996). When a high-status individual dies, his or her spirit moves away from the community, so they need to be guided back home (Figure 6.3). Memorial poles are tall, with the bottom of the tree in the ground. These poles are quite high, some of the highest in the village; they act as a guiding beacon to enable the spirit to return to the community and have a longer process of entering the ancestral realm. For example, individuals who did not die in the village (e.g., persons lost in battle or at sea) need to be guided back home, as James McGuire, Haida native artist and member of the Haida Gwaii Museum in Canada, recounts (personal communication with the authors). The living can help the dead by putting up a kind of beacon near the pole so that those lost can be brought back home. Poles are raised only at very specific times in the year. It is only during the potlatch, an ancestral ceremonial feast at which possessions are given away or destroyed to display wealth or enhance prestige, when Haida people raise their dead and give them the last push they need to enter into the ancestral realm. For decades, the potlatch was banned by the Canadian government (Weiss 2018), but now it is a continuing expression of Haida identity.

Poles from the Field Museum Exhibition

Members of the Haida Gwaii community who were interviewed during the design process of the exhibit acknowledge that the models of poles displayed in it embody and personify important Haida Gwaii leaders. The pole shown in Figure 6.2 represents a much larger mortuary pole that once stood at Skidegate. Its original version was raised to honor and contain the remains of Wiiganaad, the Eagle Chief. The model of Figure 6.3 was raised by Chief Tl'aajaang Quuna to honor his uncle, Hungo Dass. Memorial poles are raised to honor individuals who passed away, and similar to the human body, mortuary poles are intended to decay and return to the earth, so the original ones are no longer standing (MacDonald and Cybulski 1973). Poles such as the ones displayed in the exhibit are wonderful examples of local traditions and beliefs about how Haida relatives progressively leave this plane of existence, according to those interviewed. Some of them acknowledge (or hypothesize about) the relationship between the poles displayed and specific families and clans that are present today in Skidegate. McGuire, for example, acknowledges that the Wiiganaad pole is connected to Aay Aay Albert Hans, who is the chief of the Eagles of Skidegate clan and who was also interviewed. Although McGuire cannot be sure about the origin of the Sithlingun or the Salthling-ah pole, it could also be connected to Wiiganaad. The Hungo Dass pole could have been for a wife, of an opposite lineage, who was likely from a different clan. The interviewees all hold that the colonial influence of the patriarchy nowadays confuses the relationships that can normally be established between the poles, their motifs, and the clans they might represent.

Resilience and Endurance

The importance of the ancestors in the life of the Haida Gwaii people extends well beyond the extraordinary times created and reproduced during a potlatch. The ancestors are considered to walk with the Haida people every day, while the living deal with the present dangers of the everyday and remember the harms of the past. It is like "being guided by the stars," director of the Haida Gwaii Museum Nika Collison says. The poles are not meant to endure forever, the interviewees all argue. The poles eventually fall down and decompose, and so does the body of the deceased that was placed into the "mortuary box." Some poles from the 1800s are still visible, but many others are in process of returning to the earth (Jefferson 2009). Many poles (or parts of them) were taken away by Western collectors and museums, including the Field Museum, which took poles from Skidegate in 1892. Despite the cultural disruption caused by colonial regimes and then the Canadian government, poles remain a vivid expression of Haida culture, identity, and capacity of resilience (Weiss 2018).

References

Horwood, D. 2014. *Haida Gwaii: Islands of the People*, 4th ed. Victoria, BC: Heritage House Publishing.

Jefferson, W. 2009. *Reincarnation Beliefs of North American Indians: Soul Journey, Metamorphosis, and Near Death Experience*. Summertown: Native Voice.

MacDonald, G. F. 1983. *Haida Monumental Art: Villages of the Queen Charlotte Islands*. Vancouver: University of British Columbia Press.

MacDonald, G. F., and Cybulski, J. S. 1973. *Haida Burial Practices: Three Archaeological Examples/The Gust Island Burial Shelter: Physical Anthropology*. Ottawa: University of Ottawa Press. https://doi.org/10.2307/j.ctv1759b.

Malin, E. 1996. *Totem Poles of the Pacific Northwest Coast*. Portland: Timber Press.

Swanton, J. R. 1905. "Haida Texts and Myths, Skidegate Dialect." *Bureau of American Ethnology Bulletin* 29: 1–448.

Weiss, J. 2018. *Shaping the Future on Haida Gwaii: Life beyond Settler Colonialism*. Vancouver: University of British Columbia Press.

Figure 6.2. Haida Gwaii model: Wiiganaad's mortuary pole from Skidegate (FM 17839).

Figure 6.3. Haida Gwaii model: Hungo Dass's memorial pole from Skidegate (FM 17842).

With more permanent settlements and tended fields that required labor and resource investments or "sunk-costs" (Janssen, Kohler, and Scheffer 2003), individual and domestic departures from settled communities (fissioning) became a somewhat less viable option than in more mobile networks. Larger, denser settlements have a wide range of implications (Smith 2019) for human social networks, their complexity, and integration. As human density and community size increases arithmetically, the potential number of interpersonal interactions expands exponentially (Coward and Dunbar 2014; Johnson 1982). These social ramifications of such scalar increases have been widely referenced, albeit under various terms, including "scalar stress" (Bandy 2004; Johnson 1982), "social stress" (Düring 2013), "communications stress" (Fletcher 1995), "intracommunity conflict" (Ur 2014), and "density-dependent conflict" (Birch 2013).

With co-residence in larger, denser settlements, not only the number but also the nature of social ties change. The burdens of sustaining and servicing social relationships strain time-and-energy budgets, increasing demand on memory and social cognition (Roberts 2010). The specific scope of human cognitive capabilities is individually variable, and there is debate over precise capacities (Dunbar 2011). But there is little disagreement over the fact that constraints do exist and that they range around no more than several hundred interpersonal associations (Wellman 2012). That is, the biographical knowledge any one person might have of others is limited to fewer than 1000 individuals (and probably somewhat less). Thus, once proximate social networks exceed that size, the nature of relations shift (Coward and Dunbar 2014) so that ties with close affiliates (biographical) differ from those farther afield (categorical, role-based affiliations).

Similar differences in interpersonal ties were present in mobile networks as well, but the option to fission could diminish stresses. Furthermore, the proportion of people linked through weak ties (Granovetter 1973; 1983) becomes much greater as settlements expand. The size of networks and communities may grow, and still endure, only if individuals are able to cope not merely with increasingly large sets of social ties but also with a lesser familiarity and weaker links with an expanded set of contacts. The ability to stabilize weak ties represents an important adjustment for human existence in larger social formations that offsets the cognitive, temporal, and energetic costs of processing greater quantities of social information (Coward and Dunbar 2014). As the scale of population concentrations grows, personal interactions are mediated less by in-depth mutual knowledge and more through symbols and events linked to place and status, by social roles (Sterelny and Watkins 2015).

The integration of relational networks, some with weak ties, and others with strong ties, allows communities to grow and expand rather than break apart. Shared ritual practices, and the associated material culture, can help scaffold and affirm weak ties, just as drinking, feasting, and reciprocal exchanges may solidify less intimate relations (Coward and Dunbar 2014; Nettle and Dunbar 1997). As the size of social affiliations scale up, there are collective challenges and opportunities to integrate and cooperate with people who are outside the sphere of regular, intimate interaction (Coward and Dunbar 2014; Dunbar 2013). For sustainability, the potential disruptions of fissioning, distrust, disputes, and free riders have to be managed, while collective action problems, such as defense and environmental perturbations, have to be faced. Deaths also pose challenges, through the voids left in social networks, the grief spurred, and the roles and duties left open.

Globally, the most common features of funerary rituals, especially for subalterns (nonrulers), promote social cohesion, sustainability, and solidarity in the face of loss. Mortuary rituals not only reaffirm community solidarity with the most grief-stricken, but they tend to feature feasting, drinking, shared singing or chanting, collaborative tasks, coordinated movements, such as funerary processions, and the recounting of shared memories, all activities that foster and affirm individual identification with the group (e.g., Roberson, Smith, and Davidson 2018; Whitehouse and Lanman 2014). Among sedentary peoples, bodies generally are interred or dispatched proximate to descendants, whether in or adjacent to dwellings, in local cemeteries, or in other public spaces. Often these locales are returned to by the living at regular intervals for reaffirmation rituals that reenforce social ties and cohere individual identities with a larger group. In Iraq 12,000 years ago at Göbekli Tepe and 5000 years ago at Stonehenge in England (mortuary monuments), as well as 2000–1500 years ago in Ohio (Hopewell), even before mobile peoples in those regions resided in permanent settlements (villages), they created monumental ritual landscapes where the dead were integrated into places and ritual events that structured affiliations (Charles and Buikstra 2002; Gresky, Haelm, and Clare 2017), both in the past and moving forward.

Here, we can see some of the early examples of the building of mortuary monuments to the dead, in collective rather than individual settings. Places become linked to the rites of death and reaffirm the group membership of the mourners who visit. Sometimes, they become not just singular places, but entire landscapes memorializing the dead and reaffirming the living networks in which they participated. Memories of the dead, their collective inhabitance in special places, both bodily and perhaps spiritually, become places where social network ties are remade with seasonal or annual rituals. They reinforce and rebuild the networks damaged by the loss of individuals, and they create new linkages in social networks so that the death of a key individual does not cause the collapse of the social relationships. Indeed, the deads' final resting place and the rituals of memorialization over time serve to reinforce social networks through the periodic coming together to remember.

Death, Leadership, Succession, and Legitimation

As discussed, most human funerary rites conform to what Harvey Whitehouse (2021) characterizes as doctrinal forms of religiosity and ritual, involving repetition, coordination, cohesion, and the fostering of individual identities with the larger group. One exception to these practices is a subset of mortuary ritual associated with high-status individuals, rulership, succession, the accession of a new ruler, and the legitimation of the heir. Such death-related rituals are most often personalized, tinged with dysphoria, spectacle, and the creation of fear, especially when consecrated for divine kings and other autocratic rulers. For example, among Classic Maya kings, autosacrifice, drawing blood from one's genitals with a pointed tool to offer to the supernatural world, and sometimes human sacrifice, were incorporated into the sequence of rituals that began with the death of a ruler (Fitzsimmons 2009; Munson et al. 2014; Stuart 1984). Events that included the sacrifice of retainers or, perhaps, captives, dispatched with the ruler, also have been noted for the Royal Cemetery of Ur (Iraq), Early Dynastic Egypt, the Shang (China), and at Moche centers in Peru (Schwartz 2017). All of these were historic episodes when rule and governance was relatively autocratic.

Egyptian pyramids, elaborate Shang tombs, and Maya temples that housed subterranean crypts all required intensive investments of labor (see Nash in this volume). In most of these cases, constructions began for the mortuary housing of the rulers long before their deaths. Some Maya lords were buried in funerary monuments that were far removed from their palatial residences. In these cases, bodies were traversed through sites, sometimes across rivers, up and down stairs, with foreign dignitaries in attendance (Fitzsimmons 2009, 178–79). Such events were widely viewed spectacles.

Cross-culturally, the size and elaboration of funerary monuments (e.g., Binford 1971) and the degree to which succession is institutionalized (generally through customized rituals) after a ruler's death (e.g., Gerring and Knutsen 2019) is, at least to a degree, a reflection of societal scale. And yet, democratic and collective leaders and governors of large, urban societies generally do not receive the individualized treatments, rich material accompaniments, or lavish contexts afforded autocratic, personalist dynasts. A series of factors underlie this distinction. Autocratic rulers often do not merely claim to be conduits to the supernatural world, but wholly or partly divine. In consequence, a potential conundrum is raised when they are seen to be subject to a very human life crisis, death.

In addition, leaders of polities with collective or democratic forms of governance regularly change or cycle. In contrast, a principle of autocracy is the maintenance of power, and so a leader's demise presents a rare break in the sequence of rule. Furthermore, autocrats generally have a chosen successor, such as their offspring, and so in the absence of consent, the successor requires legitimation (Brownlee 2007; Helms 2020). Finally, autocrats—personalized rulers—prioritize loyalty to themselves, not to their nation or group. They aim to bind the personal identities and loyalties of their followers to themselves, and "identity fusion" is fostered through imagistic religiosity, dysphoria, fear, and spectacle (Atran 2016; Blanton 2016; Feinman 2016; Whitehouse 2021). The placement of the graves of collective or democratic leaders tends to conform more closely with general societal practices, so are positioned in domestic contexts, churchyards, or cemeteries. When monuments are erected to these collective-focused leaders, they tend to be modest and solemn as opposed to spectacular.

We should note, however, that autocratic rulers can become symbols for collectives and nation-states in the future, and their tombs or mortuary monuments may be adopted as symbols of national identity or destroyed in an effort to purge the common collectivity they represent. The Inca emperors' mummies were maintained in the palaces in which they resided during life by their relatives and heirs. They were convened in the great plaza of Cusco by the living emperor for consultation. The mummy bundles themselves and the places in which they resided were powerful institutions in Inca society. When the Spanish conquered Cusco and set up a puppet emperor, other heirs escaped to the jungle to form a resistance empire. Eventually, the Spanish destroyed or sent away the bodies of the Inca mummies to destroy the collectives of Inca power they held together. The Inca emperors were certainly powerful autocratic semi-divine rulers. Yet they represented Indigenous self-determination and became powerful symbols of native rights and a threat to the Spanish Crown in the new order.

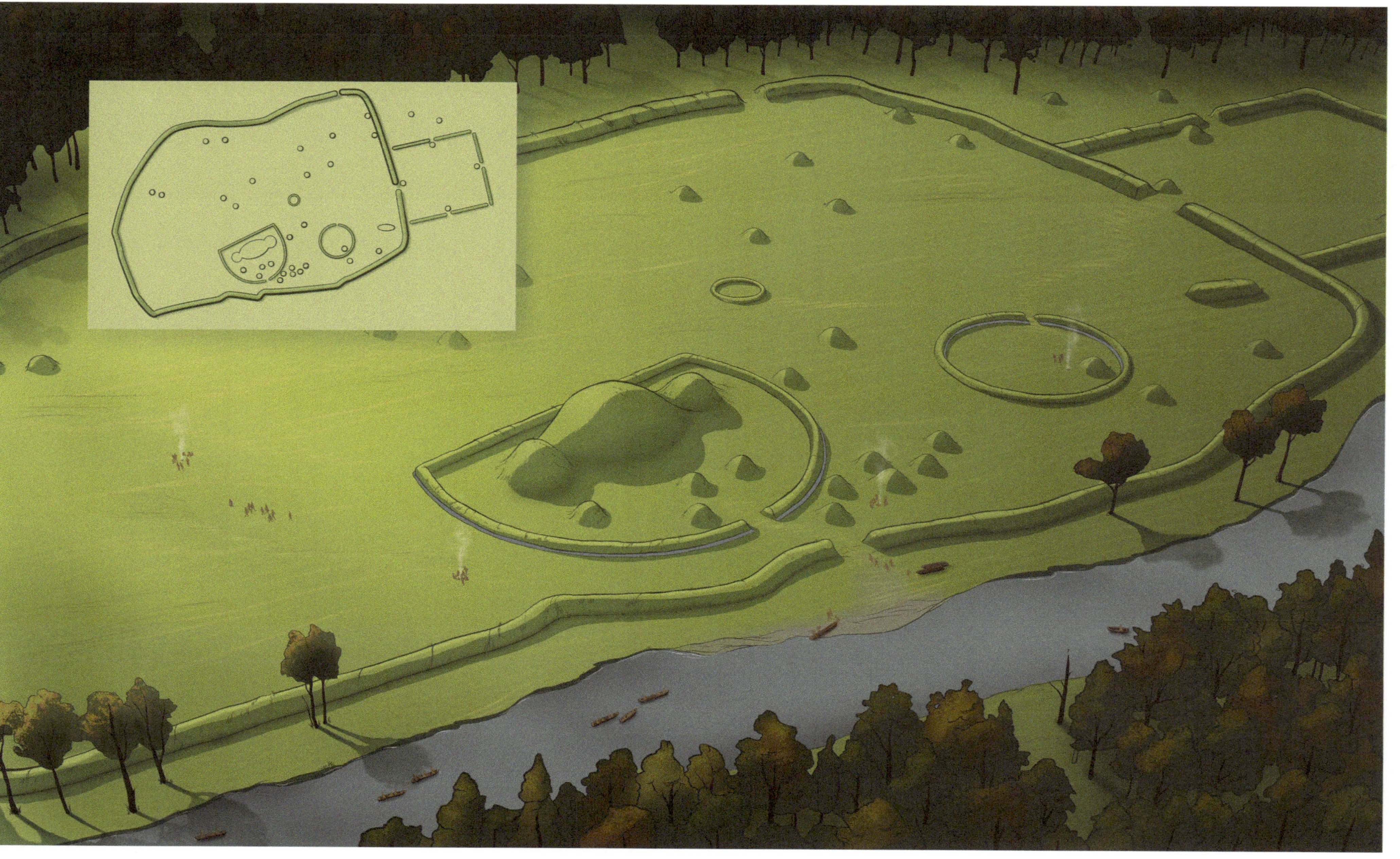

Figure 6.4. Artist reconstruction of the Hopewell Mounds site with Mound 25 in the foreground.

Figure 6.5. A set of Hopewell objects found together on Altar 2, Mound 25: obsidian biface (FM 56774.B); kneeling figure made of animal bone (FM 56747); head figure made of animal bone (FM 56735); and shark tooth from the Atlantic coast (FM 56538.1).

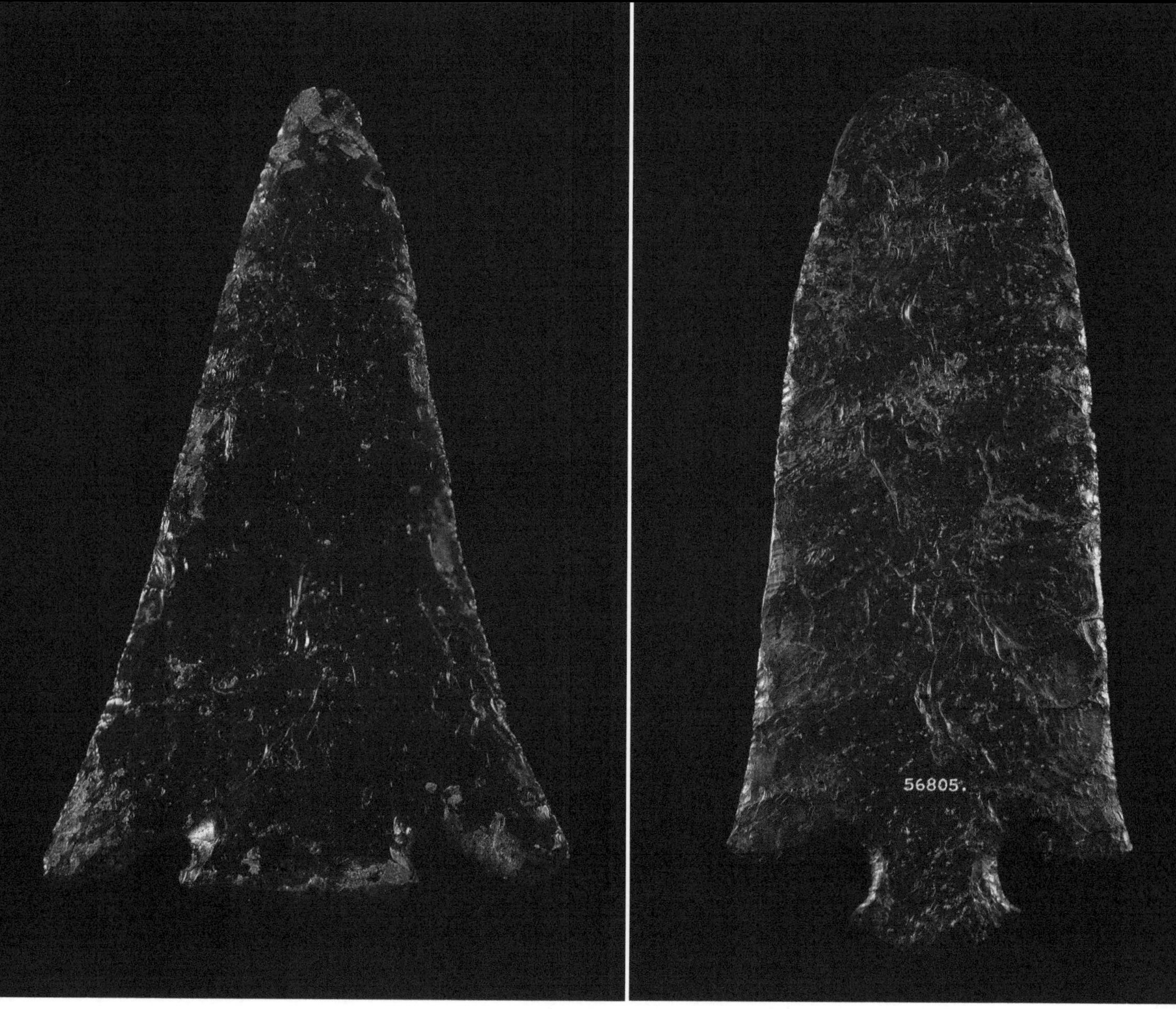

Figure 6.6. Hopewell large obsidian bifaces; obsidian sourced from Yellowstone National Park (FM 56805, 56772.C).

6C The Hopewell Collective

Brad Lepper
Ohio History Connection

The Hopewell cultural collective formed among dispersed horticultural communities in the Ohio Valley at around 1 CE (Lynott 2014). Although many of the things that have come to define the Hopewell appeared first in the Illinois River Valley, the epicenter of the "explosion" of architecture, art, and ceremony that has come to define classic Hopewell was at the Hopewell Mound Group (Figure 6.4) in the Scioto Valley (Greber and Ruhl 1989, 64). Characteristic features of the Hopewell cultural collective included monumental earthen enclosures built in various geometric shapes or in irregular shapes that followed the outlines of the hilltops on which they were constructed. The Indigenous people did not live at the earthworks, but gathered there in large numbers for periodic ceremonies.

Artifacts that appear to have reflected a Hopewell identity include copper earspools and breastplates, sheets of mica cut into varied shapes, small smoking pipes often carved into naturalistic depictions of animals, oversized spear points made from obsidian, and small blades made from Flint Ridge (Ohio) and Wyandotte (Indiana) cherts. These signature artifacts typically are found in mounds either as funerary objects or as part of large deposits, or offerings, not associated with a particular individual's burial.

Some of the more spectacular offerings were found in Mound 25 at the Hopewell Mound Group (Moorehead 1922) (Figures 6.5–6.6). Altar 2, for example, was a clay basin filled with more than 500 objects that had been placed on a roaring fire and then buried while the fire was still burning. This offering included obsidian spear points, small sculptures of humans or spiritual beings in human form, and shark teeth. Mound 25 also contained a deposit of 120 copper artifacts laid upon sheets of bark spread over an area 3 feet long and 2 feet wide, which then had been covered with more bark sheets before being buried within the mound. The artifacts in the deposit included 66 copper axes, 23 copper plates, and several cut-outs in the shape of fish (Figure 6.7), probably the river redhorse, a bottom-feeder common in the rivers of eastern North America.

The various earthworks had different, but complementary, functions. Most were not burial mounds, but the nearly universal presence of buried ancestors associated with some part of each site suggests their presence was central to what the Hopewell were doing at these sacred places. The importance of the ancestors to what took place at the earthworks is further shown by the fact that Hopewell ceremonial leaders sometimes retained and modified the bones of particular ancestors to serve as sacred relics. They crafted arm bones into flutes and lower and upper jaw bones into pendants. Priests or shamans also cut off the heads of particularly special deceased persons, which, based on a stone figurine found at the Newark Earthworks, were then brought to certain ceremonies wearing earspools and with carefully combed hair. This suggests the ancestors were perceived to be not just present, but active participants in the ceremonies that took place at the earthworks.

These ceremonies included burial rites for select men, women, and children, which were more than funerals for the deceased. Instead they were part of World Renewal ceremonies enacted at the monumental earthworks, which functioned, as James Duncan (2015, 227) has proposed for an earthwork of a later era, as resurrection engines "not only for the living community of the Middle World, but also for the entire cosmos."

Many of the Hopewell earthworks incorporated alignments to the summer and winter solstices or to the pivotal points on the horizon marking the cycle of moonrises and moonsets. Hopewell priests likely used the calendrical capabilities of the earthworks to determine appropriate times for gatherings, but the celestial alignments of the architecture meant much more than that.

The late Vine Deloria Jr., a Standing Rock Sioux writer and activist, proposed that American Indian architecture in general involved representing and reproducing the cosmos in order "to provide a context in which ceremonies could occur. Thus, people did not feel alone; they participated in cosmic rhythms" (Deloria 2001, 25–26). The alignment of the Hopewell earthworks to these cosmic rhythms, therefore, may have served as a means to provide that context.

The great earthworks also served as nodes of social integration that brought dispersed communities together to jointly mourn the deaths of family members and to activate the monumental resurrection engines with their ceremonies. Weeks in advance, caretakers prepared the sites by burning off the prairie grasses that had grown up since the last gathering. Others harvested crops and wild plant foods, captured fish with weirs and nets, and hunted white-tailed deer and other game to feed the many participants who would come.

Many came as pilgrims bringing offerings of raw or worked copper, mica, or obsidian from their homelands, such as the necklace from Hopewell (Figure 6.8). Others came with their honored dead. In stately ceremonial processions they carried the ancestors through the varied ceremonial spaces where they may have undergone a prescribed sequence of rites particular to each location, such as ceremonies of mourning, spirit release, spirit adoption, and final interment in the mounds as cremations or extended burials (Lepper 2016, 54).

The large gatherings at these earthen cathedrals allowed people to connect with others from near and far. These personal connections formed the basis for social networks that could ensure access to valued commodities or to potential sources of aid during times of trouble. In addition, the gatherings provided opportunities for participants to meet a wider pool of potential marriage partners than they could find in their small local communities.

For reasons that are not fully understood, the Hopewell cultural collective began to come apart by 400 CE, resulting in the end of major ceremonial activity at the great earthwork centers. Nevertheless, these awe-inspiring places continued to be recognized as hallowed ground by the descendants of the Indigenous people who built them. The early archaeologist Warren Moorehead (1908, 41) recounted a story he had been told by an elderly resident of Oldtown, previously the site of a Shawnee village. The man's father had said that the pioneer Simon Kenton, who was fluent in the Shawnee language, "said the Indians had no tradition of the builders of Fort Ancient [not a fort, but a Hopewell ceremonial enclosure], but that they … visited the place en route to the Ohio [River] and did homage to the spirits of its makers."

References

Deloria, V. J. 2001. "Power and Place Equal Personality." In *Power and Place: Indian Education in America*, edited by. V. J. Deloria and D. Wildcat, 21–28. Golden: American Indian Graduate Center and Fulcrum Resources.

Duncan, J. R. 2015. "Identifying the Characters on the Walls of Picture Cave." In *Picture Cave: Unraveling the Mysteries of the Mississippian Cosmos*, edited by C. Diaz-Granados, J. R. Duncan, and F. K. Reilly III, 209–37. Austin: University of Texas Press.

Greber, N. B., and Ruhl, K. C. 1989. *The Hopewell Site: A Contemporary Analysis Based on the Work of Charles C. Willoughby*. Boulder: Westview Press.

Lepper, B. T. 2016. "The Newark Earthworks: A Monumental Engine of World Renewal." In *The Newark Earthworks: Enduring Monuments, Contested Meanings*, edited by L. Jones and R. D. Shiels, 41–61. Charlottesville: University of Virginia Press.

Lynott, M. J. 2014. *Hopewell Ceremonial Landscapes of Ohio: More Than Mounds and Geometric Earthworks*. Oxford: Oxbow Books.

Moorehead, W. K. 1908. "Fort Ancient: The Great Prehistoric Earthwork of Warren County, Ohio." *Phillips Academy, Department of Anthropology, Bulletin* 4: 27–166.

Moorehead, W. K. 1922. "The Hopewell Mound Group of Ohio." *Publications of the Field Museum of Natural History, Anthropological Series* 6, no. 5: 75–185.

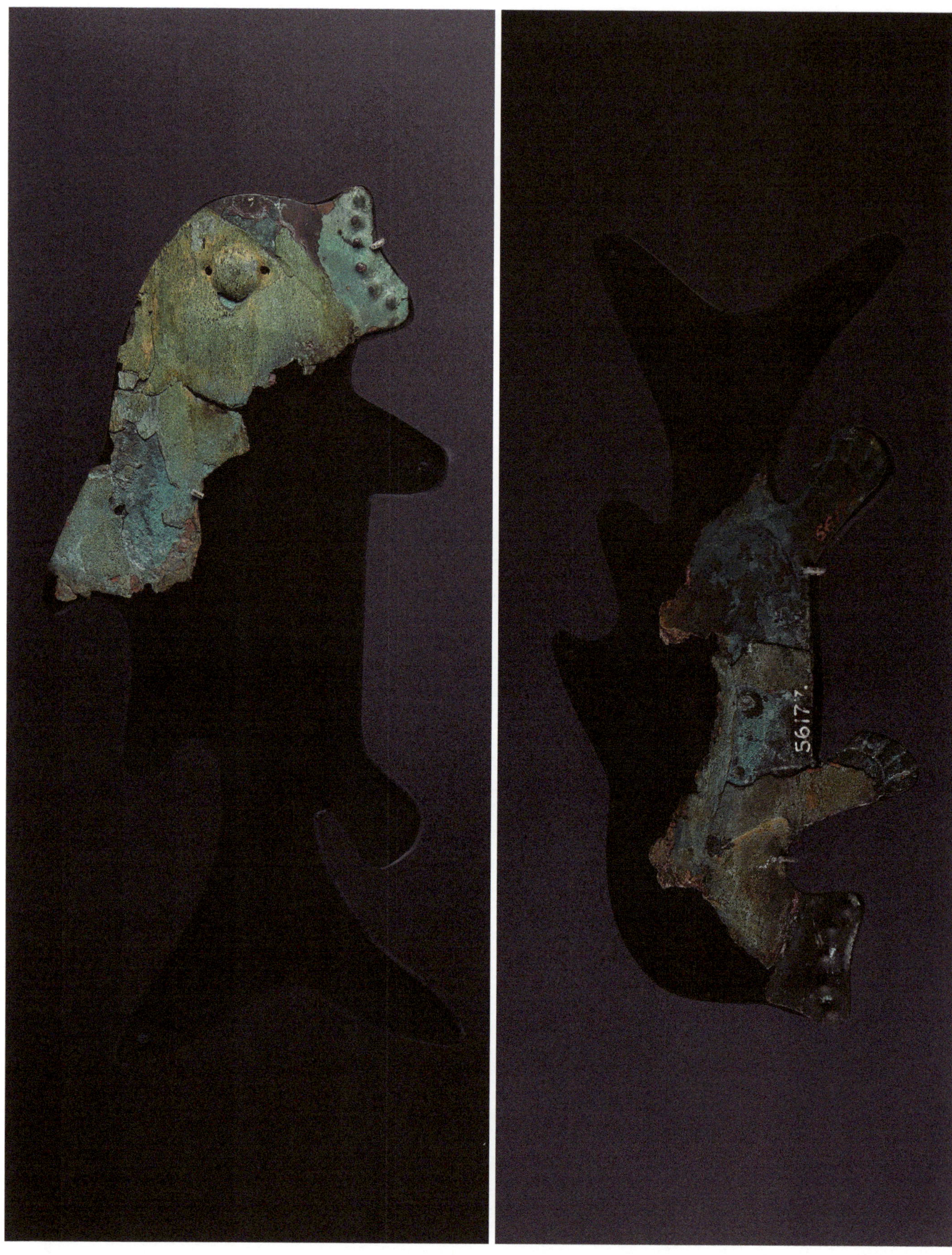

Figure 6.7. A pair of copper fish cut-outs from Hopewell Mounds site, Chillicothe, Ohio (FM 56176, 56177).

Figure 6.8. Hopewell necklace with copper pendants from Hopewell mounds (FM 56235, 56602, T2001.6.5).

Figure 6.9. Great Pyramid at Giza.

Figure 6.10. Taj Mahal, royal tomb of the Mughal ruler of India, Shah Jahan.

6D Pyramids and Standing Stones: Monuments for the Dead

Donna J. Nash
Field Museum/University of North Carolina Greensboro

Monuments dedicated to the dead hold power over the living long after they are built. Architecture can transform how people experience a landscape or city for hundreds or thousands of years. The construction of elaborate edifices meant to memorialize the dead brought many people together, represent large expenditures of labor and resources, and manifest the power of individuals or groups to shape ideals, convey conceptions of the cosmos, legitimize the leadership of particular lineages, or dominate their domain long after death. Archaeologists use the features of mortuary monuments to discern differences and understand the role of the dead among the living.

Spectacular tombs, such as the Taj Mahal in India or the pyramids at Giza in Egypt are world famous (Figures 6.9–6.10). They are synonymous with the identity of nations where they were built. Despite the millennia that passed between them, both mortuary monuments signaled their builders' wealth and power, were conceptualized as afterlife abodes, and included quarters for living attendants. The eventual "residents" of these grand palatial graves each espoused royal ideology. Shah Jahan covered his cenotaph with flowers because he viewed himself as "the spring of the flower garden of justice and generosity" (Koch 2005, 147), whereas Khufu elevated his burial chamber, a complex feat of engineering, to position himself closer to the sun god and assert identification with the deity (Billing 2011; Verner, Posener-Kriéger, and Vymazalová 2006, 180).

Towering mortuary monuments were also built in the Americas. Like those in Egypt, many Maya constructions paired temples with tombs, and kings were adored as semi-divine beings upon their death. One example is Temple 1 at Tikal in Guatemala (Figure 6.11). The nine-level pyramid, which represents Maya beliefs about the universe, started by Jasaw Chan K'awiil, ruler from 682 to 734 CE, once featured his portrait above the entrance to the temple at its top. The project was completed by his son, Yik'in Chan K'awiil, 734–746 CE (Martin and Grube 2000). Elements of Temple 1 represent the three plains of the Maya cosmos: the underworld, the Earth, and the celestial (see Feinman in this volume, on Mesoamerican Cosmologies). Jasaw's remains were found under the pyramid, dwelling in the underworld, but his image in life faced the plaza from lofty celestial heights, much like the gods. His essence as ancestor was carved on the lintels inside the shrine, which may have represented the dark interior of a cave (Orton 2015). Only a select few could enter and experience its interior. The floating kingly father depicted on the lintel may replicate images from previous centuries of rulers with a powerful ancestor hovering above their head (e.g., Stela 31, Tikal). It is quite possible that Yik'in purposely staged himself under the carved lintel to communicate with Jasaw, who legitimized his rule at Tikal. The portrait atop Temple 1 left little doubt to whom the pyramid was dedicated; such features emphasize the power of individuals and their lineages. Similar to the Taj Mahal and Khufu's pyramid, Tikal's Temple 1 required a great investment of labor and many resources, and put power on public display. The dead were not forgotten, but rather dominated the visual landscape long after their passing.

Impressive monuments built to commune with the dead can be more egalitarian in purpose when ancestors are broadly shared, or several are considered of equivalent status between lineages in a broader region. One of the earliest sites with monumental structures, Göbekli Tepe, dates to the tenth millennium BCE (Figure 6.12). It features megalithic T-shaped pillars in circular formations connected by benches and walls. Pillars depict different animals in relief, and a few are engraved with hands and clothing to represent humans. Among the 12 excavated stone circles, each is unique in its depictions. This may represent social divisions; however, the size of the stones, up to 12 feet in height, probably required coordinated efforts from several groups to put in place. Evidence indicates such gatherings involved feasting and possible beer drinking. There are no intact burials, but numerous skeletal fragments and pieces of modified skulls connect it with cultic activities celebrating the dead at smaller megalithic sites and cemeteries in Upper Mesopotamia, as well as farther afield in Israel, Jordan, and Syria (Gresky, Haelm, and Clare 2017). Like people, the enclosures were ritually buried upon abandonment. The broken heads of human statues, which lack distinctive features, were interred near the central pillars (Notroff, Dietrich, and Schmidt 2015). Decommissioning the site would have been of symbolic importance, which likely shifted the power it held over people elsewhere.

Göbekli Tepe may remind us of Stonehenge (Figure 6.13), a monument built, remodeled, and used between 3000 and 1500 BCE in Britain (Bayliss, Ramsey, and McCormac 1997). The eponymous standing stones were surrounded by a ridge and ditch etched into the chalklands and formed a circular ceremonial space of approximately 87 meters in diameter (Parker Pearson et al. 2020). Ritual constructions of this sort were created throughout the area; there was not a single, dominant place to celebrate the dead; however, Stonehenge had the greatest number of cremation burials placed between 3000 and 2400 BCE. Their presence is not obvious today but would have been

Figure 6.11. Temple I at Tikal, started by Jasaw Chan K'awiil and completed by his son Yik'in Chan K'awiil between 734 and 746 CE, reflects the power of Maya rulers.

an essential part of the sacred site. Many fragmentary remains were interred in the Aubrey Holes, which are interpreted as sockets that held the earliest standing stones erected at the site. Cremation burials were added during later ceremonies adjacent to the unfinished bluestones or elsewhere within the complex. The monument continued to be modified, the sarsen stones were added, and the blue stones were rearranged throughout the Early Bronze Age. The dead with few exceptions were interred elsewhere. A select set were buried with great labor and wealth in upland barrows on the surrounding ridges, which had a commanding view of the avenue that led pilgrims from the river Avon to Stonehenge (Allen 1997; Lawson 1997; Needham, Lawson, and Woodward. 2010). Henge monuments continued to be centers of community labor and celebration, even as the newly dead were entombed in other locales. Enduring sacred sites like Stonehenge may have been the domain of fictive forebearers described in legends and song. If this were the case, those bold enough to claim kinship with these entities could exert influence over seasonal celebrants who came from near and far in midwinter to observe the return of the sun with the barrows of leading lineages prominent on the horizon.

Monuments dedicated to remembering the dead are as diverse as the societies who built them. The tombs of Shah Jahan, Khufu, and Jasaw exemplify the ways in which the powerful expend great resources to maintain their position and that of their descendants. If the goal was to achieve immortal renown, they met it. Stonehenge and Göbekli Tepe were built by groups that chose to remember the dead for different reasons. At their inception such monuments may have mediated equality, but such omnipotent symbols in the landscape and the perceived importance of maintaining connections with the illustrious dead (real or fictional) can ultimately be a source of influence or a means to assert power through control of these places. Monumental tombs, whatever their form, make the dead impossible to forget; their role among the living may change over time, but their influence may be inescapable.

References

Allen, M. J. 1997. "Environment and Land-Use: The Economic Development of the Communities Who Built Stonehenge (an Economy to Support the Stones)." In *Science and Stonehenge*, edited by B. Cunliffe and C. Renfrew, 115–44. Oxford: Oxford University Press.

Bayliss, A., Ramsey, C. B., and McCormac, F. G. 1997. "Dating Stonehenge." In *Science and Stonehenge*, edited by B. Cunliffe and C. Renfrew, 39–59. Oxford: Oxford University Press.

Billing, N. 2011. "Monumentalizing the Beyond: Reading the Pyramid before and after the Pyramid Texts." *Studien zur Altägyptischen Kultur* 40: 53–66.

Gresky, J., Haelm, J., and Clare, L. 2017. "Modified Human Crania from Göbekli Tepe Provide Evidence for a New Form of Neolithic Skull Cult." *Science Advances* 3, no. 6: e1700564.

Koch, E. 2005. "The Taj Mahal: Architecture, Symbolism, and Urban Significance." *Muqarnas* 22: 128–49.

Lawson, A. J. 1997. "The Structural History of Stonehenge." In *Science and Stonehenge*, edited by B. Cunliffe and C. Renfrew, 15–38. Oxford: Oxford University Press.

Martin, S., and Grube, N. 2000. *Chronicle of the Maya Kings and Queens: Deciphering the Dynasties of the Ancient Maya*. New York: Thames & Hudson.

Needham, S., Lawson, A., and Woodward, A. 2010. "'A Noble Group of Barrows': Bush Barrow and the Normanton Down Early Bronze Age Cemetery Two Centuries On." *The Antiquaries Journal* 90: 1–39.

Notroff, J., Dietrich, O., and Schmidt, K. 2015. "Gathering of the Dead? The Early Neolithic Sanctuaries of Göbekli Tepe, Southeastern Turkey." In *Death Rituals, Social Order and the Archaeology of Immortality in the Ancient World: "Death Shall Have No Dominion,"* edited by C. Renfrew, M. J. Boyd, and I. Morley, 65–81. Cambridge: Cambridge University Press.

Orton, E. D. 2015. "Spaces of Transformation at Temple 1, Tikal, Guatemala." In *Maya Imagery, Architecture, and Activity: Space and Spatial Analysis in Art History*, edited by M. D. Werness-Rude and K. R. Spencer, 271–305. Albuquerque: University of New Mexico Press.

Parker Pearson, M., Pollard, J., Richards, C., Thomas, J., Tilley, C., and Welham, K. 2020. *Stonehenge for the Ancestors: Part 1: Landscape and Monuments*. Leiden: Sidestone Press.

Verner, M., Posener-Kriéger, P., and Vymazalová, H. 2006. *Abusir X: The Pyramid Complex of Raneferef: The Papyrus Archive*. Prague: Czech Institute of Egyptology.

The dead, and the monuments to them, have great symbolic power in almost every society on Earth. They continue to be touchstones for human social organization, be it political, religious, or economic power being sought by a social group. They are not always used in the way they or their descendants may have intended in life, but they hold great sway in the ways in which the world is constituted even today.

Death Is Not the End

For humans, physical immortality remains elusive (Zenou 2022), and so if our polities and groups are to remain sustainable, our social networks and institutions must continue to patch and bridge the voids left by death. Throughout human history, people have employed beliefs, memories, monuments, shrines, rituals, and other means in a sense to put the dead to work, using them to help address the problems that their absences and other factors create for the living and to foster the aims of those who endure. At this time of pandemic, loss, inequity, and war, the importance of remembrance cannot be overstated.

"Grief is the repeated experience of learning to live after loss" (Lee 2022). Collective sustenance and well-being

Figure 6.12. Göbekli Tepe's (Turkey) megalithic pillars framed communal monuments for commemorating the dead in the tenth millennium BCE.

in the face of personal and untimely tragedies requires us to provide the mechanisms to acknowledge, channel, harness, and collectively memorialize those losses. Democratic, collective forms of governance require work, not just from leaders, but from all of us. Selfish ideologies, focused on consumption and emphasizing personal choice rather than citizenship and collective responsibility are in many ways incompatible long-term with democracy (Blanton et al. 2021; Porter 2021). Now, after over two years of staring death and trauma in the face, we must redouble our commitment to do that work and build community.

References

Adam, D. 2022. "Covid's True Death Toll: Much Higher than Official Figures." *Nature* 603: 562. https://www.nature.com/articles/d41586-022-00708-0.

Apicella, C. L., Marlowe, F. W., Fowler, J. H., and Christakis, N. A. 2012. "Social Networks and Cooperation in Hunter-Gatherers." *Nature* 481: 497–501.

Atran, S. 2016. "The Devoted Actor: Unconditional Commitment and Intractable Conflict across Cultures." *Current Anthropology* 57, no. S13: S192–S203.

Balzeau, A., Turq, A., Talamo, S., Daujeard, C., Guérin, G., Welker, F., Crevecoeur, I., Fewlass, H., Hublin, J. J., Lahaye, C., and Maureille, B. 2020. "Pluridisciplinary Evidence for Burial for the La Ferrassie 8 Neandertal Child." *Scientific Reports* 10, no. 1: 1–10.

Bandy, M. S. 2004. "Fissioning, Scalar Stress, and Social Evolution in Early Village Societies." *American Anthropologist* 106: 322–33.

Bandy, M. S., and Fox, J. R. 2010. "Becoming Villagers: The Evolution of Early Village Societies." In *Becoming Villagers: Comparing Early Village Societies*, edited by M. S. Bandy and J. R. Fox, 1–16. Tucson: University of Arizona Press.

Binford, L. S. 1971. "Mortuary Practices: Their Study and Their Potential." In *Approaches to the Social Dimensions of Mortuary Practice*, edited by J. A. Brown, 6–29. Washington, DC: Society for American Archaeology, Memoir No. 25.

Birch, J. 2013. "Between Villages and Cities: Settlement Aggregation in Cross-Cultural Perspective." In *From Prehistoric Villages to Cities: Settlement Aggregation and Community Transformation*, edited by J. Birch, 1–22. New York: Routledge.

Blanton, R. E. 2016. "The Variety of Ritual Experience in Premodern States." In *Ritual and Archaic States*, edited by J. M. A. Murphy, 23–49. Gainesville: University Press of Florida.

Blanton, R. E., and Fargher, L. F. 2016. *How Humans Cooperate: Confronting the Challenges of Collective Action*. Boulder: University Press of Colorado.

Blanton, R. E., Fargher, L. F., Feinman, G. M., and Kowalewski, S. A. 2021. "The Fiscal Economy of Good Government: Past and Present." *Current Anthropology* 62: 77–100.

Bond, R. 2017. "Network Healing after Loss." *Nature Human Behavior* 1: article 0087. https://doi.org/10.1038/s41562-017-0087.

Brownlee, J. 2007. "Hereditary Succession in Modern Autocracies." *World Politics* 59: 595–628.

Carballo, D. M., Roscoe, P., and Feinman, G. M. 2014. "Cooperation and Collective Action in the Cultural Evolution of Complex Societies." *Journal of Archaeological Method and Theory* 21: 98–133.

Cashdan, E. 1980. "Egalitarianism among Hunters and Gatherers." *American Anthropologist* 82: 116–20.

Chapman, R. 2013. "Death, Burial, and Social Representation." In *The Oxford Handbook of the Archaeology of Death and Burial*, edited by S. Tarlow and L. Nilsson Stutz, 47–57. Oxford: Oxford University Press.

Charles, D. K., and Buikstra, J. E. 2002. "Siting, Sighting, and Citing the Dead." In *The Space and Place of Death*, edited by H. Silverman and D. B. Small, 13–25. Arlington: American Anthropological Association Archeological Papers 11.

Coward, F., and Dunbar, R. I. M. 2014. "Communities on the Edge of Civilization." In *Lucy to Language: The Benchmark Papers*, edited by R. I. M. Dunbar, C. Gamble, and J. A. J. Gowlett, 380–404. Oxford: Oxford University Press.

Coward, F., and Gamble, C. 2008. "Big Brains, Small Worlds: Material Culture and the Evolution of the Mind." *Philosophical Transactions of the Royal Society B, Biological Sciences* 363: 1969–79.

Dunbar, R. I. M. 2011. "Constraints on the Evolution of Social Institutions and Their Implications for Information Flow." *Journal of Institutional Economics* 7: 345–71.

Dunbar, R. I. M. 2013. "What Makes the Neolithic So Special?" *Neo-Lithics* 2, no. 13: 25–29.

Düring, B. S. 2013. "The Anatomy of a Prehistoric Community: Reconsidering Çatalhöyuk." In *From Prehistoric Villages to Cities: Settlement Aggregation and Community Transformation*, edited by J. A. Birch, 23–43. New York: Routledge.

Engelke, M. 2019. "The Anthropology of Death Revisited." *Annual Review of Anthropology* 48: 29–44. https://doi.org/10.1146/annurev-anthro-102218-011420.

Feinman, G. M. 1995. "The Emergence of Inequality: A Focus on Strategies and Processes." In *Foundations of Social Inequality*, edited by T. D. Price and G. M. Feinman, 255–79. New York: Plenum.

Feinman, G. M. 2016. "Variation and Change in Archaic States: Ritual as a Mechanism of Sociopolitical Integration." In *Ritual and Archaic States*, edited by

Figure 6.13. Stonehenge (Great Britain), built between 3000 and 1500 BCE, contained cremation burials in addition to the famous standing stones and represents communal labor and commemoration.

J. M. A. Murphy, 1–22. Gainesville: University Press of Florida.

Feinman, G. M., and Neitzel, J. E. 2019. "Perspective: Deflating the Myth of Isolated Communities. Individual Mobility at Early Settlements Raises Questions about Tenets of Culture History." *Science* 366: 682–83.

Fitzsimmons, J. L. 2009. *Death and the Classic Maya Kings*. Austin: University of Texas Press.

Fletcher, R. 1995. *The Limits of Settlement Growth: A Theoretical Outline*. Cambridge: Cambridge University Press.

Gerring, J., and Knutsen, C. H. 2019. "Polity Size and the Institutionalization of Leadership Succession." *Studies in Comparative International Development* 54: 451–72.

Granovetter, M. S. 1973. "The Strength of Weak Ties." *American Journal of Sociology* 78: 1360–80.

Granovetter, M. S. 1983. "The Strength of Weak Ties: A Network Theory Revisited." In *Sociological Theory*, edited by R. Collins, 201–33. San Francisco: Jossey-Bass.

Gresky, J., Haelm, J., and Clare, L. 2017. "Modified Human Crania from Göbekli Tepe Provide Evidence for a New Form of Neolithic Skull Cult." *Science Advances* 3: e17700564.

Hayden, B. 2009. "Funerals as Feasts: Why Are They So Important?" *Cambridge Archaeological Journal* 19: 29–52.

Helms, L. 2020. "Leadership Succession in Politics: The Democracy/Autocracy Divide Revisited." *The British Journal of Politics and International Relations* 22: 328–46.

Hobbs, W. R., and Burke, M. K. 2017. "Connective Recovery in Social Networks after the Death of a Friend." *Nature Human Behavior* 1: 1–6.

Janssen, M. A, Kohler, T. A., and Scheffer, M. 2003. "Sunk-Costs Effect and Vulnerability to Collapse in Ancient Societies." *Current Anthropology* 44: 722–28.

Johnson, G. A. 1982. "Organizational Structure and Scalar Stress." In *Theory and Explanation in Archaeology, the Southampton Conference*, edited by C. Renfrew, M. J. Rowlands, and B. A. Seagraves, 389–421. New York: Academic Press.

Jong, J. 2016. "From Mummification to 'Sky Burials': Why We Need Death Rituals." *The Conversation*, June 13. https://theconversation.com/from-mummification-to-sky-burials-why-we-need-death-rituals-60386.

Lannutti, P. J., and Bevan, J. L. 2022. "Conclusion to the Special Issue: Relationships in the Time of COVID-19. Examining the Effects of the Global Pandemic on Personal Relationships." *Journal of Social and Personal Relationships* 39: 80–91. https://doi.org/10.1177/02654075211063536.

Laqueur, T. W. 2015. *The Work of the Dead: A Cultural History of Mortal Remains*. Princeton, NJ: Princeton University Press.

Lee, M. R. 2022. "Grief, Everywhere: We Must Not Mistake a Return to 'Normal' Life as the End of Someone's Pain." *The Atlantic*, April 12. https://www.theatlantic.com/ideas/archive/2022/04/us-covid-grief-one-million-deaths/629533.

Malinowski, B. 1954. *Magic, Science and Religion*. Garden City, NY: Doubleday.

Munson, J., Amati, V., Collard, M., and Macri, M. J. 2014. "Religious Rituals: Quantifying Patterns of Variation in Hieroglyphic Texts." *PLOS One* 9, no. 9: e107982.

Nettle, D., and Dunbar, R. I. M. 1997. "Social Markers and the Evolution of Reciprocal Exchange." *Current Anthropology* 38: 93–99.

Nilsson Stutz, L., and Tarlow, S. 2013. "Beautiful Things and Bones of Desire: Emerging Issues in the Archaeology of Death and Burial." In *The Oxford Handbook of the Archaeology of Death and Burial*, edited by S. Tarlow and L. Nilsson Stutz, 1–14. Oxford: Oxford University Press.

Pettitt, P. 2011. *The Paleolithic Origins of Human Burial*. London: Routledge.

Pomeroy, E., Bennett, P., Hunt, C. O., Reynolds, T., Farr, L., Frouin, M., Holman, J., Lane, R., French, C., and Barker, G. 2020. "New Neanderthal Remains Associated with the 'Flower Burial' at Shanidar Cave." *Antiquity* 94, no. 373: 11–26.

Porter, E. 2021. *The Consumer Citizen*. New York: Oxford University Press.

Powell, A., Shennan, S., and Thomas, M. G. 2009. "Late Pleistocene Demography and the Appearance of Modern Human Behavior." *Science* 324: 1298–301.

Renfrew, C. 2007. *Prehistory: The Making of the Human Mind*. London: Weidenfeld & Nicolson.

Riel-Salvatore, J., and Gravel-Miguel, C. 2013. "Upper Palaeolithic Mortuary Practices in Eurasia: A Critical Look at the Burial Record." In *The Oxford Handbook of the Archaeology of Death and Burial*, edited by S. Tarlow and L. Nilsson Stutz, 303–46. Oxford: Oxford University Press.

Roberson, K., Smith, T., and Davidson, W. 2018. "Understanding Death Rituals." *International Journal of Childbirth Education* 33, no. 3: 22–26.

Roberts, S. G. B. 2010. "Constraints on Social Networks." In *Social Brain, Distributed Mind*, edited by R. Dunbar, C. Gamble, and J. Gowlett, 115–34. Oxford: Oxford University Press.

Schreiber, M. 2022. "What One Million COVID Dead Mean for the US's Future." *Scientific American*, March 29. https://www.scientificamerican.com/article/what-one-million-covid-dead-mean-for-the-u-s-s-future.

Schwartz, G. 2017. "The Archaeological Study of Sacrifice." *Annual Review of Anthropology* 46: 223–40.

Smith, M. E. 2019. "Energized Crowding and the Generative Role of Settlement Aggregation and Urbanization." In *Coming Together: Comparative Approaches to Population Aggregation and Early Urbanization*, edited by A. Gyucha, 37–58. Albany: State University of New York Press.

Solecki, R. S. 1975. "Shanidar IV, a Neanderthal Flower Burial in Northern Iraq." *Science* 190, no. 4217: 880–81.

Steadman, L. B., Palmer, C. T., and Tilley, C. T. 1996. "The Universality of Ancestor Worship." *Ethnology* 35: 63–76. https://www.jstor.org/stable/3774025.

Sterelny, K., and Watkins, T. 2015. "Neolithization in Southwest Asia in a Context of Niche Construction Theory." *Cambridge Archaeological Journal* 25: 673–705.

Stuart, D. 1984. "Royal Auto-Sacrifice among the Maya: A Study of Image and Meaning." *RES: Anthropology and Aesthetics* 7/8, Spring–Autumn: 6–20.

Ur, J. A. 2014. "Households and the Emergence of Cities in Ancient Mesopotamia." *Cambridge Archaeological Journal* 24: 249–68.

Wellman, B. 2012. "Is Dunbar's Number Up?" *British Journal of Psychology* 103: 164–76.

Wengrow, D., and Graeber, D. 2015. "Farewell to the 'Childhood of Man': Ritual, Seasonality, and the Origins of Inequality." *Journal of the Royal Anthropological Institute* n.s. 21: 597–619.

Whitehouse, H. 2021. *The Ritual Animal: Imitation and Cohesion in the Evolution of Social Complexity*. Oxford: Oxford University Press.

Whitehouse, H., and Lanman, J. A. 2014. "The Ties That Bind Us: Ritual, Fusion, and Identification." *Current Anthropology* 55: 674–95.

Yong, E. 2022a. "The Final Pandemic Betrayal." *The Atlantic,* April 13. https://www.theatlantic.com/health/archive/2022/04/us-1-million-covid-death-rate-grief/629537.

Yong, E. 2022b. "How Did This Many Deaths Become Normal?" *The Atlantic,* March 8. https://www.theatlantic.com/health/archive/2022/03/covid-us-death-rate/626972.

Zenou, T. 2022. "The Long and Gruesome History of People Trying to Live Forever." *Washington Post,* May 1. https://www.washingtonpost.com/history/2022/05/01/immortality-g...F596b089e9bbc0f403f8a0447%2F42%2F53%2F626ef4f8956121755a5d116d.

Appendix A

Spanish Translation of the Introduction (Chapter 1): Introducción

Patrick Ryan Williams y Gary M. Feinman

Traducido por Luis Muro Ynoñán

La muerte es universal, aunque esta es experimentada de diversas maneras por los diferentes pueblos y culturas. Desde una perspectiva global e histórica, la muerte tiene diferentes significados e implicancias para cada comunidad. A través de una reflexión sobre ella, e incorporando diversas perspectivas, podemos obtener una mejor idea del significado de la vida. La muerte es un fenómeno biológico, social y espiritual; y exploraremos en este capítulo sus diferentes significados, a través del tiempo y el espacio. La muerte se refiere al cuerpo, pero también a la esencia del propio ser; además, a los vivos quienes llevan los recuerdos y los genes de aquellos que fenecen. Se refiere al esfuerzo humano para prevenirla; a nuestra capacidad para cometer injusticias con tal de evitarla, y a nuestra humanidad para hacer frente a la pérdida. Finalmente, se trata de cómo seguimos adelante pese a ella, estando nosotros mismos íntimamente conectados los unos a los otros a través de lazos sociales, con una conexión se ve interrumpida por la desaparición de aquellos que están más cercanos a nosotros. La muerte, en su último acto, creará nuevamente vida.

Los autores de este volumen explorarán el papel de la muerte en nuestras vidas; cómo esta es entendida desde varias perspectivas; y cómo esta se cruza con la vida misma, el pasado, el presente y el futuro. Pese a que ni la exhibición ni este volumen pueden ser completamente exhaustivos en el tema, nuestro objetivo es ilustrar la diversidad de miradas, comportamientos, y creencias. Hoy en día vivimos en una sociedad que adopta una perspectiva en la que la naturaleza está separada de la humanidad; esta perspectiva mira la vida y la muerte de una forma distinta a aquellas percepciones religiosas y culturales de muchos otros grupos humanos, del pasado y presente. Para muchos en los EE.UU., la muerte es un punto final en nuestra biología. Esta representa un momento específico en el tiempo en el que la vida expira definitivamente y de una manera acotada, un camino finito con un principio y un final. Esta mirada tiene sus raíces en un empirismo que impregna nuestra visión modernista, arraigada en la ciencia y el conocimiento médico como una perspectiva generalizada de nuestro tiempo.

Pese a ello, e incluso en nuestra propia sociedad, las perspectivas alternativas de la muerte impregnan mucho de nuestro propio entendimiento sobre ella. Y en las sociedades de todo el mundo aquella perspectiva empírica de la muerte, como un momento finito en el tiempo, un final sin renovación, y un punto de vista fatalista, es desafiada tanto por el pensamiento religioso como por las realidades vividas que enfrentan los seres vivos a medida que la atraviesan y experimentan. Para muchos, la muerte no es un mero punto final, o un "gran cierre," sino tiene un significado mucho más profundo en el ciclo de la vida.

La exposición diseñada a partir de la investigación que se expresa, también, en este volumen se nutre del conocimiento de muchas culturas del mundo, y del conocimiento obtenido del mundo natural, para así abordar diversas respuestas y puntos de vistas a varias preguntas existenciales sobre la muerte (ver Miller y Whitfield, este volumen). ¿Qué es la muerte? ¿Acaso tengo que morir? ¿Qué le pasará a mi cuerpo? ¿Qué le pasará a mi espíritu? ¿Cómo afectará mi muerte a los demás? Las respuestas a estas preguntas no se abordan secuencialmente en este volumen, puesto que cada historia, en realidad, tiene múltiples respuestas a las preguntas sobre nuestra propia muerte y la de los demás. Sin embargo, ciertos temas representados en esta colección de ensayos abordan algunas preguntas de una manera más explícita que otras. El tratamiento del cuerpo, por ejemplo, resuena muchos mas en los ensayos sobre la biología del ciclo de vida y la orquestación de rituales de duelo; mientras que el potencial del espíritu tiene una invocación mucho más evidente en los ensayos sobre la religión, la vitalidad, y la fuerza de vida.

Este volumen está organizado en torno a cinco ensayos temáticos, cada uno con cuatro breves casos de estudio que profundizan en varios de los temas de la exhibición (ver Figura 1.1). Los autores de este volumen son destacados científicos, académicos con raíces indígenas, y profesionales del mundo de los museos que han contribuido a la exposición como consultores, desarrolladores, diseñadores, y co-curadores, o siendo ellos mismos los curadores de la muestra. Muchos de los objetos exhibidos en la exposición, y fotografiados de una manera exquisita por la fotógrafa, Michelle Kuo, forman parte de la colección permanente de antropología del Field Museum. Varios otros objetos fueron adquiridos para la exposición y han pasado ya a formar parte de la colección permanente del museo por medio de esta exposición. Esto incluyen el ataúd de Ghana de Seth Kane Kwei; las banderas haitianas de *Gede*; y la cerámica *govi* y *kanari* creada por el Taller de Ronald Edmunds. Estamos agradecidos por los préstamos otorgados por el Jewish Museum y el Art Institute of Chicago, así como por aquellos realizados por Mitchell Hendrickson, Tory Hambly, y Life Gem.

Los capítulos aquí representados se basan en las historias elegidas para la exposición, que a su vez fueron seleccionadas tras una extensa investigación en las colecciones del Field Museum y en cada historia y objeto seleccionado (y obtenido) especialmente para la exposición. De hecho, fueron las extensas colecciones del museo las que fueron claves para identificar qué historias podríamos contar en la muestra y, por lo tanto, en este volumen. Nos hemos esforzado por poder adoptar un enfoque global, mientras abordábamos cada una de las cinco preguntas planteadas; la mayoría de los continentes del mundo están, además, aquí representados. También, hemos intentando incorporar una diversidad de perspectivas de fe religiosa, incluidas las del pasado distante y la actualidad. Al final, esta no es una mirada integral a la visión de la humanidad sobre la muerte, pero incorpora perspectivas reconocidas desde hace mucho tiempo hasta el presente actual, desde varias experiencias culturales y desde reflexiones sobre las diversas creencias religiosas de ayer y hoy. Los cinco ensayos temáticos ayudan a sintetizar las perspectivas particulares sobre la muerte, mientras que los casos de estudios más breves elaboran sobre la diversidad de aproximaciones que diferentes pueblos aportan a las preguntas sobre la muerte.

El primero de los ensayos temáticos, por Robert Martin, explora una visión biológica del "viaje de la vida a la muerte" y nuestras reacciones a los procesos biológicos implicados en este. El autor nos lleva desde la concepción misma del ciclo de la vida humana, y cómo esta se asemeja a la de nuestros parientes animales, y explora la extensión artificial de la vida y la esperanza de algunos para alcanzar la inmortalidad. Martin se pregunta si la medicina moderna tiene la capacidad de alterar drásticamente la vida humana, o si podríamos no estar restringidos a las limitaciones físicas del cuerpo humano. Resulta que la longevidad depende, en gran medida, no solo de nuestras realidades biológicas y físicas, sino también de nuestra experiencia social vivida. Martin examina cómo los científicos estudian los cuerpos muertos para evaluar la vida y la muerte de las personas. También, reflexiona sobre cómo cuidamos los cuerpos de los muertos, tema que también es tratado por otros autores en el volumen. Es importante destacar que varios de los casos de estudio que acompañan este capítulo reflexionan sobre las injusticias alrededor de la muerte, aquellas que nuestra sociedad impone a ciertos miembros en función de su sexo, raza, y otras categorizaciones de identidad.

Acompañando al capítulo de Martin, se exploran aquellas meditaciones hechas por los monjes budistas japonesas sobre la descomposición biológica del cuerpo humano por medio de las fascinantes acuarelas de *Kusōzu (Nine Stages of Bodily Decay)*. Mientras que la exposición se enfoca en estas acuarelas como una representación de lo que le sucede al cuerpo, Chelsea Foxwell llama la atención sobre cómo las acuarelas de *Kusōzu* reflejan, además, la moral del pensamiento budista. En el siglo XIX, cuando probablemente y originalmente fueron creadas estas acuarelas, la mayoría de los budistas japoneses eran cremados. Sin embargo, las acuarelas de *Kusōzu* reflexionaban sobre la impermanencia del cuerpo y su cambio a través de las diferentes etapas de la muerte. Si bien en la exposición nos centramos en el proceso biológico de la muerte, esta historia saca a la luz la naturaleza más compleja del pensamiento budista en torno a la muerte y a su búsqueda por el *nirvana*.

La búsqueda de la inmortalidad en la China de ayer y hoy ilustra aquellas dificultades que enfrentamos cuando desafiamos a la muerte, y las maneras en las que hemos abordado este desafío. Esta historia es contada en secciones de la exposición que hablan sobre la longevidad, y Deborah Bekken cuenta la historia de las prácticas taoístas que buscaban la prolongación de la vida utilizando elixires y elementos naturales. El énfasis especial en el hongo *lingzhi*, como proveedor de la vida, ilumina la manera en cómo el cuerpo humano podía llegar a mantenerse y/o preservarse, y presagiaba el uso de medicamentos hoy en día para evitar la muerte. Las propiedades reparadoras del *lingzhi* se remontan a más de 2,000 años y están ampliamente disponibles, hoy en día, en tés, polvos o suplementos dietéticos.

Y en la sociedad moderna estadounidense, las desigualdades sociales que conducen a la muerte prematura de las madres de color, así como las muertes de víctimas del COVID 19, nos hacen comprender que la injusticia social y la muerte están íntimamente relacionadas. Kim Mutcherson detalla las sorprendentes tasas de mortalidad entre las mujeres negras en los Estados Unidos debido a las drásticas disparidades en el servicio de salud materna. Si bien los Estados Unidos tiene una de las peores tasas de morbilidad para las madres en general entre las naciones desarrolladas, las madres de color se ven afectadas aún más drásticamente. Son las formas racistas en las cuales se tratan a los cuerpos negros y la indiferencia al conocimiento mismo de la mujer sobre su propia salud y bienestar lo que crean estas tasas tan altas de morbilidad. Es una crisis que amenaza el futuro de nosotros mismos como población humana y que necesita reparación inmediata.

La pandemia del COVID 19 también ha tenido efectos vastos y diferenciales en las poblaciones mundiales, y Alaka Wali nos detalla cómo el Field Museum inició un proyecto para documentar los impactos sobre las poblaciones alrededor del mundo, y particularmente en Chicago. Un objeto en particular, un *banner* que agradecía a los trabajadores esenciales durante la pandemia, cuenta la historia de resiliencia e injusticia sobre quién estuvo expuesto al virus y cómo la raza y la clase estructuraron "quién vivió" y "quién murió." Este textil, hecho por Andrea Martinez, nativa de la ciudad Chicago, cuenta la historia de estos valientes trabajadores que continuaron ayudándonos a todos y todas pese al gran riesgo para ellos mismos durante las primeras semanas y meses de la pandemia.

Perspectivas alternativas sobre la relación entre la vida y la muerte son abordadas por Kyrah Malika Daniels y William Schweiker, quienes reflexionan sobre las tradiciones religiosas de África y la diáspora africana, por un lado, y aquellas del mundo Judeo-Cristiano, por el otro. En el primer ensayo, Daniels nos lleva a través de las formas en que las comunidades de África y su diáspora en el mundo Atlántico entienden la muerte y su lugar en la experiencia humana. Ella se basa en, y hace referencia a, varias de las historias contadas en la exhibición, con un énfasis especial en los pueblos afrodescendientes de Haití y el vudú haitiano contemporáneo, el cual enfatiza los principios fundamentales de la longevidad, la vitalidad, y el dinamismo de la vida. Examinar estos principios, en última instancia, permite revelar cómo la fuerza vital de la vida se sostiene a través del equilibrio, el ritual, y la fortificación de las almas y las energías divinas en las religiones africanas.

La perspectiva en las religiones africanas se complementa con aquellas de las culturas indígenas de América Latina. La diáspora del mundo Atlántico es a menudo vista como la explotación europea de los cuerpos africanos, y ha sido correctamente definido como tal. Pero, también, está involucrada la apropiación de las tierras de los pueblos indígenas de las Américas, así como la usurpación de sus cuerpos y su trabajo. El ensayo de Daniels y las historias que lo acompañan destacan las perspectivas sobre la muerte que los pueblos africanos, de la diáspora africana, y los pueblos nativos latinoamericanos desarrollaron, y como estas contribuye a comprender la muerte desde una manera más amplia en la humanidad.

El trabajo de Daniels, entonces, se acompaña de otras perspectivas sobre la muerte desde África y las Américas. Pertenecientes a las tradiciones Yoruba, en torno a los gemelos en África Central, las estatuas *ere ibeji* ("nacidos dos veces") encarnan las poderosas fuerzas espirituales que están presentes en el nacimiento de gemelos, los cuales son altamente valorados en la sociedad Yoruba. Las figuras de madera que representa a cada uno de los gemelos se convierten en importantes representantes del difunto durante los ritos y rituales de los vivos. Foreman Bandama examina cómo la pérdida de un gemelo, o de ambos gemelos, repercute en la sociedad Yoruba en general. Dado que el alma de un gemelo se comparte entre ambos hermanos, mantener el equilibrio requiere que el alma del difunto tenga un *ibeji* para así poder vivir. De lo contrario, podría traer consecuencias catastróficas para los vivos.

Desde el otro lado del mundo, la importancia de la *fuerza vital* es explorada en las representaciones del mundo Moche (200–900 ec) asociadas a la muerte, la sexualidad, y el ser que desafían nuestras concepciones de cómo la vida *anima* el mundo. Luis Muro Ynoñán presenta algunas reflexiones sobre la naturaleza de la vida y la muerte a través de una interpretación de las figurinas de cerámica de los Moche del Perú. Aquí, los personajes están involucrados en actos sexualmente explícitos que nos ayudan a comprender que la muerte, la reproducción, y los fluidos corporales están todos entrelazados en los ciclos de vida Moche. De hecho, no son los actos sexuales los que son el foco de las escenas, sino el traspaso de los fluidos vitales entre las entidades lo que parece ser lo más importante. Y estas entidades no son solo humanas, sino animales, seres esqueléticos, y otros seres íntimamente conectados con la constante (re)producción de la vida.

El *capac hucha* de los Incas revela una perspectiva Andina sudamericana diferente sobre el significado de la muerte, en el que el sacrificio de los niños y niñas nobles Incas nos indica que el momento preciso de la muerte no siempre es tan fácil de definir. Ryan Williams explora el significado del *capac hucha* para la comprensión de la muerte Inca (1400–1532 dc). Aquí, también se cuestiona la línea entre la vida y la muerte, como en el caso haitiano y de Yoruba. A medida que los niños y niñas son retirados de sus comunidades, se inicia una transición a su nueva existencia iniciándose semanas o meses antes de su verdadera muerte biológica. Estos infantes nobles se convierten en seres sociales diferentes por medio de esta transición, e incluso luego de que son enterrados en la cima de montañas cubiertas de nieve o en una isla en el medio del Océano Pacífico, ellos continúan desempeñando el papel de mensajeros con los antepasados. Incluso en la muerte, ellos continuarán sirviendo al Inca.

Tomando nuevamente el concepto de "trayectoria de vida," los pueblos Prehispánicos de Mesoamérica concibieron la existencia de distintos reinos habitados por seres vivos y muertos. Ciertos seres y lugares facilitaron una comunicación, así como el movimiento, entre estos reinos borrando aún mas la distinción misma entre la vida y la muerte. Gary Feinman analiza los tres reinos del universo Mesoamericano: el supramundo, el mundo del medio, y el inframundo, así como los portales que los conectan. Esta concepción no es tan diferente a aquella del universo en el mundo Andino con el *hananpacha, kaypacha* y *ukhupacha* relatada por Luis Muro Ynoñán. La vida, la muerte, y la renovación están todas conectadas en el mundo Mesoamericano, y lugares tales como las canchas Prehispánicas del Juego de la Pelota (1200 AC–1520 dc), o seres tales como los perros, asistieron en el traspaso a través de estos reinos. El maíz, también, representó una metáfora central dentro de esta cosmovisión, puesto que las semillas de la vida están "incrustadas" en el crecimiento y la muerte del maíz mismo, desde su transformación de semilla en tallo, y de tallo en maíz.

En el tercer ensayo, *Performing Death,* Luis Muro Ynoñán nos conduce a las formas en cómo el ritual y el duelo nos ayudan a enfrentar la muerte en diferentes contextos culturales y sociales. En estos ensayos vemos los profundos impactos sociales de la muerte en los individuos y en las comunidades. En el ensayo final de este volumen, Gary Feinman y Ryan Williams llevan esta perspectiva más allá examinando los impactos a largo plazo de la muerte en la sociedad más en general. En el ensayo de Muro Ynoñán, sin embargo, el duelo y el ritual ocupan un lugar central en la elaboración de cómo lidiamos con la pérdida de un ser querido en la inmediatez de su fallecimiento, tanto físico como espiritual. Muro Ynoñán destaca los comportamientos funerarios en el pasado y el presente humano, puesto que son el único y exclusivo medio por el cual los humanos lidian con el dolor, el vacío, y la frustración a través del ritual. El ritual mortuorio también involucra la transformación de la persona y el cuerpo, y ese proceso implica tanto los deseos personales del difunto, como, y especialmente, la inscripción de significados por parte de la comunidad sobreviviente en los cuerpos de los occisos. Los muertos son lavados, vestidos, agasajados, y enterrados de acuerdo con las identidades prescritas por quienes los entierran. Algunos de los difuntos se convierten en importantes ancestros y, en algunos casos, en la ausencia de sus cuerpos, las representaciones mismas de aquellos difuntos adquieren nuevos significados para sus comunidades.

El tratamiento ritual de los muertos es explorado en las varias formas en las que los cuerpos son preparados y enterrados en la Costa Peruana, y en particular, hace 600 años por la sociedad Chancay. Nicole Slovak analiza las formas en que los Chancay (1000–1400 dc) trataban a los cuerpos de los difuntos y la importancia de la preservación del mismo para esta sociedad. En particular, los fallecidos continuaban sus vínculos con los vivos, incluso después del entierro, ya que estos eran vestidos, alimentados y conmemorados varias veces luego de su entierro. Muchas otras comunidades Andinas, antes de la llegada de los europeos, también volvían a rememorar a sus muertos cuidando de los cuerpos de sus antepasados durante muchos años luego de su entierro. La vida, al parecer, no abandona por completo el cuerpo al morir, o al menos el *ser físico* continúa siendo alimentado y vestido mucho después de que se ha producido su muerte biológica.

La momificación; es decir, la preservación del cuerpo para el más allá, también fue un medio clave para *escenificar* la muerte en el Antiguo Egipto. Las circunstancias de la momificación egipcia fueron muy diferentes a las del caso Andino, como explica Emily Teeter. Mientras que el espíritu requiere un hogar terrenal, esto es, un cuerpo preservado para habitar, el espíritu, también, se convierte en un dios imperecedero que mora para siempre en el más allá. No todos los que morían eran momificados en la sociedad egipcia, y este era un proceso mucho más elaborado en su forma entre las élites y los faraones; la mayoría de los aspectos aquí descritos datan del 1000 ac. Para los egipcios, la preservación de los restos corporales era clave para que el espíritu viviera una eternidad en el más allá. A diferencia del caso Andino, el difunto momificado egipcio ya no participaba activamente en el mundo de los vivos. Pese a ello, la perturbación de sus restos terrenales podría poner en peligro su existencia en aquel más allá.

En la actual Accra, en Ghana, ha surgido una tradición de entierro en ataúdes muy elaborados los cuales representan las aspiraciones profesionales o personales, la personalidad, o el estatus del difunto, a partir de un ritual que celebra, fundamentalmente, el poder. Foreman Bandama analiza los cambios en las tradiciones funerarias bajo el dominio colonial británico en Ghana, que remueve a los difuntos de ser enterrados en sus hogares a cementerios públicos, y con ello la adopción concomitante de una nueva tradición de entierro en ataúdes elaborados de fantasía. Iniciándose en el pueblo Ga, y extendiéndose a muchos otros pueblos de Ghana, la tradición surgió de las literas de manos que usaban algunos jefes de Ghana. Hoy en día, estos ataúdes están hechos tanto para el entierro de individuos como para obras de arte específicamente para exhibiciones de museos. La tradición de ataúdes de Ghana muestra cuánto puede cambiar, en el transcurso de un siglo, una tradición mortuoria, y también nos recuerda que la muerte se trata de recordar y honrar al difunto mismo.

Y en Tsavo, Kenia, un antepasado desaparecido debido a la esclavitud, y cuyo cuerpo no puede ser reclamado para su inclusión en un santuario ancestral, es representado por un cráneo de animal. Chapurukha Kusimba describe la migración de los pueblos de las llanuras de Tsavo hacia las colinas altas mientras huían del comercio de esclavos, las sequías, y las enfermedades durante los siglos XVI al XIX dc. La comunidad de Tsavo se llevó consigo los cráneos de sus antepasados y construyeron santuarios en sus nuevos hogares ahora en las montañas, en donde vivieron una vida nómada como refugiados durante varios siglos. Entre uno de estos cráneos, había el de una oveja (o una cabra) que representaba a uno de los antepasados perdidos en una de las cacerías de esclavos, por lo que su cráneo no pudo acompañar al de sus parientes. El contacto con los restos físicos de los ancestros mantiene la continuidad entre las generaciones. Un ser querido que es arrancado de su grupo social sufre una muerte social a los ojos de aquellos quienes nunca más volverán a verlo, por lo que estos necesitan representarlo a pesar del conocimiento de su muerte corporal y la falta de sus restos físicos.

En el penúltimo ensayo, el ensayo de William Schweiker sobre la muerte en las tradiciones cristianas y judías, nos acerca a una comprensión de la muerte desde Occidente, incluyendo a dos de las religiones más prominentes del mundo indoeuropeo. Esto nos recuerda que las definiciones médicas de la muerte van acompañadas de teologías muy profundas de pensamiento acerca de la finalidad de la muerte y la continuación del ser a partir de la muerte del cuerpo. En particular, la perspectiva religiosa aquí articulada examina el por qué existe la muerte y sus orígenes teológicos; cómo se entrelazan la vida y la muerte; cómo prepararse para la muerte; y qué hay más allá de la muerte de nuestros propios cuerpos. Schweiker nos recuerda que, en la doctrina cristiana, el origen de la muerte se debió al pecado original de Adán y Eva luego de ser exiliados del Jardín del Edén, para así vivir y morir en un mundo de pecado. La muerte existe ya que todos los humanos nacemos con el pecado original, y solo a través de la expiación del pecado por Cristo podemos los humanos ser salvados. En última instancia, la resurrección de Cristo de entre los muertos es la victoria de Dios sobre la muerte.

Las tradiciones religiosas cristianas, así como las judías, también relacionan los desafíos de la mortalidad, así como el vivir como seres mortales con una moralidad especifica, y la importancia de seguir una vida moral en la iglesia. El primer sacramento cristiano, el bautismo, es visto, de hecho, como una muerte ritualizada tras la cual el individuo es resucitado a una nueva vida en el cuerpo de Cristo. Y tanto en la religión judía como en la cristiana, el ideal es el amarse los unos a otros y ser una luz para el mundo. Prepararse para nuestra propia muerte o para la muerte de un ser querido nos hace adherirnos a esta perspectiva de amor y comprensión. Permitir la confesión de los pecados antes de la muerte, acompañar a los moribundos y a los deudos en su dolor, y brindar consuelo son principios importantes de la preparación para la muerte. Finalmente, la doctrina religiosa habla de lo que existe más allá de la muerte, y Schweiker describe los peligros y las posibilidades de las diferentes perspectivas religiosas sobre el más allá. Aquí, el potencial de una "Segunda Muerte" o una "Muerte Eterna" dentro del pensamiento cristiano y judío, en el que el alma se separa para siempre de lo divino, representa un destino mucho más aterrador que la muerte misma. Estas ideas se exploran con mayor profundidad en varios de los casos que acompañan este ensayo.

Cuando el espíritu fenece, el cuerpo permanece y debe ser enterrado rápidamente según la tradición judía. Aquellos que limpian el cuerpo antes del entierro realizan un deber solemne, el *Chevra Kadisha.* Laurie Zoloth nos lleva a través de una reflexión personal sobre este rito y un análisis de su significado en la vida judía. Ella nos recuerda que una vez que se proclama la muerte médica, el cuerpo en la sociedad moderna es tratado como un recipiente vacío, enviado a una morgue como un artículo almacenado. El ritual judío, sin embargo, re-humaniza el cuerpo previo al entierro, tal y como ella lo describe con tanta elocuencia, y nos recuerda que los participantes, junto con el difunto, son parte de una comunidad con Dios. Los *Chevra Kadisha,* nos enseñan, también, sobre los rituales y los performances alrededor de la muerte y su significado para aquellas comunidades de práctica que la circundan. Esta discreta tradición nos recuerda que la muerte es una experiencia humilde y humanizadora, que también nos pone en contacto a través de una experiencia compartida.

Los Guna de Panamá traen a relucir la historia cristiana del Jardín del Edén a través de su propia interpretación usando a las elaboradas *molas* que ellos tejen. Alaka Wali comparte con nosotros el significado de estas *molas*, señalando que la historia de Adán y Eva, tal como se muestra en una particular, se basa en el concepto de "pecado original," pero que esto, probablemente, no se ajusta ni resuena con los tejedores Guna a lo largo de los últimos 150 años. Algunas denominaciones cristianas argumentarían que estar vivo espiritualmente requiere la aceptación de Cristo en la vida de uno. El rechazo de Dios, y de Cristo Su Hijo, significa que uno ya no vive en la luz del Señor; que uno está muerto espiritualmente sin Dios. Es posible que el artista Guna que creó esta *mola* no se haya comprometido del todo con esa teología, Wali argumenta, pero seguro apreció cómo los elementos del diseño concordaban con los principios de los Guna: el equilibrio de lo masculino y lo femenino, y la representación del mundo natural (manifestado por una palma nativa de Panamá, en lugar de un árbol de manzana). Los significados de las historias se pueden adaptar y cambiar para ajustarse a las realidades y tradiciones de los grupos que las adoptan.

El Día de Muertos nos hace recordar sobre otras maneras en que la religión católica, tal como es practicada en México y otras partes de América Latina, es un profundo sincretismo entre la fe cristiana y las tradiciones de pensamiento indígenas que existieron en el Nuevo Mundo milenios antes de la conversión católica. Álvaro Amat comparte su experiencia personal al crecer en una familia mexicana con una matriarca hispano-cubana en la que las contradicciones de las prácticas indígenas adoptadas por muchos Mexicanos Católicos estaban en desacuerdo con una perspectiva conservadora.

Vemos una teología alternativa a la judeocristiana, una que se practica en Asia a través de los lentes de las enseñanzas de Buda. Los budistas no ven la desaparición del cuerpo como la muerte definitiva. Para ellos, la *iluminación definitiva* llega después de vivir muchas vidas y atravesar por muchos cuerpos. Mitchell Hendrickson nos lleva a través de las enseñanzas de Buda (563–483 ac) y la representación de la muerte final por la que este atraviesa, en las muchas representaciones de su estado de *parinirvana*. El ciclo de muerte, renacimiento y sufrimiento continúa hasta que uno alcanza la *iluminación*. Uno puede experimentar muchas muertes físicas, pero todas son fugaces, ya que es la liberación espiritual definitiva (y final) en la que se obtiene la *iluminación*. Aprendemos que el momento de la muerte física (o de las muertes) no es el fin de la existencia ni del sufrimiento; eso requiere alcanzar el *nirvana*.

Finalmente, Gary Feinman y Ryan Williams exploran el papel de la sociedad como una entidad viva en la que la muerte es parte de esta, y un desafío a las redes sociales en curso que nos definen como miembros de una comunidad, y como un colectivo con una existencia que trasciende al individuo. Ambos profundizan en la historia de las conmemoraciones humanas a los muertos y su significado para las sociedades a lo largo de miles de años. Al explorar los primeros ejemplos de "memoriales" a los difuntos por parte de nuestros antepasados humanos, no se tiene una respuesta clara sobre qué precipitó estas tradiciones, aunque su creciente complejidad y escala pueden estar relacionadas con el aumento de la densidad de población. Este comportamiento es, sin duda, anterior a la vida sedentaria en aldeas, aunque puede estar relacionado, también, con el retorno habitual a ciertos lugares del paisaje que estaban asociados a nuestros ancestros tempranos. A medida que aumenta la congregación social, se van afianzando los memoriales más elaborados y, en algunos casos, se invierten grandes cantidades de recursos y mano de obra para la construcción de tumbas para los muertos.

Los orígenes de la memoria social se profundizan largamente en el pasado humano. El entierro de la *Mujer Magdaleniense* nos recuerda que mucho antes del advenimiento de las sociedades agrícolas, nuestros ancestros humanos se reunían para conmemorar a los muertos en un esfuerzo por construir "comunidad." El entierro de la *Mujer Magdaleniense* tuvo lugar en el abrigo rocoso de Cap Blanc en la actual Francia, probablemente hace entre 9000 y 17,000 años (aunque existe cierta ambigüedad en los diferentes fechados de radiocarbono procesados a partir de los restos). El abrigo rocoso contiene también un increíble friso esculpido de más de cuarenta pies de largo que representa a caballos, bisontes, y renos. Es probable que la joven haya sido enterrada aquí de manera deliberada, ya que su cuerpo estaba colocado en una posición fetal flexionada, lo que sugiere que su cuerpo estaba así dispuesto cuando fue enterrado. No hay objetos funerarios asociados con el entierro, aunque la ubicación de su cuerpo y el lugar en el que fue colocada puede sugerir una preocupación temprana con la construcción de memoria.

Los Haida Gwaii nos muestran cómo los ancestros continúan desempeñando un papel importante en la comunidad a través de la colocación de postes funerarios y postes conmemorativos, desde el siglo XIX hasta el presente. Como explican Luis Muro Ynoñán y Gary Feinman, los postes mortuorios y los postes conmemorativos ayudan a las comunidades a recordar y mantener a los antepasados conectados con aquellos parientes que aún habitan en el territorio. Los postes son manifestaciones tangibles de los derechos y las historias de las familias que los poseen, y están íntimamente relacionados con los ancestros familiares, como un puente hacia el más allá. Los postes mortuorios, por ejemplo, almacena los restos ancestrales en sus partes más altas y ayudan "a empujar" al muerto al siguiente reino. En una generación futura, esos mismos postes ayudan al alma del antepasado a regresar al pueblo en la forma de espíritu o de un ser reencarnado. Los postes conmemorativos, por su lado, tienen un propósito similar al ayudar al espíritu del antepasado a encontrar el camino de regreso a la aldea, especialmente en aquellos casos en los que murieron estando lejos o perdidos. Estos son como un "faro" que trae a los ancestros a casa y continúan rejuveneciendo la vida en la comunidad a través del regreso de los ancestros. Los Haida han perpetuado así sus comunidades durante miles de años, revitalizados por los ancestros que siempre forman parte de ellos.

Hace unos dos mil años, la sociedad Hopewell construyó redes sociales amplias e inclusivas, a través de la construcción de grandes túmulos funerarios para sus muertos (100 AC–500 DC) en lo que hoy es el Estado de Ohio. Estos no eran solo cementerios, sino que, como describe Brad Lepper, eran lugares centrales en un paisaje habitado por grupos móviles Hopewell que se dedicaban a prácticas ceremoniales de "renovación del mundo." Vinculados no solo a la renovación del mundo de los vivos, estas construcciones de tierra de los Hopewell fueron, también, los motores para la renovación de todo el cosmos. Y, por supuesto, para los vivos que vinieron a enterrar a sus muertos y participar en estas ceremonias, estas ceremonias reafirmaron sus lazos sociales con la comunidad Hopewell de manera amplia. Este puede haber sido el lugar donde se conocían las parejas, donde se confirmaban las relaciones intercomunitarias, y donde se reencontraron parientes lejanos. La muerte y la renovación se convirtieron en el centro de la red social que constituía la vida de los Hopewell. Sin estas ceremonias y sin estos lugares, Hopewell como sociedad no podría haber existido.

Y en todo el mundo, del pasado y el presente, los monumentos a los muertos aglutinan a sus descendientes y forjan la base de los lazos sociales que perduran por generaciones. Donna Nash nos ayuda a comprender la diferencia entre los memoriales colectivos y los monumentos dedicados a los gobernantes de la élite. Ella nos recuerda que los monumentos a los muertos pueden ser fuentes de inspiración colectiva que unen a sociedades como las de Hopewell, Stonehenge, y Göbekli Tepe. Los gobernantes poderosos también pueden invertir grandes recursos para conmemorarse a sí mismos y reforzar el dominio de su linaje y su descendencia durante generaciones. En ello, la pirámide de Khufu en Giza, el Taj Mahal de Shah Jahan, y el Templo 1 de Tikal construido por Jasaw Chan K'awiil son ejemplos evocadores. Independientemente de su propósito original, estos monumentos "cobran vida" propia en la sociedad, ya que son utilizados para proyectar ideas sobre la nación, el poder y la unidad social. Los muertos continúan ejerciendo su influencia sobre los vivos a través de sus impactos en las generaciones venideras.

Agradecimientos

A los miembros de nuestra comunidad y a los académicos que fueron consultados sobre cada una de las historias de la exposición: Kyrah Daniels, Laurie Zoloth, Robert DeCaroli, Chelsea Foxwell, Kostas Arvanitis, Bill Schweiker, Betsy Williams, Troy Hambly, Emily Teeter, Chap Kusimba, Kim Mutcherson, Brad Lepper, Ben Barnes, Mitch Hendrickson, Aay Aay Hans, Nika Collison, Sean Young, James McGuire, Colette Lee, Elizabeth Kvale, Fr. Eddie DeLeon, Geraldine Gorman, Jim Brown, Patrick Belligarde-Smith, Robin Wright, William Gblerkpor.

El financiamiento para el desarrollo de la exposición fue proporcionado por el *Lilly Endowment*.

Milton Keynes UK
Ingram Content Group UK Ltd.
UKHW050045160824
446953UK00006B/22

9 781407 360430